THE FALL OF
BURMA
1941–1943

DESPATCHES FROM THE FRONT

*The Commanding Officers' Reports from
the Field and at Sea*

THE FALL OF BURMA 1941–1943

Introduced and compiled by John Grehan and Martin Mace with additional research by Sara Mitchell

Pen & Sword

MILITARY

First published in Great Britain in 2015 by
PEN & SWORD MILITARY
An imprint of
Pen & Sword Books Ltd
47 Church Street
Barnsley
South Yorkshire
S70 2AS

ISBN 978-1-78346-210-0

Typeset by Concept, Huddersfield, West Yorkshire HD4 5JL.
Printed and bound in England by CPI Group (UK) Ltd, Croydon CR0 4YY.

Pen & Sword Books Ltd incorporates the imprints of Pen & Sword Archaeology, Atlas, Aviation, Battleground, Discovery, Family History, History, Maritime, Military, Naval, Politics, Railways, Select, Social History, Transport, True Crime, and Claymore Press, Frontline Books, Leo Cooper, Praetorian Press, Remember When, Seaforth Publishing and Wharncliffe.

For a complete list of Pen & Sword titles please contact
PEN & SWORD BOOKS LIMITED
47 Church Street, Barnsley, South Yorkshire, S70 2AS, England
E-mail: enquiries@pen-and-sword.co.uk
Website: www.pen-and-sword.co.uk

Contents

Introduction

The sudden, though hardly unexpected, attack upon US and British territory on 7 and 8 December 1941, almost immediately placed Burma on the front line. With Burma sharing a frontier with India the decision was quickly taken to place the defence of Burma under responsibility of the Commander-in-Chief in India, General Sir Archibald P. Wavell. This came into effect on 15 December.

When Wavell went to inspect his new command he found its defences to be wholly inadequate. This, he explains in his despatch, was entirely understandable as Burma was bordered by two friendly, neutral nations, Thailand and French Indo-China, both of which professed their intention to defend themselves against Japanese aggression. Except as a subsidiary air base, Wavell concedes, Burma hardly entered into the strategic plans of the Far East Command, which was concerned with the defence of Hong Kong and Malaya/Singapore.

The entire situation changed when Vichy France handed over control of Indo-China to Japan in 1940 and then, on 21 December 1941, Thailand signed a treaty of friendship with Japan after it had been invaded.

At the time Wavell took over there were just two British infantry battalions, two Indian infantry brigades, and eight battalions of Burma Rifles to defend a country with a land mass almost three times that of the United Kingdom. In terms of air defence, Burma possessed one squadron of Blenheims, and one of Brewster Buffaloes plus one squadron of Hurricanes which arrived in January 1941, becoming operational on the 26th of that month.

The air defences of Burma, especially of the vital port of Rangoon, would have been overwhelmed at once but for the presence in Burma of the American Volunteer Group (AVG) – an air force manned by American pilots for the defence of China which was equipped with Curtiss P-40 fighters.

The Japanese attack on Burma began on 19 January 1942, with easy initial gains through, according to Wavell, "bad handling by local Commanders, lack of training and in some instances lack of fighting spirit on the part of our troops". Wavell was informed that Rangoon was the likely objective of the enemy.

Wavell quickly moved every unit he could into the area to try and hold the Japanese advance. He had already despatched the 17th Division from India and he diverted 7 Armoured Brigade which was on its way from the Middle East to Malaya. By this time the troops in Malaya had been driven into Singapore Island and the Armoured Brigade was obviously of no use there. A regiment of field artillery was also moved into Burma as well as 46 and 63 Indian Infantry Brigades to strengthen 17 Indian Division.

Wavell's despatch outlining operations up to 20 May 1942 includes a report from Lieutenant General T.J. Hutton who assumed command in Burma on 27 December 1941. When the Japanese attack began three weeks later 16 Indian Brigade stood in the path of the enemy but, fearing it might be overwhelmed and destroyed by the Japanese, was told to undertake a fighting withdrawal.

The crucial engagement took place at the only bridge over the River Sittang on the road to Rangoon. Brigadier John Smyth, who had been awarded with the Victoria Cross in the First World War, was in charge of 17 Division. Smyth had been told to blow the bridge but around half of his men were still on the far bank of the river when the Japanese arrived. Smyth took the bold decision to blow the bridge to stop the Japanese rushing down the road to Rangoon.

Smyth delayed the Japanese advance and many of the stranded soldiers were able to subsequently swim across the river as the Japanese had moved along the river to find an alternative crossing point. The division was reduced to around 40 per cent of its strength, having lost most of its equipment. Smyth was dismissed and was never given another command.

The Japanese were soon across the Sittang and bore down on Rangoon. A stand was made at Pegu which delayed the Japanese until 7 March but already the evacuation of Rangoon was being considered. That decision was Wavell's alone.

Rangoon was given up as a lost cause by the Chiefs of Staff who chose instead not to send 7 Australian Division to Burma as previously arranged and at the last moment the East African Brigade was diverted elsewhere. That, as Hutton wrote, sealed the fate of the Burmese capital.

Already the now well-known characteristics of the Japanese had begun to be seen, as Hutton observed:

Perhaps the most important characteristic of the Japanese soldier is his ability to live almost entirely on the country and to dispense with the enormous administrative organisation in rear of the fighting troops that is required by most armies.

He achieves this by being tough. He can live for five days on the rice he actually carries and he has been taught that he must reduce his expenditure of ammunition to that which he can carry. He uses any means of transport available – porters, civilians, bullock carts, boats, captured M.T., etc., but has little in the unit. His troops do not expect to be carried everywhere in M.T. The other main point is his insistence on the offensive spirit and the tactics of envelopment. Quite small forces will work round the rear of a much larger force and may succeed in defeating it entirely by bluff ... They do not hesitate to fight in plain clothes or enemy uniform if it suits their purpose and, although they may deny any deliberate policy of committing atrocities, both officers and men often kill or maim prisoners or wounded after capture in a most brutal and coldblooded manner. They neglect enemy wounded completely – even more than they do their own.

There is no doubt that the tough, ruthless Japanese were too determined to be stopped. In time, the British and their Allies would learn how to defeat the Japanese but, in those early months of the war in the Far East the Japanese very quickly gained the upper hand.

Hutton was superseded by General Harold Alexander on 5 March 1941. On arriving in the region he was given his instructions by Wavell, which were that:

> The retention of Rangoon was a matter of vital importance to our position in the Far East and every effort must be made to hold it. If, however, that was not possible the force must not be allowed to be cut off and destroyed but must be withdrawn from the Rangoon area for the defence of Upper Burma. This must be held as long as possible in order to safeguard the oil fields at Yenangyaung, keep contact with the Chinese and protect the construction of the road from Assam to Burma.

It did not take Alexander long after reaching Rangoon to realise that all the roads out of the Burmese capital were in danger of being cut by the enemy. On 7 March all non-essential personnel were ordered out of Rangoon, leaving behind just demolition parties.

The loss of Rangoon placed Alexander's forces in a perilous situation. Rangoon was the only point of entry for supplies into the country as there was no road into India. This meant that Alexander was virtually cut off inside Burma with no hope any outside help other than what limited amounts could be delivered by air. Before the loss of Rangoon aerodrome the RAF and AVG fighters had been able to achieve superiority in the air, now this had been relinquished.

Alexander had sought to hold Upper Burma, but this soon became impracticable and he was forced to retreat to India along narrow sandy tracks and irregular footpaths. "Anyone seeing this track for the first time," wrote Alexander, "would find it difficult to imagine how a fully mechanised force could possibly move over it". Eventually, the weakened remnants of Alexander's force reached India, and Alexander's task was at an end.

Wavell's second despatch reproduced here deals with the defence of India and Ceylon. The success of the Japanese, which seemed so remarkable, now threatened to be continued into the jewel in the British Empire's crown. All available forces were sent to India's frontier with Burma as Alexander's men arrived, along with an estimated 400,000 civilian refugees.

By the middle of June the situation eased somewhat with reinforcements in the form of the 2nd and, 5th British Divisions, with the Indian 23rd Division being raised. The weather then intervened as the monsoon arrived, putting an end to fears of an imminent Japanese attack upon India. "India therefore had a breathing space," wrote Wavell, "to reorganise, train and prepare".

To lose Burma was one thing, to lose India was another altogether. Britain was determined it would not happen and after a meeting with Churchill and the Chief of the Imperial Staff in Cairo, Wavell was promised the support he needed to secure India and, eventually, retake Burma.

So significant was the increase in the forces in India, by the end of 1942 there were twenty-nine squadrons operational and another twenty forming, in addition to two squadrons of transport aircraft – and Wavell was already laying down plans for an offensive into Burma.

Wavell's third despatch takes the story up to June 1943. It deals with the Arakan campaign and Ord Wingate's first Chindit expedition. It deals mainly with the build up of forces and the logistical arrangements necessary for taking the war back into Burma.

The final despatch is from Field Marshal Sir Claude J.E. Auchinleck who took over from Wavell on 20 June 1943 and ends in November 1943 when, with the offensive developing into Burma, India no longer became the operational headquarters of the fight against the Japanese.

Wavell described the loss of Burma as "our most serious reverse of the Japanese war". He went on to add: "It has deprived our Chinese allies of a flow of munitions to continue their long resistance; it has made the establishment of air bases within effective range of Japan a matter of extreme difficulty; it has exposed India to a serious threat of invasion; and it has had a disastrous effect on British prestige in the East."

In fact this proved not to be the case. In 1943 the Fourteenth Army was formed from British, Indian and African divisions and, under the command of General Slim, it helped to drive the Japanese out of Burma in conclusive and dramatic style. Though Wavell did not see the concluding act of the war in Burma he was undoubtedly instrumental in the defeat of the Japanese and eventual re-conquest of the country lost so easily in 1942.

*   *   *

The objective of this book is to reproduce the despatches from Wavell, Alexander, Hutton and Auchinleck as they first appeared to the general public some seventy years ago. They have not been modified, edited or interpreted in any way and are therefore the original and unique words of the commanding officers as they saw things at the time they were written. The only changes that we have made are with the footnotes which are placed at the end of each despatch rather than at the foot of the respective page. Any grammatical or spelling errors have been left uncorrected to retain the authenticity of the documents. Much has changed in Burma, or the Republic of the Union of Myanmar as it is now known, including many place names, and some of the places referred to in the despatches are difficult to find on a modern map of the country.

Abbreviations

A.Tk	Anti-tank
AA	Anti-aircraft
ABDA	American-British-Dutch-Australian [Command]
AC	Army Co-Operation
ADC	Aide-De-Camp
ADMS	Assistant Director Medical Services
ADOS	Assistant Director of Ordnance Services
Adv.	Advance
AFC	Air Force Cross
AHQ	Army Headquarters
ALG	Advanced Landing Ground
AOC	Air Officer Commanding
AOC in C	Air Officer Commanding-in-Chief
Armd	Armoured
ARP	Air Raid Precautions
AVG	American Volunteer Group
AVM	Air Vice Marshal
BAF	Burma Auxiliary Force
BAFSEA	British Air Force South-East Asia
Bde	Brigade
BESA	Bengal Entertainment for the Services Association
BGS	Brigadier, General Staff
BHC	Burma Hospital Corps
Bn./Btn.	Battalion
BORs	British Other Ranks
BRNVR	Burma Royal Naval Volunteer Reserve
BT	Bomber Transport
Bty.	Battery
CAO	Civil Affairs Officer
CATF	Chinese-American Task Force
CB	Companion of the Order of Bath
CBE	Commander of the Most Excellent Order of the British Empire
CCAO	Chief Civil Affairs Officer
CCS	Casualty Clearing Station

CIE	Companion of The Most Eminent Order of the Indian Empire
CIGS	Chief of the Imperial General Staff
CinC/C-in-C	Commander-in-Chief
CGS	Chief of the General Staff
CMG	Companion of the Most Distinguished Order of Saint Michael and Saint George
COS	Chiefs of Staff
CSI	Companion of the Order of the Star of India
CVO	Commander of the Royal Victorian Order
cwt.	Centum Weight (or hundredweight)
DADMS	Deputy Assistant Director Medical Services
DCO	Director Combined Operations
DG	Director General
Div.	Division
DMS	Director Medical Services
DSO	Distinguished Service Order
DWR	Duke of Wellington's Regiment
E&ME	Electrical and Mechanical Engineers
ECO	Emergency Commissioned Officers
EI	East Indian
Fd.	Field
FFR	Frontier Force Regiment
GBE	Knight Grand Cross of the Most Excellent Order of the British Empire
GCB	Knight Grand Cross of The Most Honourable Order of the Bath
GCIE	Knight Grand Commander of The Most Eminent Order of the Indian Empire
GCO	Governor's Commissioned Officer
GCSI	Knight Grand Commander of The Most Exalted Order of the Star of India
GHQ	General Headquarters
GOC	General Officer Commanding
GOC in C	General Officer Commanding-in-Chief
GP	General Purpose
GPT	General Purpose Transport
GR	General Reconnaissance/Gurkha Rifles
GS	General Staff
HBM	His Britannic Majesty
HE	High Explosive/His Excellency
HM	His Majesty
HMG	His Majesty's Government
HMIS	His Majesty's Indian Ship

HMS	His Majesty's Ship
IAF	Indian Air Force
IATC	Indian Air Training Corps
IEF	Indian Expeditionary Force
IHC	Indian Hospital Corps
IMS	Indian Medical Service(s)
Ind.	Indian
Inf.	Infantry
Innisks.	Inniskilling
IORs	Indian Other Rank(s)
IWT	Inland Water Transport
JIC	Joint Intelligence Committee
KBE	Knight Commander of the Most Excellent Order of the British Empire
KCB	Knight Commander of the Most Honourable Order of the Bath
KCIE	Knight Commander of The Most Eminent Order of the Indian Empire
KCMG	Knight Commander of The Most Distinguished Order of Saint Michael and Saint George
KCSI	Knight Commander of The Most Exalted Order of the Star of India
KCVO	Knight Commander of The Royal Victorian Order
KG	Knight of the Most Noble Order of the Garter
KOYLI	King's Own Yorkshire Light Infantry
LAA	Light Anti-Aircraft
LCS	Landing Craft Support
LMG	Light Machine Gun
L of C	Line(s) of Communication
LRP	Long Range Penetration
Lt.	Lieutenant
MC	Military Cross
MG	Major General/Machine-Gun
ML	Motor Launch
MMG	Medium Machine-Gun
MT	Motor Transport
Mtn.	Mountain
MV, M/V	Motor Vessel
NAAFI	Navy, Army and Air Force Institutes
NCO	Non Commissioned Officer
NOIC	Naval Officer in Charge
NWFP	North-West Frontier Province
OBE	Most Excellent Order of the British Empire
OCTU	Officer Cadre Training Unit

OP	Operation(s)/Observation Post
P&T/P and T	Posts and Telegraphs
PAIC	Persia and Iraq Command
PC	Patrol Craft
pdr.	pounder
POL	Petrol, Oil, Lubricants
PRU	Photographic Reconnaissance Unit
QMG	Quartermaster General
R/T	Receiver-Transmitter/Radio Transmitter
RA	Royal Artillery
RAF	Royal Air Force
RAOC	Royal Army Ordnance Corps
RASC	Royal Army Service Corps
RE	Royal Engineers
Regt.	Regiment
RGR	Royal Gurkha Rifles
RHA	Royal Horse Artillery
Rif.	Rifles
RIN	Royal Indian Navy
RN	Royal Navy
RTR	Royal Tank Regiment
SEAC	South East Asia Command
SS	Steam Ship
SSAFA	Soldiers', Sailors' and Airmen's Families Association
SWPC	South-West Pacific Command
TB	Torpedo Bomber
Tk	Tank
Tpt.	Transport
UOTC	University Officers Training Corps
US	United States
USAAF	United States Army Air Force
WAAF	Women's Auxiliary Air Force
WAC	Women's Auxiliary Corps
WET	War Equipment Table
YMCA	Young Men's Christian Association

1

GENERAL SIR ARCHIBALD P. WAVELL'S DESPATCH ON OPERATIONS IN BURMA, 15 DECEMBER 1941 TO 20 MAY 1942

The War Office, March, 1948.
The following Despatch was submitted to the Secretary of State for War on the 14th July, 1942, by, G.C.B., C.M.G., M.C., A.D.C., Commander-in-Chief, India.

1. This despatch covers reports by Lieut.-General T.J. Hutton and by General The Honourable Sir Harold R.L.G. Alexander describing the operations in Burma between 15th December, 1941, when the defence of Burma became the responsibility of the Commander-in-Chief in India, and 20th May 1942,when the last troops of the Burma Army were withdrawn across the frontier into India. The despatch is intended to explain how the general strategical situation affected operations in Burma and to record the actions I took as the Commander chiefly responsible for them. Although the defence of Burma was three times transferred from one Command to another during the period, I remained personally responsible except for a period of about one week at the end of February, 1942.

2. The vital importance of Burma, in a war against Japan, to the Allied cause in general and to the defence of India is obvious. Through Burma lay the only route by which the Chinese armies could be kept supplied, and bases stocked for Allied air attack on Japan itself. From India's point of view, so long as Burma was in our possession, Calcutta and the great industrial centres of North-East India were practically immune from air attack, and her eastern land frontiers were secure from the threat of invasion.

BURMA BEFORE WAR WITH JAPAN.
3. Burma had been included, for operational purposes, in the Far East Command when this was established in November, 1940, with headquarters in Singapore. Administration remained directly under the War Office. So much, however, was the security of Burma of concern to those charged with the defence of India that several attempts were made by successive Commanders-in-Chief in India to have this arrangement altered and responsibility for the defence of Burma transferred to India. The recommendation to this effect made by my predecessor, General Auchinleck, was not accepted. Shortly after my appointment as Commander-in-Chief, India I paid a visit to the United Kingdom and personally pressed this change on the Chiefs of Staff, who again refused to alter the existing arrangement, on the grounds that the question had been fully considered when the Far

East Command was established. The Japanese had by this time invaded Indo-China and thus brought danger to Burma much closer, but this fact was not held to justify the change.

On returning to India I paid a visit to Burma and Malaya and discussed the question with the Commander-in-Chief Far East, Air Marshal Sir Robert Brooke-Popham, and with the Governor of Burma, Sir Reginald Dorman-Smith, and with the G.O.C. Burma, Lieut.-General D.K. Macleod. As a result I cabled to the C.I.G.S. on 11th November, 1941, again recommending the transfer of Burma to the Indian Command. I understand that my recommendation was supported by the Governor of Burma.

I was very greatly concerned by the extent of unpreparedness in Burma's defences of which I became aware during my visit. I realised that the number and training of the troops, their equipment, the Intelligence lay-out, the size and organisation of the staff, the administrative system and the defensive arrangements were quite inadequate. So dangerous to India did I consider the situation to be that on my return I initiated the despatch to Burma of an additional Indian Infantry Brigade and battery and arranged for a senior administrative staff officer to visit Burma and to ascertain their most pressing needs. Though the administration of Burma was the responsibility of the War Office, it was obvious that, if Japan entered the war, it would be quite impossible for Burma's requirements to be met in time from the United Kingdom; and since any failure in Burma would endanger India, it was essential for the India Command, in spite of its own grave shortages, to put the defence of Burma on a reasonable basis. I also took up the question of the construction of an all-weather road from Assam to Burma as a matter of immediate urgency. (See also paragraph 39.)

4. The neglect of Burma's defences during the early part of the war was understandable. There seemed little pressing danger even should Japan decide to attack Great Britain. Burma was protected on the east by two neutral states, Thailand and Indo-China, both of which professed their intention to defend themselves against Japanese aggression, and by the natural difficulties of the mountainous undeveloped country on her border. So long as Singapore remained in British possession, there was little danger of a threat from seaward. Troops, equipment and staff were badly needed elsewhere, and it was only natural that Burma's requirements were placed by the War Office very low in the scale of priority. When Japan entered Indo-China in July, 1941, and her aggressive intentions became obvious, Burma became more nearly threatened and more attention should have been paid to her deficiencies. The cardinal mistake seems to me, however, to have been in placing Burma in the Far East Command instead of under India. Except as a subsidiary air base, Burma hardly entered into the strategical plans of the Far East Command, which was concerned with the defence of Hong Kong and Malaya; whereas for India Burma was a vital bulwark. Similarly in administration the War Office was too far away and too occupied with other matters to concern itself with, or even to understand, the needs of Burma, to

which India would have given sympathetic consideration as part of her own defence problem.

In Burma itself more might have been done, in spite of all the deficiencies, to place the country on a war footing. Political considerations, the climate, under-estimation of the enemy, over-estimation of the natural strength of the frontiers, the complacency of many years of freedom from external threat, all combined to prevent the defence problem being taken sufficiently seriously.

BURMA PLACED UNDER COMMANDER-IN-CHIEF, INDIA.

5. On 12th December, five days after the entry of Japan into the war, I received a telegram from the Prime Minister placing Burma under the Commander-in-Chief, in India for defence. In this telegram I was allotted the 18 British Division, then on passage to Mid-east, for the defence of India and Burma; I was from the commitment to send 17 Indian Division to Iraq; and I was promised a special allotment of anti-tank and anti-aircraft guns. I was also told that four squadrons of fighter aeroplanes would be diverted from Mid-east to India. In a later tele-gram I was informed that Mid-east had been instructed to prepare plans to send six squadrons of Blenheim IVs to India for Burma.

I at once prepared to despatch to Burma the leading brigade group of 17 Indian Division which was about to embark for Iraq. I had asked the C.I.G.S. at the end of November to consider sending me some African troops for Ceylon or Burma, now that Gondar had fallen and the campaign against Italian East Africa was over; he replied on 16th December that two Brigades could be made, available, the first of which could be ready to embark at the end of January. Thus when I visited Rangoon on 21st December I had, as I thought, ample forces in sight for the defence of Burma.

6. In Burma itself there were at this time two British infantry battalions, two Indian infantry brigades, and eight battalions of Burma Rifles (four of which had been raised since the beginning of the war). The Burma Rifles who composed practically half the available force were of doubtful fighting quality (see para. 4 of General Hutton's report). The artillery in Burma comprised only four mountain batteries and one four-gun 18 pr. battery. The Administrative services were so inadequate that they might almost have been termed non-existent.

There was also the Burma Frontier Force, the equivalent of approximately six battalions, divided into a number of detachments. They were composed not of Burmans but of Indians enlisted from the same classes as the Indian Army. This should have been a most valuable force but in actual practice proved disappoint-ing and had little fighting value. It was normally under the control of the Civil Power and only came under army control for operations shortly after the out-break of war with Japan, whilst remaining for other purposes subject to their own Inspector-General.

It should be realised that the Burma Army had had a very short existence and only dated from the separation of Burma from India in April, 1937. The inhabi-tants of Burma have shown themselves brave and tough fighters in defence of their country but as irregulars in guerilla warfare. Regular soldiering and discipline make no appeal to them.

7. The air forces nominally available in Burma at the outbreak of war were one fighter squadron equipped with Brewster Buffaloes and one bomber squadron of Blenheims. Actually the aircraft of the bomber squadron were in Malaya for armament training and were taken by Far East Command for Malayan operations. None ever returned to Burma. It may be noted that this Blenheim squadron was one of two borrowed from India by Far East Command (the only modern aircraft India possessed). There was thus only one squadron in Burma, with a type of fighter which proved unable to compete with the Japanese fighters. The War Cabinet's proposals for air reinforcements were an immediate programme of four Fighter Squadrons, six Bomber Squadrons, two Army Co-operation Squadrons and one G.R. Squadron. On the 1st January Air Vice-Marshal Stevenson arrived to command in Burma. The forward elements of three Hurricane Squadrons – aircraft and personnel – began to arrive on 21st January. It was not, however, until 26th January that a Squadron built up from these elements became operational. The total reinforcement of bombers arriving in the country before the decision to evacuate Rangoon was reached comprised the aircraft and personnel of 113 Bomber Squadron and the aircraft and crews of 45 Bomber Squadron.

India, after parting with her Blenheims to Far East, had no modern aircraft of any kind and could contribute only a flight of 4 Wapiti and 2 Audax aircraft (both completely obsolete types) to form a Coast Defence Flight. This was later replaced by a flight of Blenheim I aircraft. Later India sent the 1 Indian Squadron and No. 28 Squadron R.A.F. with Lysander biplanes. These squadrons, in spite of their out-of-date equipment, did much valuable work, and 1 Indian Squadron acquitted itself gallantly in the first service in this war of an Indian air squadron. No. 31 Bomber Transport Squadron equipped with Valencia and Douglas aircraft was also placed by India at the disposal of Burma.

The air defences of Burma, especially of the vital port of Rangoon, would have been overwhelmed at once but for the presence in Burma of the American Volunteer Group (A.V.G.), an air force manned by American pilots for the defence of China. It was equipped with P-40 fighters and led by Colonel G. Chennault. One of its two squadrons was alternately made available by the Generalissimo for the defence of Rangoon, and the pilots together with the R.A.F. Buffalo Fighter Squadrons saved the situation by their dash and skill.

8. In an appreciation about the middle of December, General Macleod estimated the maximum scale of Japanese attack at one or two divisions against Southern Shan States and one division in the south against Tenasserim. He stated that two infantry brigades, one field regiment and one field battery were the additional land reinforcements necessary to deal with the situation. He considered three bomber squadrons and two fighter squadrons were required.

Both Far East Command and War Office informed me that an attack in force against Burma was unlikely until the Japanese had completed their campaigns in Malaya and the Philippines.

9. After discussing Burma's defence problems with the Governor and G.O.C. I cabled from Rangoon on 22nd December to the C.I.G.S. an appreciation in which I emphasised the weakness of Burma's defences, the lack of an Intelligence system, and the need for air forces. I said that the *immediate* requirements of Burma were two bomber and two modern fighter squadrons, a divisional head-quarters and two brigade groups, apparatus for a warning system and anti-aircraft artillery.

10. In view of the extensive re-organisation of the whole defence system of Burma, which was essential, I decided that it would be necessary to replace Lieut.-General Macleod, who had done his best with the very little available to him, by a commander with more experience of the organisation and administration of troops on a large scale. The Governor of Burma was anxious, for political reasons, to have an officer of the British Service if possible, and I decided to appoint my Chief of the General Staff in India, Lieut.-General Hutton, to the command in Burma. His powers of effective organisation had been amply proved in India. He assumed command on 27th December, 1941.

OFFER OF CHINESE TROOPS FOR DEFENCE OF BURMA.

11. From Rangoon I flew to Chungking with General Brett of the United States Air Force to discuss the Japanese war with Marshal Chiang Kai-Shek. I wished to ensure that at least one of the A.V.G. Squadrons, which Colonel Chennault wished to remove to China, remained in Burma for the defence of Rangoon; also to obtain the temporary use of some of the Lease-Lend material for China, which was stacked in large quantities in the Rangoon docks and could not quickly be removed, to make good the most serious deficiencies in the Burma Army. To neither of these requests did I get a definite reply, though in the end one squadron of the A.V.G. always did remain for the defence of Rangoon, and some of the Lease-Lend equipment was placed at the disposal of the Burma Army. On the other hand, the Generalissimo offered to send to Burma the Fifth and Sixth Chinese Armies. Since it has been alleged that my refusal of this offer was a main contributing factor to the loss of Burma, I will state the facts of the matter from my point of view. I accepted at once the 93 Division, part of which was already approaching the Burmese border from Puerh, and the 49 Division as a reserve on the northern frontier of Burma at Wanting. These two Divisions constituted the Sixth Army, with a third Division, the 55th, which General Dennys, head of 204 Mission in China, informed me was very scattered and would take some time to collect and was of poor quality. The Fifth Army, of good quality, was collecting round Kunming. I asked that it should not at present be moved into Burma, but should be held in reserve in the Kunming area. I considered that it would be well placed here either to move into Burma if required; or for the

defence of Yunnan if the Japanese made an advance north from Indo-China against the Burmese road, a contingency which the Chinese had not long before represented as the enemy's most probable move; or for offensive operations into Indo-China in co-operation with an advance from Burma if all went well.

The Generalissimo made it perfectly clear that it was a condition of the acceptance of his offer that a separate line of communications should be available for his troops and that they should not in any way be mixed up with British troops. It was impossible at the time to provide a separate line of communication for the Fifth Army though it was possible to keep the communications of the 93 Division from Puerh separate from that of the British troops in Burma. I had at the time every reason to suppose that I should have ample British, Indian or African troops available to defend Burma, which did not seem immediately threatened: obviously it was desirable that a country of the British Empire should be defended by Imperial troops rather than by foreign. The Chinese who had no administrative services of their own would have complicated the already difficult administrative problem in Burma. These were the reasons that were the motive of my qualified acceptance of the Generalissimo's offer. It should be noted that a Chinese "Army" was approximately the equivalent in numbers of a British division but with a much lower scale of equipment.

I am quite satisfied that my decision was justified by the military situation as it appeared to me at the time. Nor had I any reason to know that the Chinese attached great political importance to the acceptance of the offer. The Generalissimo himself showed comparatively little interest in the matter and made no attempt to press me; three-quarters of the lengthy discussions I had with him were devoted to the question of the establishment of an Allied Council at Chungking and to consideration of an ambitious plan for defeat of the Japanese in 1942.

From subsequent experience of the slowness of Chinese troop moves, I think that even if I had accepted the whole of the Fifth and Sixth Armies at once they would actually have reached Burma very little, if any, sooner than they eventually did.

As things turned out, I admit that it would have saved much criticism in China and in the U.S.A. had I accepted the Generalissimo's generous offer wholeheartedly and at once. I do not, however, think that it would have made any difference in the end to the defence of Burma.

12. When I returned to India, I found that the troops I was counting on for Burma were being taken from my control for the reinforcement of Malaya. Already the War Cabinet had ordered one brigade group of the 18 British Division and two brigade groups of the 17 Indian Division to Malaya, as well as anti-aircraft and anti-tank artillery. The remainder of the 18 Division was also put under orders for Malaya shortly afterwards. Thus of the two complete divisions on which I had reckoned one divisional headquarters and one brigade only remained. I still believed the African brigades available and expected the first to arrive in Burma

by the middle of February. It was not until that date that I received a cable to say that the leading brigade was delayed. Actually it did not embark in East Africa till after Rangoon had fallen.

13. On 23rd December and 25th December the Japanese made two large scale air raids on Rangoon. They caused practically no military damage but civilian casualties in the first raid were high, and the flight of the population from Rangoon began. From now to the final evacuation of the city, the working of the essential services, the provision of labour to unload ships and the cessation of all business became a major problem for the Government and a serious military embarrassment. The presence on all routes leading towards India of many thousands of refugees, which soon grew to hundreds of thousands, was another problem that occupied both civil and military to the end of the campaign.

TRANSFER OF BURMA TO A.B.D.A. COMMAND.

14. On 30th December, 1941, I received a telegram appointing me to the newly constituted South-West Pacific Command (afterwards known as A.B.D.A.). Burma was included in this Command. I at once recommended that the defence of Burma should remain the responsibility of Commander-in-Chief, India, for the same reasons for which I had previously urged its transfer to India from the Far East Command (see paragraph 3). I was, however, overruled on the grounds that Marshal Chiang-Kai-Shek must feel himself connected with the new South West Pacific Command. I think that this decision was a serious error from the military point of view. From my headquarters in Java, 2,000 miles distant from Rangoon, and concerned as I was with an immense area and many international problems, it was impossible for me to give as close attention to the defence of Burma as was desirable; nor had I any reinforcements at my disposal to aid Burma. They must come almost entirely from India. Moreover, administration of the forces in Burma had necessarily to be conducted from India; and it is always wrong to separate operational and administrative responsibility.

General Sir Alan Hartley who succeeded me as Commander-in-Chief, India, did everything possible to meet Burma's requirements. What was lacking was the close personal touch of the responsible commander. During the five weeks that Burma remained under A.B.D.A. Command, I was only able to pay two hurried visits; and owing to faulty signal communications, messages and reports from Burma sometimes took several days to reach me in Java. It was during these five weeks that the fate of Burma was decided.

15. I took over control of South West Pacific Command on 15th January, and established A.B.D.A. Command Headquarters in Java, near Bandoeng, a few days late. During the first half of January there had been little sign of enemy activity against Burma. The maximum scale of Japanese attack was still estimated as one division against Moulmein and one division against Kentung with possibly brigade groups against Toungoo and Mongpan. I admit that I did not at this time consider the threat to Burma serious; I over-estimated the natural difficulties of

the wooded hills on the Burmese frontier. Nor did I realise the unreliable quality of the Burma units nor the lack of training of the British and Indian troops.

I was certainly guilty of an error of judgment in minimising the danger to Burma, but it is doubtful whether, even if I had appreciated it thoroughly, I could have done much more to help Burma. India had been sucked dry of trained troops by the requirements of Middle East, Iraq and Iran; and those most nearly approaching completion of their training had been sent to reinforce Singapore. Such as could be extracted from frontier garrisons and internal security duties were being sent to Burma as rapidly as possible. The same applies to administrative units. India was deficient of equipment for her own needs and could not meet those of Burma as well. Finally, and most important of all, India had no modern air force with which to support the Burma Army.

JAPANESE ATTACK ON BURMA.

16. The Japanese advance on Burma began with engagements in the neighbourhood of Tavoy which was occupied by the enemy on 19th January. Meanwhile the garrison at Mergui further south was withdrawn without being attacked. On 20th January, fighting began in Northern Tenasserim with an attack on the 16 Indian Brigade near Kawkareik. These engagements are described in General Hutton's report. It is quite clear that the enemy were allowed to gain cheap initial successes through bad handling by local Commanders, lack of training and in some instances lack of fighting spirit on the part of our troops. It was an unfortunate beginning to the campaign and had serious results in raising the morale of the enemy and depressing that of our own troops. It became clear that the battalions of Burma Rifles, which formed so large a proportion of the army in Burma, were undependable.

From my point of view I received in Java telegrams indicating that the threat to Rangoon was considered to be imminent and that without additional and earlier reinforcement the G.O.C. did not think that Rangoon could be held. I knew that General Hutton was prepared for the loss of Mergui and Tavoy, but I had not received any information indicating the probable appearance of a Japanese force large enough to imperil Rangoon.

I flew from Java to Burma during the night 24th–25th January, spent the 25th at Rangoon and returned during the night 25th–26th January. I found the situation better than I had expected and, after discussing the situation with the G.O.C. I reported to the Chiefs of Staff that I did not consider the situation immediately serious, provided that the reinforcement of Burma with land and air forces proceeded without delay, and that some naval force was provided to prevent a landing near Rangoon from the Tenasserim coast. I had already on 19th January authorised General Hutton to accept any Chinese troops available. It may be remarked that those I had originally accepted on 22nd December, the 93 and 49 Divisions, had not by this date yet reached Burma.

17. On the night of 4th–5th February, I again flew to Rangoon and spent two days there. My purpose was partly to meet the Generalissimo who, I had been

informed, was passing through Rangoon on his way to India. He went, however, straight from Lashio to Calcutta, and I did not see him. General Hutton had a very cordial and satisfactory interview with him.

I visited the troops, who were then holding a front west of the Salween River opposite Moulmein, and all commanders expressed themselves to me as confident of their ability to deal with the Japanese advance. I was impressed with the suitability of the dry paddy fields for armoured troops and decided to divert to Burma the 7 Armoured Brigade which was on its way from the Middle East to Malaya. By this time the troops in Malaya had been driven into Singapore Island and the Armoured Brigade was obviously of no use there, while Java also offered little scope for armoured troops, I therefore ordered the Brigade to be diverted to Rangoon. It played a very prominent part in all the fighting in Burma after its arrival in Rangoon on 21st February. The air situation over Rangoon was satisfactory, Hurricanes had begun to arrive and these, with the A.V.G. P.40s, had established and were maintaining air superiority over the enemy.

18. The battle at the Sittang River bridge-head on 22nd and 23rd February, which is described in General Hutton's report, really sealed the fate of Rangoon and Lower Burma. In the withdrawal from the Bilin River to the Sittang and the action east of that River almost the whole of two brigades were lost.

BURMA RETURNED TO INDIA COMMAND.

19. By the time the Sittang River battle took place, two changes of importance in the control of the operations in Burma had been decided. I had ceased temporarily to be responsible for Burma, and the War Cabinet, in view of the proposed expansion of the forces in Burma, decided to place Lieut.-General Alexander in command of the troops in Burma. Lieut.-General Hutton remained as Chief of the General Staff to General Alexander.

The Chiefs of Staff had telegraphed me on 18th February asking my views on the desirability, in view of the loss of Singapore and Sumatra, of Burma reverting to the control of Commander-in-Chief, India. I replied that I had never varied in my recommendation that Burma should be under Commander-in-Chief, India, for defence. On 21st February I received orders that Burma was to come again under the command of Commander-in-Chief, India.

20. Soon after the middle of February I realised that it was most unlikely that Java could be held against the impending Japanese attack and that in view of the enemy command of the air it would be impossible to land the Australian Corps, which was on its way from the Middle East, in Java. I considered it absolutely essential that Rangoon and Burma should be held and recommended that the Australian Corps, or at least the leading Division of it, should be sent to Burma. My recommendation was supported by the Prime Minister but was not accepted by the Australian Government.[1] When this convoy changed course for Australia, the last hope of holding Rangoon practically vanished.

21. On 23rd February I was ordered to close down A.B.D.A. Command Headquarters and to reassume my appointment as Commander-in-Chief, India. I thus
against became responsible for the defence of Burma within a few days of having
handed it over. I left Java on the night, of 25th–26th February. Realising that the
situation in Lower Burma must be critical I wished to fly direct from Java to
Rangoon. In view of the prevailing weather conditions, however, it was doubtful
whether even a Liberator could make the distance direct, and the aerodromes
in Southern Sumatra were in enemy hands. I had therefore to fly to Ceylon. I
arrived at Colombo on the morning of 26th February, intending to take a flying
boat on to Rangoon. I found, however, a cable from General Hartley advising
that I should first go to Delhi. I arrived in Delhi on the evening of 27th February
and was informed that there was a proposal in Burma, if no instructions were
received to the contrary, to evacuate Rangoon. Since from the information available this proposal appeared to me premature, I cabled that action should be suspended till I could reach Burma, I also ordered that the convoys containing
reinforcements which had been turned back from Rangoon should again be
diverted towards that port.

I arrived at Magwe in Upper Burma on the morning of 1st March and held a
conference with the Governor, General Hutton and Air-Vice Marshal Stevenson.
There seemed to me no reason why Rangoon should not continue to be held at
least long enough to enable the reinforcements on the way, 63 Indian Infantry
Brigade and a field regiment, to be landed. There was no evidence of any great
enemy strength west of the Sittang, the 7 Armoured Brigade was still intact, and
Chinese troops were moving down towards Toungoo. I therefore gave instruc-
tions that any orders that might have been issued with a view to the evacuation of
Rangoon should be cancelled and directed that all ships with troops or stores for
Burma should proceed.

I flew during the afternoon with General Hutton to Rangoon. On arrival there
we found a telegram from the G.O.C. 17 Division recommending the immediate
evacuation of Pegu. I motored with General Hutton to Divisional Headquarters
at Hlegu and found that the report on which the Divisional Commander's
recommendation was based had proved a false one. The Divisional Commander
was obviously a sick man, and I replaced him by Brigadier Cowan, who commanded the 17 Division with success for the remainder of the campaign.

On 2nd March I visited the troops of the 17 Division and 7 Armoured Brigade
on the Pegu front and then flew to Lashio, since I had heard that Marshal
Chiang-Kai-Shek would be there. I had two satisfactory interviews with him that
evening and next day returned to India. At Calcutta I met General Alexander,
who was on his way to take over command of the Burma Army, and instructed
him to hold on to Rangoon for as long as possible.

While my intervention on this occasion postponed the evacuation of Rangoon
for a week and enabled reinforcements of an Infantry Brigade and a field regiment
to be landed, it eventually placed General Alexander in a difficult position and led

to his forces being nearly cut off, as described in his report. On balance I am satisfied that we gained by the delay.

OPERATIONS AFTER FALL OF RANGOON.

22. Once Rangoon had fallen, there was comparatively little that G.H.Q. in India could do to influence the operations in Burma. Until the road from Assam was completed, reinforcements of personnel and stores could only be sent in by air, and the number of transport aircraft was extremely limited.

The chief requirement of the forces in Burma at this time, British and Chinese, was air support, which India was unable to provide in the necessary strength. At first it was hoped to maintain the ascendancy which our air forces in Burma had so far held over the Japanese in spite of great numerical inferiority. The loss of the port of Rangoon, however, stopped the flow of R.A.F. personnel and equipment planned by the Air Ministry, and the loss of the airfield organisation in Southern Burma greatly affected air operations. Once Rangoon had gone, the maximum force that could be maintained in Upper Burma from the resources available was one Bomber Squadron, one Fighter Squadron and one Army Co-operation Flight, in addition to one A.V.G. Fighter Squadron. It was decided to form also a mixed Wing of one Fighter, one Bomber and one G.R. Squadron at Akyab. Shortage of aircraft, however, prevented this Wing being fully formed and with the exception of a few obsolescent fighters, all the serviceable operational aircraft – fighters and bombers – were absorbed by the formation of the Wing in Upper Burma. This Wing was based at Magwe, the only airfield left in Burma with any degree of warning. On the 21st and 22nd March, over a period of some 24 hours, it was attacked by the enemy in force. The available Hurricanes and Blenheims had been engaged in the early morning of the 21st against an enemy concentration of aircraft at Mingaladon on which they had inflicted severe losses. When the enemy retaliated only 12 of our fighters were serviceable and able to take off to engage the first raid. Although four of the enemy were shot down and two were damaged, the weight of attack got home. In his attacks the enemy made Magwe temporarily untenable for first-line aircraft and destroyed or rendered unserviceable 17 bombers and fighters on the ground. The cause of this reverse was our weakness in fighters, the failure of the warning system and an almost complete absence of aircraft pens and dispersal arrangements. The loss of these aircraft, which constituted practically the only air force available at the time, and the withdrawal of the R.A.F. to Lashio on the northern frontier of Burma and Loiwing in China, several hundred miles further north, made the support of the Burma Army an extremely difficult problem. Aircraft were only reaching India in small numbers, and it was essential to organise the defence of Calcutta and of Ceylon. I had reluctantly to decide that I must use the air forces reaching India to build up a defence in that country, and that I could not afford the heavy losses that Japanese numerical superiority, the lack of training of our air squadrons, the absence of a warning system and the difficult flying conditions in Upper Burma were bound to cause in an attempt to give air support to the forces in Burma. The

Japanese air arm had therefore almost a free hand in the later stages of the Burma campaign, and it was fortunate for us that they failed to take full advantage of their opportunity.

23. I had little confidence in being able to prevent the Japanese from reaching the Burma oilfields at Yenangyaung or from occupying Mandalay if they made a determined attack on these objectives. We could not relieve or reinforce our troops of whom the majority had been fighting continuously for some months in difficult conditions, while the enemy had practically unlimited powers of reinforcing his land and air effort. During March and April he increased his forces in Burma by three divisions and gradually drove back the Chinese and ourselves.

I hoped that we might still manage to retain a hold on Upper Burma north of Mandalay and a common front with the Chinese. I discussed with General Alexander during a visit which I paid to Burma at the end of March his dispositions in the event of a withdrawal north of Mandalay being necessary, and we decided that a part of the Imperial Forces might withdraw with the Chinese on Lashio and possibly even into China.

In the end the sudden break through of the enemy into the Shan States and quick capture of Lashio, together with the enemy threat up the Chindwin against the road into Assam, led to the whole of the Imperial Forces withdrawing by Kalewa and Tamu into India. This was agreed with the Chinese who decided to withdraw the Fifth Army up the Irrawaddy valley on Bhamo and Myitkyina.

24. The defence of the Andaman Islands was included in the defence of Burma during most of this period. Its military importance lay in its seaplane base, in the possibility of establishing an aerodrome there, and in its potential value to the enemy as a submarine base. The original garrison was one British company. For security against a Japanese raid a battalion of Gurkhas was added early in January. When it became obvious that Rangoon could not be held, it was decided to withdraw the whole garrison, which was successfully carried out on 12th March. On 23rd March the Japanese occupied Port Blair.

Akyab was held till early in May when Japanese infiltration by land and sea and attack by air made it obvious that it would require an effort disproportionate to its military value to hold it any longer, since it could no longer be used as an air base. The garrison and naval patrol were therefore withdrawn.

SUMMARY OF BURMA CAMPAIGN.

25. The loss of Burma has been from a strategical point of view our most serious reverse of the Japanese war. It has deprived our Chinese allies of a flow of munitions to continue their long resistance; it has made the establishment of air bases within effective range of Japan a matter of extreme difficulty; it has exposed India to a serious threat of invasion; and it has had a disastrous effect on British prestige in the East. The reasons for this reverse merit some examination.

26. The unpreparedness of Burma for war and its causes have already been mentioned; and I have recorded my conviction that to place the control of operations

in Burma under a Far Eastern Command instead of under India was an error from the military point of view which it would require strong political reasons to justify.

27. From a geographical point of view the defence of Burma against an attack from Thailand was an awkward commitment. The fact that there was practically speaking only one means of entry into the country, by the port of Rangoon, was a source of weakness; and this port lay within a comparatively short range of enemy airfields in Thailand. The long narrow strip of Tenasserim, over 400 miles long and nowhere much more than 40 miles broad, was not easily defensible, while in the enemy's possession it was a threat both by air (there were several excellent aerodromes) and by sea.

If Moulmein in Upper Tenasserim fell, and here again the ground gave little scope for defence in depth, Rangoon was very closely threatened; while a force defending Rangoon against an enemy advancing from the line of the Salween River had the disadvantage of fighting on a front parallel to its communications and with its base close behind, almost outside, its right flank.

If ever there was a country where attack was the best form of defence it was Burma. Unfortunately the means were not available.

28. Such plans and preparations as had been made for the defence of Burma suffered from three misconceptions:

(*a*) that the main attack would be directed against Kengtung in the Southern Shan States, the only place to which there were good communications in Thailand – a motor road from a railhead at Lampang. Actually the Japanese made no attempt to use this obvious route.

(*b*) that our air force would be able to prevent the enemy using the limited approaches to the frontier. The whole experience of this war is that air forces cannot prevent the use of a road or railway; and anyway there were no bombers in Burma.

(*c*) that the natural difficulties of the country on the frontier, few and indifferent tracks, hills and thick jungle and the formidable natural obstacle of the Salween River, would restrict the numbers the enemy could employ and dictate the direction in which he used them. Actually, we found ourselves up against a new feature in warfare – an enemy fully armed, disciplined, and trained on the continental model using the mobility, independence of communications and unorthodox tactics of the savage in thick jungle. It was perhaps little wonder that our troops were out-manoeuvred and became bewildered.

29. British military authorities have seldom realised that an Intelligence system cannot be improvised and requires to be built up over a period of years. The study of Intelligence in peace is not encouraged and officers who specialise in it are apt to be regarded with suspicion. The operations in Burma are a striking example of the penalty we pay in war for this neglect.

30. There was never sufficient naval force to give any effective naval support during the Burma Campaign; and its absence made the G.O.C. always anxious about a landing near Rangoon. Actually the Japanese made no attempt at sea-borne invasion nor were any ships from convoys to Rangoon ever lost from enemy action.

Commodore Graham, R.N., with small forces did some good work in the protection of Akyab and the coast to the south in the later stages of the campaign.

The situation as regards air support has been sufficiently indicated in the narratives of General Hutton and General Alexander. I constantly endeavoured to obtain air reinforcements for Burma but they were not available.

The operations are a striking example of the importance of an adequate warning system, which conditions in Burma made it extremely difficult to organise.

The Japanese air force did not show itself particularly efficient or formidable in Burma, either in bombing or fighting. Our small air forces, skilfully and boldly handled, were more than a match for the enemy as long as good airfields and warnings were available.

Casualties and material damage from air attack were small but the moral effects were considerable. This should not be so with well-trained and disciplined troops.

I should like to express my grateful thanks to Colonel (now Brigadier General) G. Chennault and to all the officers and men of the A.V.G. who did such skilful and gallant work in the defence of Rangoon.

I should also like to record the good services of Air Vice-Marshal Stevenson, who commanded the air forces in Burma from January, 1942, onwards, and of his predecessor Group-Captain Manning.

32. The troops who fought in the Burma campaign were subjected to a very severe strain. They were opposed by a well-trained, vigorous and determined enemy, usually superior in numbers; they had to fight in a type of country and under conditions quite unfamiliar to the majority; they had no relief and very little rest during more than five months, in the later stages they were almost entirely deprived of air support. After the fall of Rangoon they felt themselves cut off from outside help and from all amenities. Every effort was made to send mails and a supply of stores to Burma, but the limitations of air transport made it impossible to meet the full needs. Rations, however, thanks to the efforts of the administrative staff, were not short.

The importance of the Fifth Column in Burma has been exaggerated; the number of actual rebels who took arms against us or assisted the enemy was probably small. But the moral effect on the soldier of the knowledge that a proportion of the population was potentially hostile and treacherous was considerable. The defection of large numbers of the men of the units of the Burma Army also had a depressing effect.

In the circumstances the troops put up a remarkable performance and showed a fine fighting spirit.

Particular mention should be made of the 7 Armoured Brigade under Brigadier J.H. Anstice (7 Hussars, 2 Royal Tank Regiment, 414 Battery (Essex Yeomanry) R.H.A., A Battery 95 Anti-Tank Regiment), who, from their arrival in Burma in the third week of February till the end of the campaign, formed the mainstay of the Burma Army and kept up a very high standard of morale and efficiency. Owing to the fact that no tanks had been available in India, the infantry in Burma had had no practice in co-operation with armoured forces, which was in consequence elementary.

The 1 Indian Field Artillery Regiment, which went straight into action on landing at Rangoon and was continually engaged to the end of the campaign, greatly distinguished itself.

33. Lieut.-General Hutton did most valuable work in placing Burma on a war footing so far as could be done in the very limited time available. To reorganise the whole military system and to endeavour to create an administrative lay-out practically from nothing, while at the same time controlling difficult operations in the field, threw a very heavy strain on him. As C.G.S. to General Alexander he continued to give most valuable service till the arrival of Major-General Winterton.

I should like also here to pay a tribute to the work previously done by him as C.G.S. in India during the expansion of the Indian Army, which owes much to his organizing ability.

34. General Alexander took over an extremely difficult situation and a somewhat shaken and disorganised army. By his cool and inspiring leadership he did everything possible during the remainder of the campaign to check the Japanese advance and to keep the army together. He also succeeded in establishing and maintaining good relations with the Chinese, though, as he says, a real combined command, owing to the difference in outlook and methods, was not possible.

35. Generally speaking, the standard of leadership of the Army in Burma was high. Lieut.-General Slim, Commanding the Burma Corps, Major-General Cowan, Commanding the 17 Indian Division, Major-General Bruce-Scott, Commanding the 1 Burma Division, were all good and resolute commanders; and it was largely due to their efforts that the enemy's superior numbers were kept at bay for so long and the final withdrawal so skilfully conducted. The majority of the brigade and battalion commanders also showed themselves competent and determined leaders.

36. Of the staff officers Major-General Goddard in charge of administration under both General Hutton and General Alexander, did outstanding work and was quite untiring. On the General Staff side Brigadier Davies, first with General Hutton and later under General Slim in the Burma Corps, did work of a high order.

The work of Major-General Wakely in charge of the lines of communication also deserves special mention.

37. The bearing and endurance of the Chinese troops who fought in Burma created a favourable impression. General J. Stilwell of the United States Army, who was placed by the Generalissimo in command of the Chinese troops in Burma, and General Lo Cho-Ying, who commanded the Fifth and Sixth Armies, were always ready to co-operate, although Chinese methods usually resulted in considerable delay in the execution of orders to put into effect the plans that had been concerted.

I should like to record the great impression that the Generalissimo, Marshal Chiang Kai-Shek, made on all commanders who met him; and to express my gratitude for the wholehearted assistance he gave in the attempt to hold Burma.

38. The Civil Administration in Burma was faced suddenly by a series of most difficult problems due to the rapid Japanese advance, the bombing of Rangoon and the flight of a large part of the population. As might have been expected, parts of the administration stood the test well and parts collapsed. The Governor, H.E. Sir Reginald Dorman-Smith, was always whole-hearted in his co-operation with the military, and his Counsellor, The Honourable Mr. John Wise, was also extremely helpful. But some of the executive branches, such as the Police, tended to break down under the strain.

Denial of essential materials to the enemy was on the whole effectively carried out. The oil refinery at Syriam, just outside Rangoon, and the oilfields at Yenangyaung were very thoroughly destroyed.

39. As will have been seen, much depended in the later stages on how quickly the process of driving a road from India to Burma could be accomplished. The project of a road between Assam and Upper Burma had been the subject of discussion for some years previous to the war, but no action had been taken. As a military necessity, it began to take shape in the late autumn of 1941; the actual orders to begin work at all speed were issued in the middle of December. India was to widen the metalled road already existing from Dimapur to Imphal in Manipur State (135 miles) and to make a road from Imphal to Tamu (65 miles) where only a bridle track existed. Burma Government was to make an all weather road from Tamu to Kalewa and thence to Ye-U (approximately 190 miles) between which places only a fair-weather cart track existed.

Up to February work inside India proceeded somewhat slowly, but thenceforward was pushed on with all possible speed. A motor road, not metalled, reached Tamu just in time for the withdrawal of the Burma Army. Maintenance by this road during the wet season would, however, have been impossible. Great credit is due to Major-General Wood who was specially placed in charge of the project in March, 1942, for the energy with which he furthered the completion of the road, and to Brigadier Gilpin, R.E., and the engineers under him for a fine piece of work in difficult conditions.

Owing to various difficulties, little work was ever done by the Burma Government on the Tamu-Ye-U sector and eventually India had to undertake to complete it. The withdrawal took place before work on an all-weather road could be begun; but some very good work was done in a very short time to facilitate the withdrawal by improvement of the existing cart track.

Report by Lieut.-General T.J Hutton, C.B., M.C., on Operations in Burma from 27th December, 1941, to 5th March, 1942.

I. SITUATION ON ASSUMING COMMAND.

1. *Staff and Services.* I arrived in Rangoon on 27th December and assumed command forthwith. I should like here to pay a tribute to the endeavours made by my predecessor, Lieut.-General D.K. MacLeod, in spite of an inadequate staff and inadequate resources, to prepare the country for war.

Briefly, the position was as follows. The H.Q. staff was totally inadequate and a few overworked staff officers were struggling to compete with problems quite beyond their powers. This was especially the case with the General and Administrative staffs on whose shoulders rested the responsibility for the direction of policy. There was no intelligence staff worthy of the name. For a time there was a serious shortage of cipher personnel and clerks. This was eventually remedied by the employment of a number of women who were organised early in January in an enrolled unit of the Women's Auxiliary Service, Burma.

Such nucleus of services, base or L. of C. organisations as existed consisted of units raised in Burma, partially trained and very weak in Governor's Commissioned Officers (G.C.Os.) and N.C.Os. and with few trained reserves. While these units did useful work for a time they eventually became unreliable and there were a considerable number of desertions.

2. *Intelligence.* No arrangements had been made to provide for external intelligence before the war and as a result we were usually in complete ignorance of what was happening just over the Thailand border. The same applied as regards internal intelligence. The possibility that the country might be invaded and that it might be desirable to "leave behind" a suitable organisation to give us information had not apparently been considered. Efforts were of course made at once to remedy the defect but it is not a thing that can be done in a hurry.

3. *Responsibilities of Army Headquarters (A.H.Q.).* A H.Q. Army in Burma was at the same time a War Office, a G.H.Q., a Corps H.Q. and a L. of C. H.Q. (owing to the absence of any L. of C. staff). A.H.Q. had, as such, responsibilities which covered exactly the same field as G.H.Q. in India.

This organisation, or lack of it, clogged the whole machine. It also imposed an intolerable burden on the G.O.C. It was impossible for me with my vast responsibilities to keep detailed control of operations on 17 Indian Division's front and it was necessary to allow wide discretion to the Divisional Commander. Unfortunately on practically every occasion when a serious situation arose, I happened to be away visiting some other part of my command. A Corps H.Q was essential from the first, it was eventually formed after the loss of Rangoon.

4. *The Burma Rifles.* The fighting troops consisted mainly of Burma Rifles. This force was in the process of expansion, a process which greatly accentuated its former weaknesses. Consisting of four different races, Chins, Kachins, Karens and Burmese, speaking different languages which few of the officers understood, it was of very limited value in serious warfare. The G.C.Os. and N.C.Os. were all very junior and inexperienced, some of the former having only two years' service. The language commonly used in the Army was Hindustani which was a foreign language to all the personnel, including of course the officers; of the latter it was hardly likely that the best regular officers would be attracted by service in the Corps – though many of them did good work. The Emergency Commissioned Officers (E.C.Os.) who formed the majority were of exceptionally good quality and consisted mostly of members of big firms, who had had extensive experience of conditions in the jungle. Their knowledge of local languages was in most cases good and many also had a smattering of Hindustani.

It was soon discovered that while these units were of considerable value for reconnaissance and patrol work in the jungle, they were not as a whole fit to stand the test of serious operations against an enemy like the Japanese. Eventually a large proportion of the Burmese and some of the Karens deserted, and the active battalions had to be reconstituted without them.

The Sappers and Miners, Army Service Corps, Hospital Corps, etc., were all of similar personnel, mostly Burmese, and the results were similar.

This question has been dealt with in some detail because it vitally affected the campaign. Instead of Indian battalions stiffening, as was hoped, the Burma Rifles, the effect was exactly the opposite. However, as more than half the forces available consisted of Burma Rifles there was no alternative to making use of them even after their lack of training began to be disclosed. The possible failure of the attenuated services behind the Army, especially M.T., was a source of constant anxiety. As regards equipment and transport the situation was equally serious and no units had their full scale and some, such as signal units and A.A. batteries, had practically none. The force, such as it was, was quite unprepared for war. Reserves were of course practically nil.

5. *Levies.* As regards levies or guerrillas, efforts had already been made to start an organisation in the Shan States. This was now extended to the Karen country of North Tenasserim. Although started very late in the day it was undoubtedly of value in providing a foundation for larger scale operations in the future, a deterrent to Japanese infiltration of the hills in that area and a valuable threat to the so-called free Burmese of the plains below.

6. *Burma Frontier Force.* There was also the Burma Frontier Force of the equivalent of six battalions which had only just been taken over by the Army from the Civil Administration, but the Inspector-General remained responsible for the administration of the force. It consisted for the most part of good Indian personnel but was numerically weak in officers and neither its organisation nor its training really fitted it to take part in active operations against a first-class enemy.

7. *British and Indian Troops.* The remainder of the troops available consisted of two British battalions, two Indian infantry brigades and one Mountain Regiment.

8. *Enemy Forces.* Very little was known about the enemy owing both to the lack of intelligence and of aircraft for reconnaissance. The thick jungle country rendered air or even ground reconnaissance very unproductive. It was known, however, that there were three or four Japanese divisions available in Thailand of which at least two could probably be made available for operations against Burma. In view of the weak state of our forces and the approach of the monsoon there appeared to be every reason why the Japanese should invade Burma as early as possible.

9. *Appreciation.* A full appreciation of the defence problem of Burma was completed by me on 10th January. It formed the basis of policy throughout the period of my command. I should like here to refer to the valuable help and assistance given me throughout my tenure of command by my B.G.S., Brig. H.L. Davies, whose judgment and military knowledge proved invaluable in dealing with a most difficult situation.

10. *Bombing of Rangoon.* On the 23rd December and again on the 25th December just before I arrived, Rangoon was bombed by a large force of enemy aircraft. These attacks were directed against the dock area and in the neighbourhood of the power station. Extensive damage was caused by fires among the crowded wooden houses and huts in the bombed area and civilian casualties due mainly to anti-personnel bombs were very heavy indeed, amounting to approximately 1,700–2,000 people killed. Very little damage of a military nature occurred and the only damage to the docks was the destruction of one transit shed.

11. *Effects of Bombing.* The bombing had, however, a very serious repercussion as servants, menials, all subordinate employees, and coolies including the dock labourers, at once commenced to leave the town. As there were many ships loaded with military stores for the Army and with Lease and Lend stores for China waiting discharge, the results were serious.

Practically all Government offices, shops, markets, hospitals etc., lost almost the whole of their subordinate staffs as also did the Ordnance, Military Works, Transportation services, etc. For a time there was in some cases great difficulty in obtaining and preparing food as almost all servants, cooks, etc., had also departed.

Rangoon town was not raided again; thereafter the enemy directed all his efforts against the aerodrome at Mingaladon and that neighbourhood. As a result of this policy labour gradually regained confidence and a useful proportion returned to work.

Taken as a whole, however, the situation was never restored. Military units for essential work became available only on a very limited scale and the working of all transportation, works, labour, etc., for services was most precarious throughout the period prior to the fall of Rangoon.

12. The organisation of the A.R.P. services in Burma was carried out by Mr. de Graff Hunter who did most excellent work in spite of great difficulties in securing suitable personnel. This organisation, like others based on locally recruited personnel, soon showed a tendency to disintegrate in face of attack.

13. *Fighter Successes.* During the first two air raids over Rangoon the R.A.F. and A.V.G. fighters were most successful and not less than 61 enemy first-line bombers and fighters were claimed as destroyed on these two days. A further large number were shot down during subsequent raids.

It is significant to note that on no occasion were the oil installations in the Rangoon area attacked and later we were able to remove with confidence for use elsewhere a proportion of the A.A. artillery detailed for the defence of Syriam.

14. *Observer Corps.* I should here like to draw attention to the fact that until the Central Telephone Exchange in Rangoon closed down on the 28th February no enemy air raid reached the Rangoon area without warning passed by the Observer Corps posts. Until Tenasserim was lost the average period of warning was forty minutes but this of course gradually decreased as the enemy closed in on Rangoon.

In all cases the Observer Posts were manned by local inhabitants who passed the warning by pre-arranged codes over the Posts and Telegraphs or Railway systems, the average time taken to pass a warning message being about two minutes. The success of the system depended on the wholehearted support of the Posts and Telegraphs officials and in particular thanks are due to Mr. Nesbitt-Hawes the D.G., P. and T., who devised the communication system and who until the last was always ready to give his personal attention to any demand made on his Department, also to Major Taylor who was the officer in charge of the whole of the warning system in Burma.

15. *A.A. Artillery.* When I arrived in Burma some A.A. equipment for the locally raised Burma Auxiliary Force (B.A.F.) units had just come from India. Later on, both British and Indian light and heavy batteries arrived and it was possible to organise a thin scale of defence for vital points. All units acquitted themselves well and a very considerable number of enemy aircraft were shot down – including one by the third shot fired by the 1 Heavy A.A. Regiment B.A.F.

II. REINFORCEMENT POLICY.

16. *Reinforcements.* The first reinforcement to reach Burma was the 46 Indian Infantry Brigade which arrived towards the end of January in time to take part in the fighting west of the River Salween. It consisted of young troops and had been destined for Iraq where it was intended it should complete its training. It was not really fit for active operations without further training and had no experience in jungle warfare.

The only other reinforcements in sight from India consisted of six Indian battalions which it was intended to withdraw from the frontier and equip on the lower scale for service overseas.

These eventually constituted the 48 Indian Infantry Brigade, consisting entirely of Gurkhas which arrived about 1st February, and did very good work on the Bilin River, and the 63 Indian Infantry Brigade, which arrived just before the fall of Rangoon. Two East African Brigades which had done excellent service in the Italian campaign, were accepted by India for service in Burma, one to arrive at the end of January and one a month later. Neither of these materialised, though it was only late in February that Burma was informed that they had been diverted elsewhere. There is no doubt that they would have been invaluable at a critical period.

17. *British Battalions.* A further reinforcement sent in response to my urgent demands for British troops, both for internal security, as reinforcements to 17 Indian Division, and for reasons of morale, consisted of three British battalions taken from the garrison of India. One, the 2 D.W.R. (Duke of Wellington's Regiment), arrived in time to take part in the battle of the Sittang, and the others, 1 Cameronians and 1 W. Yorks (West Yorkshire Regiment) did very good work during the fighting near Pegu. These battalions had been given only a few days notice of mobilization and embarkation and some were incomplete in transport, but none the less showed magnificent spirit throughout the operations – a tribute to the value of trained and experienced British troops even though not specially trained for jungle warfare conditions.

18. *Armoured Troops.* A further reinforcement, which proved invaluable, was the 7 Armoured Brigade whose fighting spirit and efficiency were the admiration of the whole Army. Unfortunately it only arrived after the battle of Sittang when it was instrumental in enabling the 17 Indian Division to reorganise round Pegu.

19. *Summary.* It will be seen, therefore, that the reinforcements provided for Burma after the outbreak of war consisted of an Armoured Brigade, three British battalions and three Indian brigades. Of these only two infantry brigades arrived before the battle of the Sittang, which, as will be seen later, practically settled the fate of Rangoon.

The three Indian Brigades, though good material, all suffered from the weakness of having a large proportion of inexperienced officers and recruits in their ranks, and also from having had no training in jungle warfare. The 48 Indian Infantry Brigade did especially well, and also some of the Battalions of the 46 Indian Brigade. As regards the 63 Indian Infantry Brigade, I was informed by General Hartley that it required a period of training before being employed in operations.

III. CO-OPERATION WITH THE CHINESE.

20. *Situation on Arrival.* On my arrival in Burma one regiment of 93 Division "Force Trellis" was already moving towards the Southern Shan States with the object of taking over the defence of the Mekong River, west of the road Kengtung – Mongpayak, with H.Q. at Mongyawng.

The rest of the Division was located about Puerh in China and we were responsible for supplying it with rice.

The remainder of the Sixth Army, which included the 49 and 55 Divisions was stationed near Paoshan on the China road. The Fifth Army was on the Yunnan – Kweichow border. Shortly afterwards the 49 Division, "Force Zigzag," moved up to the border of Wanting in reserve.

21. *Command.* It had been laid down by the Generalissimo that all Chinese troops were to be under my command and he was most insistent that all breaches of discipline were to be reported to him personally. He was anxious, however, that they should be given their own area and not be mixed up with our own troops. We were to be responsible for the supply of rice and any other requirements that could be spared including if possible medical stores and mosquito nets.

On about 15th January, 1942, I visited Kengtung and discussed the possible move of the remainder of the 93 Division from China to the Kengtung area. On 19th January when the situation in Tenasserim area became serious, the move of this Division was ordered and 1 Burma Brigade gradually withdrew from their positions south-east of Kengtung.

It was laid down in my directive that no additional Chinese troops were to be brought into Burma without reference to H.Q. South-West Pacific Command (A.B.D.A. Command). On 21st January, 1942, however, I obtained General Wavell's permission to bring in another Chinese Division, the 49; the Governor was consulted and agreed.

On 29th January it was decided that the 49 Division should come into the Southern Shan States via Lashio, and take over the area east of the River Salween about Takaw, and that 55 Division should move forward to Wanting (Chinese frontier) to complete training and equipment.

22. *The Fifth Army.* On 31st January I sent a personal cable to General Wavell saying that the Chinese appeared anxious to send us the Fifth Army and requested permission to make arrangements with General Hou for moving them to Lashio where they would be readily available either for the defence of Burma or for offensive operations against Thailand. I pointed out that such an arrangement would enable us to concentrate all our own forces for the defence of Rangoon, and to refute any accusations by the Chinese that we were unwilling to accept the assistance offered.

23. *Stores and Equipment.* Up till now, war stores for 93 Division had been brought in by the Puerh route. It was now suggested that everything should in future be brought via Lashio and an ordnance dump be established at that place.

About this time there was considerable difficulty over "Lease and Lend" stores. A crisis was precipitated by a number of Chinese lorries etc. being requisitioned by the Army and R.A.F. in Rangoon, with the agreement of the U.S.A. representatives who discussed the matter with General Wavell. This was unfortunate but quite accidental, those concerned being unaware of the political importance of this material. The Chinese eventually agreed to a number of stores vital to the defence of Burma being released to Burma Army.

24. *Meeting with the Generalissimo.* On 2nd February I started for Chungking by air to meet the Generalissimo, but unfortunately my aircraft crashed at night on the way to Lashio. On arrival I heard that General Wavell was expected at Rangoon to meet the Generalissimo, but owing to the lack of any definite news of his date of arrival the latter, who had arrived at Lashio, decided to proceed direct to India and to settle with me the policy to be pursued in respect of co-operation. Our discussion was in every respect most satisfactory and he agreed to all my proposals and in particular to take over the front about Toungoo with the Fifth Army which was in readiness to enter Burma for that purpose.

The Chinese Minister for War issued orders for the move of the rest of the Sixth Army (less 93 Division already there) on 3rd February. In that order it was stated that "H.Q. Sixth Army after moving into Burma will come under orders of G.O.C. Burma."

On 11th February I visited Taunggyi and met the Chinese representative there. At that meeting it was decided that 55 Division would go to area Bawlake and not remain in reserve at Loilem. Chinese Fifth Army started moving to area Toungoo on about 29th February but only 200 Division arrived in Burma before the loss of Rangoon.

It will be seen from the above summary that every effort was made to get more Chinese reinforcements into Burma. It is unnecessary here to go into the reasons for the delays that occurred. Many of them, due to administrative reasons, were inevitable, others were due to the Chinese system of command and administration which involved getting confirming orders from the Generalissimo before any move of importance could be carried out.

25. *Liaison Arrangements.* I was greatly assisted in these arrangements by General Dennys whose untimely death in an air accident was a serious blow to the cause of co-operation with the Chinese. As the Chinese had no transport and no administrative or medical services, and our own resources were already inadequate, we were forced from the beginning to improvise an organisation for them. A liaison staff was built up on the basis of one officer and one civil representative to be attached to each division and Army; these were added to later as occasion required. Each was supplied with W/T taken from our own meagre resources.

At H.Q. it was proposed to have General Dennys as Chief Liaison Officer, with Brigadier J.C. Martin as Chief Administrative Liaison Officer, and another Brigadier, who did not join till later, as G.S. Liaison Officer. The H.Q. staff consisted mainly therefore of Brigadier Martin, Colonel Hobson and Colonel Holmes who did magnificent work with most inadequate resources and spared no pains to smooth the way for our Chinese Allies. The fact that eventually we were able to move, feed and maintain an army of some 95,000 men including 28 and 38 Divisions, without the help of any regular administrative units at all, either British or Chinese, is a remarkable example of successful improvisation.

26. *Medical.* We were fortunate in being able to secure for the use of the Chinese an American Missionary Ambulance Unit under Dr. Seagrave. It was supplied by us with a certain amount of medical stores and did very good work. We were also able eventually to place a certain number of our own medical units at the disposal of the Chinese. There was in fact no possible alternative.

27. *Armament.* It should be noted here that while the Chinese units were fairly well equipped with L.M.Gs., mortars, etc., they had very little artillery. They had on the average only one weapon for three men so that the fire power of a division was about equal to that of one of our brigades. The balance of men were used as porters, for employments or for digging but were always available to replace casualties. The results of this organisation were not therefore as bad as might be expected.

28. *Air Support.* It was a great disappointment to the Chinese that throughout the operations we were unable to provide them with any effective air support. After their experience in China they placed great reliance on this factor and its absence undoubtedly affected their morale.

29. *Policy as regards Employment of Chinese Troops.* It was my general policy to concentrate as early as possible the whole of the Imperial Forces available in the south of Burma with the object of holding up the Japanese advance in the area where they had the best communications and presented the greatest threat to Rangoon and the communications with China. Sooner or later I hoped to develop an offensive into Thailand based on Moulmein.

At the same time I hoped that the Chinese forces would advance into Northern Thailand and keep occupied a considerable number of the enemy forces. Although communications were poor according to our standards the fact that an abundance of rice was available in Northern Thailand made this region particularly suitable for an offensive by the Chinese. Unfortunately this offensive, though practicable, never took place. The Generalissimo did not consider the Sixth Army by itself to be strong enough to undertake it, and the course of operations in the south rendered it more important to use the Fifth Army to relieve 1 Burma Division towards Toungoo than to deploy it further north on the chance that an offensive would be undertaken in time to relieve the situation. Actually the last division of Sixth Army had only just begun to reach its forward positions in the Northern Shan States at the time of the fall of Rangoon.

30. *Relations with the Chinese.* Finally I should like to pay a tribute to the Generalissimo for his wholehearted support and co-operation throughout the operations and to the senior officers of the Chinese forces under my command whose fighting spirit and appreciation of the problems involved, and the difficulties under which we laboured, evoked my warmest admiration. In particular I should like to mention-

Lt.-General Kan Li Chu, Commander, Sixth Army.
Lt.-General Lu Kuo Ch'uan, 93 Division.

Major-General Fisher T. How, Chief Liasion Officer at my H.Q.

Colonel Gordon W.K. Chu, Assistant Liaison Officer at my H.Q.

It may be desirable to mention in conclusion that we treated the Chinese throughout on a basis of complete equality and did everything possible to overcome the difficulties arising from lack of mutual confidence in the past and from the series of military reverses we suffered in Burma and elsewhere, which natually lowered our prestige.

IV. AIR SUPPORT.

31. *Preparations.* It is unnecessary here to refer in detail to air operations which will no doubt be described by Air Vice-Marshal D.F. Stevenson, who arrived in Burma to assume command on about 1st January. His predecessor, Gp. Capt. E.R. Manning, R.A.F., had done everything possible to prepare aerodromes and to ensure the successful employment of the large air force it was hoped would be made available in this theatre.

32. *Weakness of Air Forces.* Actually, however, these forces never arrived in sufficient strength materially to affect operations on land, though the outstanding successes of the fighters of the A.V.G. and our own forces achieved a very considerable mastery of the air over Rangoon. The air battle of Rangoon was a brilliant example of the achievement of well trained personnel and aircraft of high performance against vastly superior numbers. This success has perhaps led to the impression that during the operations covered by this report we were in the happy position of having air superiority. This is definitely incorrect and in the battle zone our troops were subject to frequent attack from the air throughout the operations.

Had a sufficient number of bombers been made available a very effective use of these might have been made against the enemy's communications with Malaya. Unfortunately the weakness of our land forces resulted in the loss of the aerodromes which were so well placed for the purpose of offensive air operations and in the end lost us much of the warning system, already referred to above, to which our successes in the air were very largely due.

33. *Close Support.* As regards the close support of our land forces every effort was made by the A.O.C. to make the best use of the small forces available. Their inferiority in numbers, however, rendered it necessary to employ most of them in operations against the enemy air forces or in "beating up" enemy aircraft on the ground. These latter operations were conducted with very marked success. In addition to keeping in check the enemy's aircraft which endeavoured to attack our troops on the ground, very successful co-operation was given during the period immediately after the loss of Moulmein. Subsequent intelligence reports show that very considerable casualties were inflicted on the enemy. Co-operation with the Army was made especially difficult by the thick jungle and lack of intelligence which rendered it almost impossible to indicate suitable targets even when aircraft were available. Owing to the thick country, air reconnaissance was

seldom instrumental in obtaining information of positive value, except of movements on the rivers or coastal waters and on certain roads which were visible from the air.

34. *Withdrawal of R.A.F. from Rangoon.* Owing to the loss of the ground warning system after the battle of the River Sittang, it was decided to withdraw a good deal of the R.A.F. to Akyab or Calcutta and the remainder to Magwe. This, while based no doubt on sound operational grounds, was naturally disheartening to the troops and resulted in some unfair criticism of the R.A.F. The aerodrome at Highland Queen close to Rangoon was in fact retained in use until just before the arrival of the enemy forces in its immediate vicinity. Finally I should like to pay tribute to the unfailing support and encouragement I received throughout from Air Vice-Marshal D.F. Stevenson and to the assistance he gave me in the appreciation of military problems.

V. NAVAL CO-OPERATION.

Close co-operation with such naval forces as were available, the control and escort of shipping, and the appreciation of naval problems, was obtained through the medium of Captain J.I. Hallet, R.N., and subsequently of Commodore C.M. Graham, R.N.

35. *The Burma Royal Naval Volunteer Reserve.* The B.R.N.V.R., then in its infancy, consisted of a few armed launches. Its officers were British and Burman and the ratings were almost wholly Burman. It maintained an examination service at the mouth of the Rangoon river, carried out minesweeping and furnished a Mergui Archipelago patrol. During the operations on the Tenasserim Coast every possible assistance was given by these craft both in reconnaissance and in the withdrawal of our forces from Mergui, Tavoy, and Moulmein which is referred to elsewhere. In spite of their inadequate numbers they undoubtedly proved a considerable deterrent to coastal operations of the type employed by the enemy with so much success off the coast of Malaya. Eventually, owing to desertions, and other causes, the Burma Navy, like the "Burma Army" largely disappeared but not before it had done most valuable work.

36. *Naval Assistance.* Except for one visit by a sloop of the R.I.N. sent by Commander-in-Chief East Indies in response for an urgent request for naval assistance, and the despatch of a most welcome reinforcement of 100 Marines, naval operations proper were almost entirely confined to the escort of convoys. Towards the close of the period, however, another sloop of the R.I.N. was successful in intercepting and capturing off the mouth of the Rangoon River a party of some 35 of the Free Burma Army under the leadership of a Japanese officer.

37. *Evacuation.* The successful evacuation by sea of the whole of the rear parties and protection troops left to carry out the demolitions in Rangoon, carried out under the very nose of the enemy, was highly creditable to all concerned,

including the R.A.F., who afforded air cover during the passage of the dangerous waters south-west of Rangoon.

38. *Enemy Action.* The fact that not a single transport was ever attacked by either surface craft, aircraft or submarine during the whole of the operations is a proof of the success achieved in timing the arrival and departure of convoys and the provision of air cover and seaward reconnaissance. This was not of course achieved without detriment to air operations elsewhere, and imposed a severe strain on the small air forces available.

That co-operation was so successfully achieved was largely due to the practice of holding daily, or twice daily, meetings of the three commanders and to the effort to ensure that as far as possible all communications with higher authority on major policy were sent either as from the combined commanders or else were the subject of inter-service agreement before despatch.

39. *Higher Command.* Finally it is necessary to point out that the fact that Burma was included in the sphere of the Commander-in-Chief Eastern Fleet and subsequently transferred to that of Commander-in-Chief East Indies rendered it especially difficult to obtain naval support or guidance as to naval policy. For a considerable period the exact definition of responsibility was very vague.

40. *Inshore Operations.* A further matter that deserves future consideration was the absence of any organisation, or of suitable craft, for inshore operations on the coast line from India to Malaya. The possibilities of such action, in close co-operation with troops or marines especially trained in boat work, was very considerable, and it is suggested that it should in future be recognised as a special branch of naval activities. Attempts were made to develop an organisation of this kind based on the detachment of 100 marines referred to above. Before they had completed their training, however, the evacuation of Rangoon rendered it necessary to withdraw them up the River Irrawaddy where they have since done most valuable work.

VI. ARMY ADMINISTRATION.

41. *Lack of Preparation.* The following remarks are virtually a summary of administrative difficulties and of the reasons for administrative shortcomings during the period of the campaign under review. That there has not been an administrative breakdown is, in my opinion, entirely due to the efforts of my Major-General in charge of Administration, Major-General E.N. Goddard, and his staff, to keep the machine working in circumstances of almost insuperable difficulty which persisted throughout the campaign.

A gloomy picture is portrayed, which is nevertheless considered to be accurate. If the campaign had been an advance, instead of a withdrawal, many of the defects and shortcomings would not have been evident (e.g. poor discipline) and others would have been of less importance.

The course of the campaign should be a warning that the civil and military administration must come on to a war footing before hostilities commence. It is unfair to the troops, to the civil population, in fact unfair to everybody, to expect our loosely knit peace time system of civil and military administration to adapt itself quickly to war conditions.

The main administrative lesson of the campaign during the period is to prove once again that unless the administrative conception from the outset is sufficiently broad operations will be hampered. This is particularly true in a withdrawal.

42. *Basis of Administrative Plan.* After I arrived in Burma, the War Office laid down that administrative preparations were to be made on the basis of a force of four divisions. Demands were made therefore for L. of C. administrative and ancillary units, including a Corps H.Q. on this basis, but owing to the passage of events none of them materialised before the loss of Rangoon. Large amounts of equipment and personnel which had been urgently demanded by Burma before my arrival, were also sent out by the War Office, but practically all failed to arrive in time. Administrative difficulties were greatly accentuated by the necessity of giving fighting units the preference in the allotment of shipping, and also by the fact that certain ships had to be turned back owing to inability to handle them in Rangoon.

43. *Insufficiency of Administrative Units.* At no time during the campaign has there been an adequate number of administrative units; transport, supply, medical, transportation, provost, rest camps and mess, ordnance, and labour units have all been less than the number required to administer the force. Improvisation has been necessary on a scale which has made confusion inevitable. The problem would have been less complicated if the administrative layout had been set up before active operations commenced.

44. *Civil Departments.* The whole conduct of the military administration has been complicated by A.H.Q. having to deal with numerous civil departments and agencies who do not realise how quickly events move in war and are thus unable to realise that it is necessary to have unified control well ahead of any likely emergency. The civil railway and inland water transport agencies could not be persuaded, until it was too late, that it was vital to have unified control and to form some military operating units. The result was a breakdown in railway transportation which prevented the backloading of valuable and vital stores from Rangoon to the extent that would otherwise have been possible; and great confusion and waste of effort in the Irrawaddy Flotilla Company.

45. *The Base.* The base must be far enough in rear of the zone of operations to obviate the need to move it. Rangoon was too far forward. Base installations should have been sited in Upper Burma before the outbreak of war.

The force was too highly equipped with M.T. for the terrain which in the main demanded a very comprehensive employment of pack transport.

The tendency of many Burma units, including administrative units, to disintegrate has caused administrative confusion and inefficiency apart from the effect on operations. Owing to demands for administrative units in the Middle

East and elsewhere, Burma was advised to raise as many of such units as she could from available indigenous material. This is not generally possible under war conditions and the personnel available were quite unreliable.

46. *Transport.* Units landed without their transport which had to be improvised. Improvised transport impaired fighting efficiency and was instrumental in lowering morale. As the theatre of operations approached Rangoon it was essential that transport should sail in the same ship (or the same convoy) as the unit to which it belonged. As it was troops had to go into battle as soon as they landed, without transport, and much equipment was lost in consequence.

Transport has been very short and but for 620 lorries presented by the Generalissimo from Lease-Lend the force would have been immobilised.

Transport for supplying the Chinese armies was obtained by taking up large amounts of civilian transport employed on the Burma road. A complete firm with its staff, workshops, spares and lorries was eventually taken over as an army unit and proved invaluable. The drivers, however, were local civilians who proved of very doubtful quality.

47. *Discipline.* The continued withdrawal and the inevitable straggling resulting from fighting in thick jungle undoubtedly affected discipline to a considerable extent. The presence of a large number of young officers and soldiers accentuated this.

It is a mistake to "make units up" with recruits and young officers just before they go on service. It would be better to send them into their first battle below strength and to make them up gradually later when the trained men have become accustomed to war conditions. Similarly it would be better to send units into battle on a low scale of equipment and transport than to make them up to a new scale to which they are unaccustomed, when they are just on the point of embarkation.

48. *Provost, etc.* The lack of Provost, Rest Camps and Mess Units has all tended to break down administration and, therefore, to impair discipline.

The units from India were undoubtedly handicapped owing to the lack of interpreters or liaison personnel who could speak the local language. Every effort was made to remedy this deficiency which had not been foreseen in pre-war plans.

The composition of brigades and divisions has constantly been changed which is not conducive to the maintenance of an esprit de corps. Great stress is laid in India on this factor during training, and it is regrettable that owing to unavoidable causes, the shortage of troops and of reinforcements, and heavy casualties, brigades and even units had to be broken up.

49. *Disembarkation.* One of the best administrative achievements during the period has been the disembarkation arrangements, especially during the period subsequent to the 21st February. Lack of civilian dock labour, frequent changes of orders, a virtual breakdown of transportation all tested the embarkation staff to

the full. Lieut.-Colonel Hallett, the chief embarkation staff officer, is to be congratulated on a very fine achievement in that disembarkation was so quickly and successfully carried out under most difficult conditions.

50. *Medical.* Medical staff had to be created and although medical conscription had been accepted it had not been enforced to any considerable extent by a committee appointed by the Burma Government. Many potential medical officers were thus lost.

The Indian Hospital Corps (I.H.C.) have been satisfactory. The Burma Hospital Corps (B.H.C.) poor originally in quality and quantity, has failed badly in the time of stress owing to mass desertions. The B.H.C. was eventually in danger of disintegrating altogether.

Sweepers, cooks, water carriers and washer-men were difficult to find after the bombing of Rangoon.

Lack of transport has been a serious handicap. Two Motor Ambulance Sections arrived with no cars. One improvised Motor Ambulance Section has never had more than 15 cars. All were Fords and all broke their backshafts. Field ambulances arrived without transport.

Every medical unit must have transport of some kind included in its War Equipment Table (W.E.T.). Field medical units must be self mobile. It is impossible to get transport from any pooled sources in a crisis, and so valuable equipment is lost.

All existing medical services were badly handicapped by the cheeseparing policy adopted when they were raised. Burma Army units were raised on a reduced scale totally inadequate for their work.

Two improvised Ambulance Trains were provided initially. They were not good, being non-corridor, but they have been of great value and have saved the situation many times. Number 3 Train was made up just before the crisis and was fortunately kept where it was intended, on the Prome line. This has time and again proved its value. Without these trains medical evacuation would have collapsed.

The initiative and resources of some members of all classes of the medical services, especially British, Indian and Karen, have been excellent on many occasions, and have frequently surmounted considerable difficulties and kept the service going.

Partly owing to the above mentioned difficulties and partly owing to the conditions of the campaign, there is no doubt that the wounded have suffered very considerable hardship. The D.M.S., Colonel Treffrey Thomson, and his staff, have made every effort to improve matters but would be the first to agree that there has been much in the medical situation to cause them very serious concern.

Apart from the difficulties met in dealing with our own casualties the virtual breakdown of the civil medical services has imposed considerable additional strain on the military organisation. Furthermore, the arrival of Chinese troops with practically no medical organisation at all has rendered it necessary to provide not only stores and equipment that could ill be spared but also medical units, staff and beds in our own hospitals.

51. *Amenities.* A great deal has been done in the face of much difficulty by Lieut.-Colonel A. Campbell, Chief Amenities Officer, to provide some small amount of amenities to the troops.

52. *Canteens.* No canteen organisation existed before the war, and although a Defence Services (Burma) Canteen was set up in January or February with the assistance of India, it never really got started.

As will easily be realised the canteen situation was a potent contributory factor in lowering the morale of both officers and men.

53. *Transportation.* The Director of Transportation arrived in the country on 29th January. There were no military transportation units whatsoever, except a Docks Operating Company which did very good work.

The railway administration was not to be convinced of the necessity of raising some military units, operating under military control, to run the railways in the operational area. India was unable to provide them and it was not found possible to raise them locally. Experience elsewhere suggests that if this had been done, the railways would have stood up to the strain better than they did. The same remarks in general apply to the Irrawaddy Flotilla Company, but the personality of the Manager, Mr. Morton, assisted by some British officers enabled the organisation to do some excellent work in the later stages after it had been taken over by the military. The lesson is that transportation must be organised for war.

VII. THE INTERNAL SITUATION.

54. *Civil Officials.* In view of the fact that I and most of my staff were entirely new to Burma we were naturally dependent on civil officials for assistance in those cases where local knowledge was required. I should like therefore to pay a tribute to the unfailing support and assistance I received throughout from the Honourable Mr. John Wise, Defence Counsellor, and by Mr. Potter, head of Military Finance.

55. *Internal Situation.* As regards the internal situation there were from the beginning, many alarmist reports. There is no doubt that the enemy had thoroughly organised their sympathisers in Burma before the outbreak of war, and received very great assistance from them. On the other hand, a larger proportion of the population and subordinate officials remained loyal than many of the British officials expected, and though there were many treacherous attacks on our troops there were also many cases of willing assistance being given to stragglers and others.

The worst feature of the situation was the attitude of undisciplined elements towards the unfortunate Indian population who were robbed and maltreated in a most shameful manner, inspite of the efforts of many well disposed Burmans to help them.

With the progress of invasion and the organisation of the so-called Free Burma Army, the situation naturally grew worse, but it is fair to say that during the period covered by this report, the traitor forces achieved remarkably little, though their presence was a constant threat which imposed a corresponding strain on our military organisation.

56. *Martial Law.* Throughout the period covered by the Report, the Government were opposed to the institution of Martial Law, partly owing to its association in the minds of the people with the civil rebellions of former years.

During the last days of Rangoon when looting, arson, etc., were already rife, it was decided to hand over the town to the military. A military commandant was appointed, but this was too late in the day to enable him to make any material improvement in the situation.

57. *Policy as regards Evacuation.* The policy of H.M.G. as regards evacuation was quite clear. If it proved to be impossible to hold Rangoon it was essential that the demolition of the oil refineries, oil storage and other important installations should be as complete as possible. It was also laid down that it was not desirable that the Army should become bottled up in Rangoon, which was in itself indefensible, but that it should if necessary withdraw in order to carry on the war in Upper Burma.

This would in any case retain for a time the possession of the oilfields, cover the projected road to India, protect important aerodromes, and perhaps most important of all, ensure our continued co-operation with the Chinese forces. A considerable period was also required to complete the necessary arrangements for the denial of the oilfields to the enemy. As regards the oil it was found possible by moving certain plant from Rangoon to develop a very considerable output of M.T. petrol and 87 octane spirit in the oilfields – amounting possibly to about two million gallons a month – a most valuable example of foresight on the part of my staff.

58. *Demolitions.* At that time all the information available pointed to the fact that if it was not possible to hold Rangoon and the oilfields, the greatest service that could be rendered to the Allied cause would be a complete denial of the oil and refinery resources of Burma. It had been suggested that the Japanese war effort might collapse for lack of oil.

This involved very detailed planning and a vast amount of highly technical preparatory work. This was carried out under the general supervision of Mr. Forster, whose enthusiasm and drive combined with his previous experience, was most valuable. He was most ably assisted by Captain Scott, R.E., and members of the various oil companies who had undertaken the work. This work, to which I gave considerable personal attention, was very fully justified by results both in Rangoon and in the oilfields. The destruction of the refineries and oil tanks was remarkably complete and all the personnel involved, military and civil, were successfully evacuated.

As regards other demolitions considerable planning and preparation was also necessary. Arrangements were made to destroy all port facilities and to sink a number of ships in places where they would prevent the use of the jetties. The power station, port and the telegraph installations, workshops, bridges, fixed defences, etc., were also successfully destroyed.

In view of the hardship involved for the civil population, without any material military advantages, of destroying the Rangoon water supply, this was left intact. The widespread destruction of rice mills or boats was avoided for similar reasons. A wholesale "scorched earth" policy was not practicable and would probably have created more problems for us, in the form of refugees, than it would for the Japanese.

59. *Refugees.* A considerable number of people, especially women and children, and including a large number of Indians, left Rangoon by sea during the early stages of the campaign. In order to provide increased facilities I took action to ensure that returning transports should be made available for this purpose. In view of subsequent events it is fortunate that evacuation on a large scale did take place.

A large number of Indians evacuated by walking across the hills from Prome to Taungup, whence they could be cleared to Chittagong in small craft. Lack of food, water and medical attention on the route caused much suffering and many deaths including a large number from cholera. Cholera was also present in the area south of Prome and a serious epidemic was anticipated.

60. *Evacuation Plans.* The arrangements for evacuating Rangoon were in three stages. The warning stage during which all non-essential personnel would be encouraged to depart leaving only those required to run essential services. The second stage in which the final arrangements for demolition, etc., would be completed and all civilians not required in connection with this work would be evacuated. Finally, the demolition stage on completion of which all the personnel concerned and the military for guarding them were to depart in transport for which special arrangements had been made.

61. *Route of Evacuation.* The route of evacuation for the majority of the population was inevitably the main Mandalay road and railway. The proximity of the enemy to this line after the battle of the Sittang and the small forces available to cover it rendered it very important that the first stage should not be left too late. The unreliability of the railway transportation personnel was another factor and it was only by the closest margin that the last few trains succeeded in getting away. Evacuation by the Prome route was of course possible, but the fact that the railway ended at that point and the presence of cholera and serious unrest made it undesirable to use it more than necessary. Another factor was the importance of avoiding serious congestion on either route both of which were of course essential for military purposes.

A further difficulty arose from the fact that Rangoon was only 80 miles southwest of Pegu and that the Pegu road joined the Prome road 21 miles north of

Rangoon. Unless therefore personnel were moved out of Rangoon City in good time they might well find themselves cut off from the north.

The preparation of the above measures naturally took considerable time and imposed a severe burden on an already overworked staff. In the event the interval between stage 1 and stage 2 was considerably longer than was anticipated, partly owing to lack of pressure on the part of the enemy after the battle at the Sittang and partly owing to the anticipated arrival of reinforcements which made it possible even up to the last moment that the position might be retrieved. During this period a certain number of people evacuated understage I were brought back to keep essential services and transportation services in action till the last moment. During this period large quantities of personnel and stores were disembarked and moved up-country to Prome and Mandalay.

VIII. OPERATION IN THE SOUTHERN SHAN STATES AND IN TENASSERIM.

62. *Dispositions.* The dispositions when I arrived in Burma were as follows:-

Mergui, 2 Burma Rifles and two companies 3 Burma Rifles with a Frontier Force Detachment and an aerodrome guard.

Tavoy, 6 Burma Rifles, Tavoy Company of the Tenasserim Battalion B.A.F. and aerodrome guards.

Moulmein, 1/7 Gurkha Rifles, 8 Burma Rifles and the remainder of the Tenasserim Battalion B.A.F. also one Indian Mountain Battery.

Near Kawkareik, 4 Burma Rifles watching the Thai frontier. All the above were under the command of Commander 2 Burma Brigade in Moulmein.

Rangoon, the 1 Glosters and 3 Burma Rifles (less two companies) were under the Brigadier commanding Rangoon Area.

Southern Shan States, the 1 Burma Division consisting of an Indian Mountain Regiment, one 18-pounder Battery B.A.F (4 guns), 13 Indian Infantry Brigade and 1 Burma Brigade consisting of the 2 K.O.Y.L.I. and 1 and 5 Burma Rifles. There were also some Frontier Force Detachments.

Mandalay Area (in reserve), 16 Indian Infantry Brigade (less one Battalion) and 7 Burma Rifles.

63. *Minor Operations in the Southern Shan States.* There were no serious operations undertaken in the Southern Shan States during my period of command. A raid into Thailand up the River Kemapyu obtained useful information and there were several encounters between our Frontier Force columns or guerrilla detachments and the enemy on the frontier in the neighbourhood of the Kengtung – Chiengrai road. The Chinese 93 Division also undertook some raids across the Mekong River which inflicted considerable casualties and obtained valuable information.

Although the enemy was not very active during this period, there were known to be considerable numbers of Japanese as well as Thai troops in Northern Thailand and there were persistent reports indicating early invasion on this front. The distance from our junction with the Chinese on the Indo-China border to the mouth of the Salween was some 300 miles and to guard this we had only one division consisting of two infantry brigades and a few of the Frontier Force Detachments already referred to. The road from the River Salween through the valuable Mawchi mines to Toungoo was practically unguarded. The situation was therefore one which caused me considerable anxiety, especially when it became necessary to withdraw troops from the Southern Shan States to deal with the more threatening situation in Tenasserim.

64. *Tavoy and Mergui.* A few days after my arrival on 27th December, I visited Moulmein and Kawkareik and shortly afterwards Mergui and Tavoy.

The forces at these latter places were primarily for the defence of the aero-dromes and though Mergui was to some extent defensible against land or sea attack Tavoy certainly was not – with the forces available. Mergui was, however, 300 miles from Moulmein and communications consisted of the road Ye – Tavoy – Mergui which crossed many ferries and was for the most part through thick jungle. There were a considerable number of known tracks from the Thai border, only a few miles away, by which the road could be intercepted. From Ye to Moulmein there was a railway and no road. Withdrawal from either of these places would obviously be difficult, especially as the total naval forces available consisted of two small motor launches, and other suitable craft were manned by native crews who were not likely to face any operations in the presence of the enemy. In any case there were not enough of such craft to enable the Mergui garrison to be evacuated in one lift. In view of these circumstances and the certainty that sooner or later the Japanese would begin to work up the coast or across the border from Thailand, it was decided that in event of a serious threat the Mergui garrison would be evacuated to Tavoy which would then be capable of defence. Furthermore, provided a stop could be put across one track leading in from Thailand it should be possible for the Tavoy force, if necessary, to withdraw by land towards Moulmein.

65. *Kawkareik.* One battalion of the Burma Rifles north-east of Kawkareik was watching the Thai border at Myawaddy and holding the pass over the Dawna Range which was covered throughout its length with thick jungle. In face of any serious attack its position was obviously very isolated. Although only 45 miles from Moulmein as the crow flies the only road available was 90 miles in length. It traversed two wide rivers by ferries and ran for 30 miles parallel to the Thai frontier and toward the Three Pagodas Pass into Thailand – a very likely avenue for any enemy invasion. The supply route was by launch up to Kyondo on the Gyaing River.

In view of these circumstances I decided to move H.Q. 16 Indian Brigade and one battalion then in reserve, down to Tenasserim as early as possible both to strengthen the Kawkareik position, watch the Three Pagodas Pass, and garrison Moulmein. With this accession of force it became possible to push a detachment down to the Ye – Tavoy road with a view to keeping open communication with Tavoy.

66. *Lack of Intelligence*. Information at this time, as ever, was practically nil. The thick jungle prevented any considerable information being obtained from air reconnaissance for which resources were very limited, and for political reasons no attempt had been made before the war to organise any source of intelligence in Thailand. There was therefore every prospect of an attack without warning coming at any time. Any offensive action beyond that of patrols or attacks upon isolated posts, was with the forces available, quite out of the question.

67. *Formation of H.Q. 17 Indian Division*. On the 5th January the senior staff officers of the 17 Indian Division having arrived an advanced headquarters was established at Moulmein and Brigadier Bourke assumed the command.

The Commander of the 17 Indian Division arrived on 10th January and then assumed command although the remainder of his headquarters did not arrive until serious operations were already in progress. Although he had little time to study the problems involved he entirely agreed with the plans and dispositions proposed.

68. *Enemy Activities*. During the early days of January many reports were received indicating that the Japanese were concentrating in some strength between Raheng and the frontier at Myawaddy, and on the 11th January the total was given as 5,000 in this area.

On the 3rd some interesting information was received from some police agents who had been arrested in Thailand and subsequently released. They stated that while in captivity they had overheard some Japanese officer discussing future plans which included plans for an advance on Tavoy which was to take place in three weeks time. The information which these men brought back proved to be substantially correct.

69. *Troop Movements*. In consequence of a decision to move the whole of the 16 Indian Infantry Brigade to the Moulmein area, the troops in this area were disposed on the 14th January as follows:-

The Commander 16 Indian Infantry Brigade took over responsibility for the defences about Kawkareik, where 1/7 G.R. and 4 Burma Rifles (which was very weak) were now joined by 1/9 R. Jats and a mountain battery. One company of 1/7 G.R. was posted about Kyungyaung to watch the Three Pagodas Pass into Thailand.

The 4/12 F.F. Regiment of this Brigade was left in Moulmem under the 2 Burma Infantry Brigade with the role of keeping open the road from Ye to Tavoy as far south as the road and track junction at Migyaunglaung.

The 7 Burma Rifles was at this time also ordered to Moulmein.

70. *Operations at Tavoy*. On the 16th January two companies of the 6 Burma Rifles came in contact with a Japanese force, estimated at about 100, at Myitta on the track leading from the north of Tavoy to the frontier. The companies apparently withdrew for the night with the intention of attacking the next day. Reports had been received that further enemy forces were coming down the river and there is

little doubt that they were correct. The following day the two companies supported by a company of the 3 Burma Rifles (the two companys of this Battalion having been transferred from Rangoon) advanced again to the attack. It is hard to get a clear picture but the attack failed and meanwhile the Japanese had worked round the flanks and ambushed the transport. For the time being the force was broken up into small parties, most of whom eventually made their way back to Moulmein through the jungle.

It should be mentioned here that the 6 Burma Rifles was a newly raised Battalion which had had no opportunity for carrying out higher training in any form, and in the absence of any definitely appointed commander the action of these three companies was probably not too well planned or directed.

During the next two days a good deal of useful information was forwarded to Tavoy regarding the movements of Japanese troops by men of the Tenasserim Battalion and by mine managers and so on. In some cases these reports were passed through by telephone after the Japanese had passed by.

However, early on the morning of the 19th the enemy appeared near the Tavoy aerodrome and commenced to attack it. At first the detachment of the Kokine Battalion, The Burma Frontier Force put up a spirited defence but were eventually forced to withdraw and the aerodrome was lost.

The remainder of the troops in Tavoy now completely disintegrated. The enemy had established himself astride the road leading to Ye and most of the troops eventually found their way back to Moulmein moving in small parties through the jungle.

In these operations round Tavoy, parties of the Tenasserim Battalion B.A.F. did excellent work under their officers in blowing up bridges and roads and many of them remained behind for long periods after the other troops had left, eventually getting back through the jungle or by boat and bringing with them much useful information.

71. *Southern Tenasserim.* Before recording the main operations which started at Myawaddy and ended at the River Sittang it is convenient to dispose of the remaining event in Southern Tenasserim.

The Japanese were in occupation of Victoria Point and it was known that patrols were working up towards Mergui. With the possibility of Tavoy falling into the hands of the enemy Mergui would be in a very precarious position. Consequently on the 18th January, it was decided, during my absence in Kengtung, to evacuate Mergui while there was yet time and to transfer the troops to Tavoy and to make every endeavour to hold the aerodrome at that place. I confirmed these orders on my return.

Before this move could be completed Tavoy had fallen, so the garrison and civil officials, etc., were evacuated direct by sea to Rangoon where the last parties arrived on the 24th January.

72. *Effect of Operations.* The results of the action at Tavoy were unfortunate. It had caused the withdrawal from Mergui and it is possible that in the light of after

events that it might have been wiser to hold on to Mergui even if the eventual withdrawal of the garrison or part of it were thereby prejudiced. Its retention would have enabled our air forces, small as they were, to have carried out effective bombing attacks along the L of C supplying the enemy's forces in Malaya. It should be remembered, however, that at the time the plans were made our air forces available for this purpose were practically nil and that if the plan actually made had succeeded it might have ensured the retention of Tavoy for a considerable period.

Another and perhaps more serious effect of the operation at Tavoy was that the units of the Burma Rifles involved suffered a serious loss of morale from which they did not entirely recover. The enemy received a corresponding encouragement to undertake similar enterprises in future.

73. *Operations in Northern Tenasserim.* Before dealing with the operations in Northern Tenasserim it is desirable to draw attention to the fact that nearly all the fighting took place in dense jungle for which form of warfare the Japanese were especially trained while our troops were not. Communications were very limited and in the jungle runners had to be almost entirely relied upon.

The mobility of the Japanese brought home the fact that our troops had far too much baggage and reserves of all sorts with them which often in the end were either lost or had to be destroyed.

Throughout the operations leading up to the Battle of the Sittang I had constantly in mind the necessity for fighting as far forward as possible so as to have room in which to deploy the expected reinforcements. I therefore took every unit I could from elsewhere, including 1 Burma Division, to strengthen our forces on this front. This involved taking considerable risks in the Southern Shan States, on the Karenni front and in Rangoon. There was also an internal security problem that might become critical at any time.

74. *First Japanese Attack.* Active operations on a larger scale commenced on the 20th January when 1,000 Japanese troops, reported to be Thais but probably Japanese, attacked the post of the 1/7 G.R. at milestone 48 on the Myawaddy road. Other positions were heavily bombed and machine gunned at intervals throughout the day. There was every indication that a large scale attack was about to take place.

The following morning the attack developed as expected and most of the forward troops were forced out of their positions.

By midday the enemy were severely pressing the main position of the 16 Indian Infantry Brigade about Kawkareik. As they appeared to be in considerable strength (it was later estimated from the information that became available that there were about 2,500 enemy troops in the initial attack) and no reinforcements or reserves were available, it was possible that if 16 Indian Infantry Brigade tried to fight it out on this position it might be overwhelmed. Orders were therefore issued that this Brigade was not to get so involved as to render withdrawal impossible. The Divisional Commander was told at the same time not to give up more ground than necessary and that an intermediate position should be occupied.

It appeared afterwards that the attack was not, in fact, nearly so heavy as had been originally reported and there seems little doubt that more seasoned troops could have maintained their position for the time being.

75. *Withdrawal commenced.* On the 22nd January the withdrawal commenced and unfortunately there was a certain amount of confusion.

The Brigade, however, managed to disengage and during the succeeding day withdrew without further molestation from the Japanese to Moulmein not, however, without losing most of its animal transport, its signal equipment, many of its weapons and all its M.T.

Part of the losses in transport etc. was due to the ferry boat being sunk which rendered impracticable a withdrawal by road and necessitated a move across country by a track impassable to vehicles. The operation, as the small number of casualties showed, was not a very happy start to the operations for the defence of Burma. The company of 1/7 G.R. that the enemy attacked in the first instance did especially good work and the 4 Burma Rifles showed up very well.

On the 23rd January in view of the disorganised state of the troops at his disposal and the fact that the enemy were believed to be in considerable strength the Commander of the 17 Indian Division represented the view that he considered it desirable to move his Division right back to the area Bilin – Kyaikto – River Sittang where he could concentrate his troops in a strong position and establish a secure base from which to deliver a counter stroke.

76. *Decision to hold Moulmein.* In my opinion a withdrawal on this scale was quite unjustified and I decided that at any rate Moulmein should be held and if time permitted I proposed to move up the 2 K.O.Y.L.I. from 1 Burma Division to reinforce it. I did not, however, intend to have a brigade closely invested in that place. Arrangements for a withdrawal were therefore to be planned. The first requirement was to regain touch with the enemy, which had been entirely lost as a result of the withdrawal and was not really regained until the enemy attacked Moulmein on 30th January.

By the 25th, H.Q. 16 Indian Infantry Brigade was established at Martaban with 1/7 G.R. less two companies, one of which was still missing from the Kawkareik position, two companies of the 4 Burma Rifles and the 1/9 R. Jats. The 46 Indian Brigade was ordered up to the area about Bilin. This Brigade which consisted of 7/10 Baluch, 5/17 Dogras, 3/7 Gurkhas had arrived in Burma on the 16th but without its transport which did not arrive till 30th. It was, as already explained in Part I, by no means fully trained.

On the following day 100 men of the 1/7 G.R. turned up having marched across country to the Salween.

The enemy did not press forward his advance with any great speed and it was evident that he was bringing forward more troops and probably deploying on a wider front. Reports were received to the effect that they were in some strength just east of Paan and this was confirmed the following day.

77. *Attack on Moulmein.* Early on the morning of the 30th January the Japanese started an attack on the aerodrome situated about four miles beyond Moulmein and held by the detachment of the Kokine Battalion, The Burma Frontier Force. This detachment fought well and continued to hold on to the aerodrome until ordered to withdraw at midnight.

Moulmein itself was held by the four Battalions of the 2 Burma Brigade, 3 Burma Rifles, 4 Burma Rifles, 7 Burma Rifles and 8 Burma Rifles, with the 12 Mountain Battery R.A.; extended along a seven mile perimeter. 4/12 F.F.R. less one company was in reserve. At noon Brigadier Ekin took over the command and at that time found the situation to be in hand, but having visited the units and seen something of the position he came to the conclusion that in the face of a heavy enemy attack it would be very doubtful whether this extended line could be held. Orders were therefore issued by the Brigadier for the line to be withdrawn towards Moulmein in order to form a "Box" which it was hoped would be proof against penetration.

During this operation a battalion of the Burma Rifles failed to take up their allotted position with the result that there was a gap between the 8 Burma Rifles and the 4/12 F.F.R. and this latter unit was soon at close grips with the enemy and had a difficult time.

At 1900 hours the situation was certainly serious and as no reinforcements were yet available for sending into Moulmein it looked as though it would be necessary to withdraw from the town. As he estimated that there were probably not more than a thousand Japanese attacking, the Brigadier thought that there was still a possibility of holding the town and told the Divisional Commander on the telephone that he would make a final decision later.

The Brigade Commander, however, made preparations for withdrawing if necessary and sent Major Ward, R.E., commanding the 1 Field Company Burma Sappers and Miners, to collect all available launches alongside the jetties. He managed to collect fifteen and to keep them there until they were required. These boats were manned by local crews and in charge of serangs and they worked extremely well under very trying conditions.

78 *Decision to Withdraw.* During the night it became increasingly obvious that a withdrawal would be necessary and on this being reported to the Divisional Commander he agreed and considered that it should be carried out as soon as possible.

At about 0730 hours on the 31st January the embarkation began and by 1000 hours eleven ships had left with troops. Throughout this time the Japanese were closing in round the jetties and considerable fighting was in progress. However, the bulk of the troops got away although the ships in their passage over to Martaban were subject to machine gun fire and shelling.

The month of January therefore ended with our troops west of the River Salween with the exception of small parties of men who did not get away with the ships or who had got separated from their units. Many of these turned up later having managed to cross the river in native boats or rafts, etc.

79. *Reasons for Withdrawal.* The question may well be asked as to whether it was necessary to evacuate Moulmein. While the initial attack was probably carried out by only one enemy regiment there was every reason to suppose that the remainder of a division was moving up and this afterwards proved to be correct. With the enemy established to the north and south of the town and probably on the island of Chaungzon to the west, no communication with the town would have been possible and in the absence of any naval or military boat crews, etc., operations for relief, even if troops had been available, would probably have been impossible. The area had not in any way been prepared for defence and required at least two infantry brigades to hold a secure perimeter. Furthermore the water supply came from outside the only line which it was possible to hold. In view of these considerations it is quite clear that a decision to hold Moulmein any longer would almost certainly have involved the loss of the garrison and possibly have hastened the fall of Rangoon.

At one time I hoped that the arrival of reinforcements would enable me to establish a strong force across the River Salween at Paan. This would have covered the northern flank of Moulmein and secured its communications across the River Salween. It would also have secured the most promising jumping off place for a counter-offensive.

80. *Request for Naval Assistance.* About this time a signal was despatched to G.H.Q. South West Pacific Command (A.B.D.A. Command) pointing out that Moulmein would probably fall and requesting that warships should be sent to protect the coast as otherwise the enemy would be able to move up the coast from Malaya at will.

81. *Casualties.* The casualties suffered by our troops up to and including the evacuation of Moulmein amounted to 617 all ranks, a considerable proportion being "missing." It should be noted, however, that in jungle fighting involving a withdrawal, practically all dead and wounded are likely to be counted as missing in addition to prisoners and those who, getting separated from their units, may turn up later as stragglers. There is no doubt that the enemy suffered considerable casualties at Moulmein though probably very few at Kawkareik.

Although the Divisional Commander was still anxious to withdraw to the Bilin River and to give up Martaban, I issued orders that the Division was to fight hard to hold the line of the River Salween and to give no ground. As far as possible, however, the Division was to be dispersed in depth so as to be able to deal with enemy infiltration.

The general plan was now to hold Martaban securely and the line of the River Salween to the north of Paan, with the remainder of the 17 Indian Division distributed back in depth along the road to Kyaikto.

Two companies of the 3/7 Gurkha Rifles held Martaban while the 1/7 G.R. were about Paan. The 4 Burma Rifles watched the river between these two places and the 5/17 Dogras were ordered to Duyinzaik and to carry out active patrolling.

82. *Reorganisation.* A good deal of reorganisation was now necessary within the Division and it was decided to reconstitute the Brigades so as to include a battalion of the Burma Rifles in each Brigade as it was felt that these battalions would be of greater value when brigaded with other troops.

83. *Reinforcements.* On the 3rd February the 48 Indian Infantry Brigade which had arrived in Rangoon on 31st January without its transport and had been held in Army Reserve, was ordered forward to Bilin to join the 17 Indian Division. The Divisional Commander was instructed to keep this Brigade concentrated and not to use it until there was a real necessity to do so.

84. *Enemy Action.* Martaban was now subjected to a good deal of shelling and bombing and small parties of the enemy succeeded in crossing the Salween at different points. In view of the enclosed country and long distances involved it was very difficult to locate them, especially as no information was forthcoming from the local inhabitants. Apart from this there was a lull on the front which gave our troops a much needed breathing space for reorganisation. The 1/7 G.R., however, showed a greater activity in the Paan area. They maintained a post and patrols on the far side of the river and had several very successful encounters with the enemy. Eventually, however, his increasing strength in this area forced their withdrawal across the river.

On the 5th February 7/10 Baluch relieved the 1/7 G.R. opposite Paan who then moved to Bilin. The 2 K.O.Y.L.I. which had been transferred from the 1 Burma Division in the Southern Shan States moved to Thaton while the 8 Burma Rifles and 1/9 R. Jats moved into reserve at Bilin.

85. *Martaban Road cut.* On the 9th a Japanese party which had no doubt infiltrated through the jungle led by local guides cut the road at milestone 8 a few miles south of Paung and established a strong road block there. Two carriers of the 5 Dogras failed to force a passage and two armoured cars of the Rangoon Battalion B.A.F. which came on the scene a little later were put out of action. In spite of further attacks the enemy was not dislodged from his position here. The 3/7 G.R. later succeeded in opening a way through Thebyugon and thence across country to Thaton.

86. *Martaban.* On the following day (10th) Martaban was again subjected to a considerable amount of shelling and a good deal of enemy activity was observed, all of which indicated that the enemy were likely to make a renewed effort in the near future. It was also known that some parties of the enemy were on our side of the river.

In view of the situation the Divisional Commander represented his desire to evacuate Martaban and to withdraw his line in order to get on to a less extended front. For the reasons given already I did not wish to give up more ground than was necessary and moreover as soon as the enemy got possession of Martaban it would have been easy for him to pass over troops and stores from Moulmein. I therefore issued orders that Martaban must continue to be held.

87. *Loss of Martaban.* The reports received on the 11th disclosed a somewhat confused situation but did indicate that the enemy had started the next phase of his plan.

About six hundred Japanese were now in the area about Martaban and a further 2,000 were reported to have landed on the swamps and mud flats further up the coast and would no doubt be working their way in towards the road.

The 3/7 G.R. were forced to withdraw from Martaban but were still covering the exits of that place; they inflicted very heavy casualties on the enemy and at one time charged them with the bayonet which caused them to run for cover throwing away their arms as they did so.

On this day also, about a battalion of the Japanese crossed the Salween near Paan and were believed to have surrounded the 7/10 Baluch. To restore the situation in this area the 5/17 Dogras were ordered to counter-attack from the direction of Duyinzaik.

By the evening of the 13th the situation was a little clearer. The 5/17 Dogras, only one hundred strong and much disorganised arrived back from Duyinzaik where they had been heavily engaged for the past two days, but there was still no news of the Baluch, who it was believed must have been surrounded.

88. *Condition of Troops.* The Divisional Commander now reported that, while he still had the 48 Indian Infantry Brigade intact and in hand, in the 16 and 46 Indian Brigades there was only one battalion, the K.O.Y.L.I., in a fit state to fight.

In view of the extent of his front and the condition of his troops he wished to withdraw to a better defensive position with a less extended front. While again pointing out the necessity for fighting as far forward as possible I gave him permission to withdraw if and when he considered such a course essential.

On 13th February I sent an appreciation to General Hartley, Commander-in-Chief, India, which emphasised that the situation for the next month, until more troops became available, was likely to be critical and envisaged the possibility that we might be forced back to the line of the River Sittang. The difficulties likely to be encountered in an event of a forced withdrawal across this river were especially stressed. It also pointed out that the loss of Pegu would be likely to seal the fate of Rangoon and referred to the policy of stocking bases in Central Burma with a view to continuing the campaign and covering the road to India in the event of Rangoon being lost. It ended with an appeal for more troops, especially British, as early as possible.

89. 7/10 *Baluch.* On the 14th February, the news was received that some survivors of the 7/10 Baluch after 48 hours of heavy fighting had managed to fight their way out and were withdrawing to Duyinzaik. The following day this Battalion was

visited by the Divisional Commander who found that its strength was about six officers and 250 men. There is no doubt that this Battalion fought most gallantly whilst completely surrounded by superior numbers and that it was only after all ammunition was exhausted that a small remnant was forced to surrender. The survivors consisted for the most part of a company that was detached from the Battalion and men who were away with the transport.

90. *Withdrawal to Bilin*. At midday on the 15th February, the Divisional Commander reported that, in view of the pressure on his front, he proposed to withdraw to the River Bilin which he felt confident he could hold. Accordingly as a first step the 46 Indian Infantry Brigade commenced to withdraw behind the Bilin.

On the 16th, H.Q. 2 Burma Infantry Brigade was ordered to move to Nyaunglebin together with the 7 Burma Rifles as soon as transport could be made available. A reconnaissance party started off at once. The object of this move was to ensure that the line of the River Sittang to the north should be at any rate patrolled, and also, if posssible, prepared for defence. Most units of the Burma Rifles were no longer fit for further fighting without rest and re-organisation, and certain Indian battalions were in a similar condition. It was hoped, therefore, as reinforcements became available, to withdraw these battalions into reserve across the River Sittang.

About the same time the 1 Burma Rifles which had reached the front from Mergui via Rangoon and which had not been engaged, were sent up to Papun to cover the left flank. This Battalion carried out its task very well and after several weeks in the jungle eventually joined 1 Burma Division near Toungoo. Two detachments of about a company each were also placed to watch likely crossings over the River Salween between Papun and Paan and a Burma F.F. column was detailed to protect the left flank of the 17 Indian Division.

At 12.05 hours a report was received to the effect that a party of Japanese estimated at being from 300 to 1,000 strong, had crossed the Salween at Yinbaing and were advancing on Mepli. A company of the 8 Burma Rifles were sent to investigate and contacted the Japanese at Kuseik.

In the evening Thaton was evacuated and the bridge at Yinnein was demolished, and on this date the 1/4 G.R. of 48 Indian Brigade were put into the line and carried out a counter-attack to restore the situation on the left flank.

Heavy fighting took place on most parts of the front on the 17th February and it was evident that the enemy were trying to work around the left flank of the Division. The remainder of the 48 Brigade was now brought up into line on the right of 16 Indian Brigade, where both 5/17 Dogra and 8 Burma Rifles were found to have vacated their positions. To protect the right flank an organisation of watchers backed up by Burma Military Police was put in operation along the coast.

The 2 K.O.Y.L.I. now became heavily engaged with the enemy about Danyigon and were out of touch for some considerable time.

91. *Pegu Force.* The possibility of the Japanese crossing the estuary of the River Sittang by boat and cutting off our communications with Pegu or of going further afield and landing near the Rangoon River had been considered for some time past, but beyond small detachments of the Burma Frontier Force and Burma Military Police, there had been no troops spare for this task. The arrival of reinforcements now made it possible, however, for more effective steps to be taken, and on the 18th February, the Pegu Force was formed. This Force consisted of the 1 W. Yorks, F.F.6 and detachments of the Burma Military Police, and was given the role of protecting Pegu from the south east linking up with the 17 Division at the Sittang Bridge. An armoured train was provided to operate in the Delta area. A similar organisation consisting of a company of the 1st Glosters, F.F.7 and some Military Police were responsible for the approaches to Syriam from the sea.

92. *7 Armoured Brigade.* In anticipation of the arrival of the 7 Armoured Brigade every effort had been been made, to strengthen bridges, and to convert railway bridges for the passage of tanks in order to give them as large an area in which to operate as possible.

All possible steps were also taken to ensure that the disembarkation of the Brigade could be carried out as quickly as possible after its arrival, and that there would be no delay in moving the units to their concentration areas. It was obviously doubtful whether the Brigade would be in time to assist in the defence of the area east of the River Sittang, but the Brigade arrived in Rangoon on the 21st and, thanks to the excellent work of all concerned, it was got forward in time to impose considerable delay on the enemy west of the River Sittang and to relieve the pressure on the tired troops in the Pegu area.

93. *Bilin Position.* It is now necessary to turn back to the operations on the Front of the 17 Indian Division which was occupying the Bilin position.

During the 18th the enemy definitely increased his pressure against our troops and succeeded in crossing the river to the south of the village of Bilin.

In this area a counter attack was delivered by the 48 Indian Infantry Brigade which, while succeeding in holding up the enemy advance, did not succeed in pushing him back over the river. Further to the north the enemy were working round the flank of the 16 Indian Infantry Brigade. The 2 K.O.Y.L.I. which had put in a gallant counter attack, had suffered heavy casualties, but was holding its own. It should also be mentioned that on this date some very effective bombing was carried out by the R.A.F. on enemy troops south of the Bilin River. The night passed with our troops in close contact with the enemy along the north bank of the River.

On the 18th a wide turning movement was initiated by 4/12 F.F.R. with the object of attacking the enemy's right flank. The operation achieved considerable success and heavy fighting ensued. It left the Division, however, without any reserves and weak along the coast. The troops were becoming very weak and exhausted. The enemy also established himself in the rear of the right flank – presumably by landing from the sea. In view of the situation, I ordered up the 2 D.W.R., the only unit I had in hand, to protect the rear of the Division.

94. *Question of Withdrawal.* During the morning of the 19th I visited the Division. A counter attack by 2/5 R.G.R. had not altogether succeeded in driving the enemy out of Thattkyon in rear of the right flank. The enemy was well established in the centre of the position and there was every indication that he was bringing up strong forces against the left flank. The situation was, therefore, such that there appeared to be grave risk of not being able to disengage the troops unless a further withdrawal was ordered.

In view of the strong position on the River Sittang in rear, the anticipated arrival of reinforcements and especially tanks, a decision "to fight it out" on the River Bilin had little to recommend it. In view of subsequent events there is little doubt that had the withdrawal been further deferred the Division would have been practically destroyed and Rangoon left open to the enemy.

I, therefore, told the Divisional Commander to make all necessary preparation for withdrawal and to judge for himself when the necessity for doing so had arrived. Subsequent orders were issued to the effect that all transport should be got across the River Sittang at an early stage of the withdrawal, and that the 2 D.W.R. should be sent back to guard the bridgehead as early as possible. I myself had personally ordered the retention of one company at that place, in view of the weakness of the garrison.

On 18th February, I sent to A.B.D.A. Command and the War Office an appreciation which after referring to the severe check that had been inflicted on the enemy on the Bilin River indicated that if, as appeared probable, he was able to renew his attack with fresh troops, it might not be possible to continue to hold the position. It also pointed out that if the battle went badly, the enemy might succeed in crossing the River Sittang without much difficulty which would render the evacuation of Rangoon an imminent possibility. After reviewing the meagre resources of troops available, and future reinforcements, it is stated that probably the best that could be hoped for was that it would be possible to hold up the enemy on the line of the River Sittang. This would, however, involve an immediate threat to the main road and railway from Rangoon to Mandalay which was the main route of supply of China and for the evacuation of civilians, stores and base installations from Rangoon. After referring to the difficult problem of whether to start evacuation of non-essential personnel at once, with its obviously bad effect on morale, or risk congestion and confusion at a later stage, it concluded by stating that five divisions in all were essential to the defence of Burma of which two would be required for the defence of the River Sittang. It expressed doubts, however, as to whether sufficient troops could arrive in time to save Rangoon and said that unless they could do so more quickly than was at the time visualised, the risk of losing Rangoon within the next few weeks was considerable.

The accuracy of this was very fully borne out by events. On the 20th February, after the decision to withdraw to the River Sittang, a further telegram was sent which, after describing the condition of the troops, dealt in some detail with the necessity for taking preliminary measures for the evacuation of Rangoon. It stated that after consultation with the Governor and Combined Commanders, it had been decided to commence certain measures under the evacuation scheme which would not, however be detrimental to the actual defence of Rangoon. These included the diversion of certain ships carrying administrative units which would be very difficult to unload in the existing conditions and whose presence would seriously complicate the evacuation problem. It made it clear that fighting troops should be continued to be sent as reinforcements and that every effort would be made to hold Rangoon. It also dealt with the evacuation of women and children and the denial of the oil refineries. It concluded with emphasizing once again the need for a Corps Commander and also for a Senior General Officer to undertake liaison duties with the Chinese Armies.

There can be no doubt now that the timely adoption of these measures was amply justified, without them there would have been chaos.

95. *Withdrawal begins.* On the 20th February after three days of almost hand to hand fighting, the forward troops managed to disengage from the enemy and the first stage of withdrawal commenced. The withdrawal was co-ordinated by the Commanders of the 48 and 16 Brigades. The only unit that had any difficulty in getting away was the 1/9 R. Jats, which was partially surrounded and owing to a delay in receipt of orders to withdraw was caught by a pre-arranged bombing attack intended for the enemy. This delayed the withdrawal of 48 Brigade till 1500 hours and it was eventually ferried to Kyaikto by M.T., reaching that place at about 2030 hours.

The intention now was for the 17 Indian Division to form a strong line on the west bank of the River Sittang, and it was hoped that, if any enemy managed to cross in any strength, the 7 Armoured Brigade would be able to deal with them. It may be mentioned here that while the paddy land looked most suitable for the employment of tanks, it was found that the small bunds between the fields necessitated the tanks slowing down to take them, and thus making them vulnerable and slow.

96. *Plan of Withdrawal.* The 17 Indian Division's plan for the withdrawal was for 48 Brigade to move back first, going into divisional reserve. It was to pass through 46 Brigade which was already in the Kyaikto area. 46 Brigade was to act as rearguard to the 17 Division, On 21st February the leading battalion of 48 Brigade was only to go as far as the quarries, two miles east of Mokpalin. The remaining battalions were to halt on positions some four or seven miles further back along the main road. To strengthen the bridgehead defence consisting of the 3 Burma Rifles and one company 2 D.W.R., the Divisional Commander subsequently ordered the 4/12 F.F.R. to the Sittang bridge area.

The 2 D.W.R. less one company remained with 46 Indian Infantry Brigade and it was also decided that units should retain their transport.

97. *Communications.* The withdrawal across the river was bound to be a difficult operation as only the one bridge existed, but a power ferry, for M.T. with three boats had been placed in position as an alternative means, and was provided with landing stages of elaborate construction.

It should be noted here that in this area communications were extremely difficult, apart from the railway there was a road only as far as Waw some 10 miles west of the Sittan Bridge, on the east side there was no road until reaching Kyaikto 16 miles beyond the River. Every effort had been made to complete the road, and to deck over the railway bridge. By excellent work on the part of Mr. Stewart of the Burma Railways, the latter and the power ferry were completed, but the "road" was still a very dusty and rough track through the jungle. It may be added, that the River Sittang at this place was nearly 500 yards wide and very swift. The rapidity of the current, the enormous rise and fall of the tide (40 feet) and the existence of a bore, were considered to render it unsafe for navigation, and nobody but a very strong swimmer could hope to cross it by that means.

98. *Visit to Lashio.* As the withdrawal of 17 Indian Division on 20th had been successfully begun, I felt able on 21st to fly up to Lashio to meet the Generalissimo on his way back to China. It was obviously most desirable that I should do so in order to hasten as far as possible, the arrival of the Chinese troops in Burma. Unfortunately he decided at the last moment not to land, and flew straight on to Chungking. I returned to Rangoon by air on 22nd to find a very serious situation had arisen on the River Sittang. It is necessary first however, to describe what had taken place on 21st during my absence.

99. *Events of 21st.* By 12.00 hours on the 21st both 48 and 16 Indian Infantry Brigades had passed through 46 Brigade at Kyaikto. During the afternoon 46 Brigade commenced its withdrawal and although bombed from the air it was not followed up. The order of march was 48 Brigade leading, followed by 16 Brigade M.T., 46 Brigade M.T. and then 16 Brigade followed by 46 Brigade. One battalion of 46 Brigade moved by the railway line, all the remainder by the road and track.

Between 12.00 and 15.00 hours the troops between Kyaikto and Mokpalin were very heavily bombed and machine gunned by aircraft which were considered by many people to be our own. Whether this was the fact and whether the fault lay with the Army or the R.A.F. was not satisfactorily cleared up at the time.

By 18.30 hours on 21st H.Q. 48 Brigade and 1/4 G.R. were established in Mokpalin with the remaining battalions of the Brigade supporting them and seven miles further south as laid down by Divisional H.Q.

The 16 and 46 Brigades spent the night 21/22nd on the road between Kyaikto and Mokpalin and the time of start for the 22nd was fixed between the Brigadiers concerned. It was agreed that 16 and 46 Brigades M.T. should start at about 03.00 hours, in that order, followed by 16 Brigade and 46 Brigade. By 06.00 hours the whole of the troops in the rear of the column were on the move.

100. *Situation about the Sittang Bridge.* We must now return to the head of the column. The movement from the Quarries started at 04.00 hours on 22nd February with the 1/4 G.R. leading, followed by Divisional H.Q. and H.Q. 48 Indian Infantry Brigade.

The 1/4 G.R. were given the task of protecting the west bank of the bridge against parachute attack and the bridgehead was still therefore dangerously weak. The passage of M.T. across the river was completely held up for three hours by a 3-ton lorry which got off the roadway. Movement did not therefore start again till 06.30 hours.

At 08.30 hours, as the 7/10 Baluch was marching through the railway cutting immediately east of the bridge, the enemy put in a heavy attack from the north-east of the bridgehead. One and a half companies of the 3 Burma Rifles holding that sector were forced back and the attack went through almost to the end of the bridge itself. An Advance Dressing Station north of the bridge was overcome. The A.D.M.S., D.A.D.M.S. and all medical personnel were taken prisoner. Two companies of the 4/12 F.F.R. at once counter attacked and re-took the original position on the north and north-east of the perimeter. The Battalion was supported by the 7/10 Baluch. The bridgehead was again lost and re-taken later. D Company 2 D.W.R. then on the west bank was ordered across the River and took up a position on the south-east of the bridgehead perimeter. The ferries immediately above the bridge were destroyed in view of the situation and there was no communication with the remaining battalions or brigades which were still a considerable distance on the far side of the river.

At about 14.00 hours the bridgehead was shelled. About this time two platoons of 1/3 G.R. reached the bridgehead. It transpired later that the 2/5 R.G.R. and 1/3 G.R. had staged an attack on the enemy between them and the bridgehead. These platoons, whilst taking part in the attack, had lost direction in the dense jungle. They were subsequently employed in the defence of the bridgehead. During the remainder of 22nd and during the night heavy pressure continued on the bridgehead. The original garrison had had considerable casualties and 1/4 G.R. less one company were brought up to reinforce it. In spite of heavy fire stragglers started to come in via the river bank from the south – all telling the same story of troops ambushed, cut up and scattered. It seemed as if no unit of the Division remained intact, and as the enemy pressure gradually increased the Commander 48 Brigade after consulting the Divisional Commander by telephone and obtaining his consent, decided to blow the bridge before daylight on the 23rd.

At 05.30 hours on the morning of the 23rd, after very heavy fighting, the bridge was blown.

The destruction of the bridge left the other two Brigades and two battalions of 48 Brigade on the far side of the River in a very precarious position and it is necessary now to return to the story of their action on 22nd.

At about 08.45 hours on 22nd heavy fire was opened on 3/7 G.R., the leading battalion of 46 Brigade, an immediate counter attack failed to dislodge the enemy and further attacks developed on both flanks. 5/17 Dogras and one company 2 D.W.R. endeavoured to deal with these attacks but while doing so a further attack was made on the rearguard – 2 D.W.R. Severe casualties were sustained on both sides.

101. *Bridgehead recaptured.* About 10.00 hours Brigadier Ekin, Commander 46 Brigade, organised a sweeping movement through the jungle which enabled the troops on the road to move forward and join 16 Brigade, three miles further on. This Brigade was also by this time heavily attacked. This action continued till dark on 22nd and the column under the Brigadier 46 Brigade encountered about 20.00 hours a large enemy force moving up the railway line on Mokpalin. By now the forces involved were much split up and various elements eventually made their way through the jungle and crossed the river higher up. Meanwhile Brigadier Jones, 16 Indian Infantry Brigade had been fighting hard and a number of gallant counter attacks had been carried out by battalions of that Brigade and the Gurkha battalions of 48 Brigade which were cut off from the bridge. By 09.00 hours on the morning of 23rd he had cleared the enemy from the bridgehead and organised its defence with his own Brigade, two battalions of 48 Brigade and portions of all three battalions of 46 Brigade. He also had the Divisional Artillery and most of the M.T. with him. By this time, however, the bridge had been blown and there were no boats.

Very determined attacks supported by artillery and air bombing were still being made by the enemy from the south and east and there was no hope of organised withdrawal. Brigadier Ekin now succeeded in joining 16 Indian Infantry Brigade and after discussion it was decided that the only course possible was to start withdrawal by every means possible before disorganisation became complete.

Great credit is due to those officers and men who held their positions to the last to cover the withdrawal of the others and the evacuation, so far as it was possible, of the wounded. Many men swam the River, a most formidable undertaking involving nearly an hour in the water. A large number who attempted it were unfortunately drowned in the attempt. Others crossed, under fire all the time, on improvised rafts on which they carried such of the wounded as they could collect. Others with the aid of ropes collected in Mokpalin crossed the gap between the remains of the bridge, also under fire. A number of others who could not swim, forced their way through the jungle and crossed some miles higher up, where the River is narrower, in boats or rafts. Quite a number did not get back to our lines for many days, or in a few cases weeks, afterwards.

It has only been possible to obtain the names of a few of those who performed outstanding acts of gallantry on this day. Many swam the River again and again under fire bringing over parties of wounded and the whole episode, disastrous as it was, is a magnificent example of heroism on the part of all ranks of the forces engaged. The fact that a large proportion of men eventually rejoined their units shows that at no time was there any disposition to surrender to the enemy. Brigadier Ekin swam the River about 15.00 hours and Brigadier Jones about an hour later. Although many of the troops were able to make good their escape few were able to bring back their arms and practically all transport and equipment had to be abandoned. Many of the transport mules which had been turned loose swam the River on their own and joined up with other units which had mules.

102. *Condition of Troops.* From this date onwards none of the Infantry Brigades concerned could be regarded as more than remnants, ready to defend themselves doggedly but otherwise unfit for any of the normal operations of war. If they could have been pulled out for a few weeks to rest and refit, and if it had been possible to provide their deficiencies in personnel, equipment and transport, no doubt they would have recovered. In existing conditions this was of course impossible and after only a short pause they were again engaged in the severe fighting at Pegu which eventually culminated in the loss of Rangoon.

It was afterwards ascertained that the enemy had brought up for this action part at any rate of another Division – the 33rd. This Division moved via Paan and jungle tracks north east of the Thaton – Bilin – Kyaikto road and was no doubt intended to annihilate our forces east of the River Sittang. Our timely with-drawal, however, prevented his carrying out his plan in full. By forced marches he was able to launch an attack on the bridgehead at the Sittang and thus bring about its premature destruction. He was also able to ambush our columns on the march and inflict heavy casualties. The success of the latter operation was no doubt partly due to the disorganisation caused by the bombing already referred to. It is interesting to note that it was reported by stragglers that the tracks used by the enemy were most carefully marked with paper arrows and that the enemy un-doubtedly had the assistance of local guides.

There is no doubt that the battle of the River Sittang was nothing less than a disaster. Except for about two battalions which both suffered heavy casualties the Division had lost practically all its equipment, transport, guns and ammunition. The men that were eventually collected had in some cases retained their rifles but many had lost them in crossing the River Sittang and others had had in addition to discard some of their uniform including even their boots. Their morale was naturally low and many were utterly exhausted. Steps were of course immediately taken to distribute such transport, arms, clothing and equipment as could be made available, though this amounted to little. A large number of men who were unarmed had to be put on trains and evacuated to reinforcement camps up country where they could be rested, re-armed and equipped. Owing to trans-portation difficulties many of them did not rejoin their units until after the loss of Prome. The 46 Indian Infantry Brigade had to be broken up and many units were amalgamated or re-distributed, among these were 5/17 Dogras, 7/10 Baluch,

1/7 Gurkhas, 3/7 Gurkhas, 1/3 Gurkhas. The following table shows the state of battalions of 17 Indian Division on the evening of 24th February.

STATE OF INFANTRY OF 17 INDIAN DIVISION
(EVENING 24TH FEBRUARY)

Bde.	Bn.	B.Os.	V.C.Os	O.Rs.	Rifles	Brens	T.S. M.Gs.
16	2 K.O.Y.L.I.	6		200	50	2	2
	1/9 R. Jats	8	10	550	50		2
	1/7 G.R.	6	4	290	50	2	
	8 Burma Rifles	3	3	90	60	2	
	Total 16 Bde.	23	17	1,130	210^2	6	4
46	7/10 Baluch	5	3	200	90		2
	5/17 Dogra	1	3	100	70		
	3/7 G.R.	5	5	160	30		
	2 D.W.R.	16		300	150	4	6
	Total 46 Bde.	27	11	760	340^2	4	8
48	1/3 G.R.	3	4	100	40	5	8
	1/4 G.R.	12	18	650	600	30	30
	2/5 R.G.R.	6	6	215	30	2	2
	4/12 F.F.R.	9	13	480	200	9	16
	Total 48 Bde.	30	41	1,445	870^2	46	56
	Total Div.	80	69	3,335	$1,420^2$	56	68
Approximate deficiency		100	65	4,500	5,800	300	300
Immediate deficiency of weapons					1,700	120	100

IX. – PEGU AND THE LOSS OF RANGOON.

103. *Troops available.* On the 23rd February, I met the Commander 17 Indian Division near Pegu and was able to ascertain the state of the Division. One squadron of tanks was now available for operations and as it could not get across the Sittang – Rangoon River canal at Waw it was decided to concentrate and reorganise the remnants of the 17 Indian Division in the area Waw – Pegu.

In addition to the 17 Indian Division the forces that now became available were 7 Armoured Brigade which included 7 Hussars, 2 R. Tanks and 414 Bty. R.H.A. The Cameronians were attached to the Armoured Brigade as a motorised regiment and the 1 W. Yorks were still watching the coastal area to the south of Pegu.

104. *Fighting in front of Pegu.* On 26th February and succeeding days there was considerable fighting about Waw where for the first time Burma Traitor forces took an active part in operations. The enemy, unwilling to meet our tanks in the open now attempted to work across the plains by night with the object of infiltrating into the jungle to the west of the main road from Pegu to Toungoo. This

road was cut at Pyinbon on the 25th but the situation was restored by the Armoured Brigade. Unfortunately there were not sufficient troops available to close the gap between 17 Indian Division and the Burma Brigade at Nyaunglebin so that this gap of some 30 miles remained open to enemy penetration.

In view of the convincing reports of enemy infiltration through the Yomas with the object of cutting the Prome road and also the bad reports about the internal situation in that area, one squadron of tanks and a company of 1 W. Yorks were sent back to Tharrawaddy on 27th February. This place held a very important dump of supplies and petrol which at this time was quite unguarded. In view of subsequent events it was fortunate that this move was carried out. About the same time the remnants of 16 Indian Infantry Brigade, which was very weak, was withdrawn to Hlegu, the location of Divisional H.Q. A further appreciation dealing with the probable course of enemy action was despatched on the 27th February. This dealt with the probable future action of the enemy and foretold the probability of his infiltrating across the open country west of the Sittang by night into the close jungle of the Pegu Yomas, and eventually cutting the Rangoon – Prome road. It went on to describe the action taken or proposed to be taken and finished up by stating that the prospects of the successful defence of Rangoon in the absence of the early arrival of the 7 Australian Division (which was at that time expected) were not good.

In view of the general situation at this time the question of carrying out the demolition and evacuation of Rangoon had to be kept under constant review. This was especially necessary as the 1 W. Yorks which had been covering Syriam refineries from the sea had had to be withdrawn to assist in the defence of Pegu. The coast line was therefore undefended and except for some small detachments close to Syriam there was nothing to prevent the enemy landing a force to seize the refineries. A final decision was, however, postponed in view of the anticipated arrival of reinforcements and the probability of a visit from General Wavell to discuss future policy. He arrived on 1st March.

On 1st March, Brigadier Cowan assumed command of 17 Indian Division. On 2nd and 3rd March the enemy occupied Waw in some strength and an attack by the Armoured Brigade and Cameronians, though partially successful, failed to clear it completely.

On 4th March I flew to Toungoo where H.Q. 1 Burma Division had just arrived. 2 Burma Brigade was still in Nyaunglebin and a successful little operation had recently been carried out by Brigadier Bourke against Shwegyin where there was a considerable number of Burmans led by Japanese officers. In accordance with my instructions, the Divisional Commander was to concentrate as many of his troops as possible south of Toungoo but it must be remarked that in addition to two battalions of the Burma Rifles and some Frontier Force columns he had only a total of three Indian battalions in his Division. Some of the Burma Rifles had already deserted with their arms (under an officer) and others were known to be shaky.

On 3/4th March the enemy had occupied Kyaikhla (south-west of Waw) and Payagyi 12 miles north of Pegu on the Toungoo road. An attack by tanks and infantry was launched in the late afternoon of the 4th against the latter. Considerable casualties were inflicted and a gun and mortar were captured, but the force available was insufficient to prevent further penetration in this area. Meanwhile the enemy had occupied Tandawgyi close to Payagyi.

105. *Pegu Road cut.* On the 5th I visited H.Q. 17 Indian Division at Hlegu intending to go on to see 48 Indian Infantry Brigade at Pegu but the road was cut by the enemy and I was unable to proceed. The position at that time was that the 48 Brigade was holding the outskirts of Pegu while the Armoured Brigade with the Cameronians and 1 W. Yorks were acting in a mobile role in the open country to the east. Owing to the presence of many water courses and the fact that the small bunds surrounding the rice fields proved an unexpectedly serious obstacle to the tanks, their operations were much restricted.

106. *Enemy Infiltration.* The enemy, under cover of darkness, had now succeeded in passing a considerable number of troops across the open country to the north of Pegu whence he was able to cross the Pegu River and enter the thick jungle. It was no doubt his advanced troops which had cut the road west of Pegu at a place where there is thick jungle on both sides of the road. Attempts to drive back the enemy had failed and the 48 Brigade was still in no condition for offensive action.

107. *Landings on the Coast.* Meanwhile landings had been reported on the Coast west of the Rangoon River and although one shipload of 55 well-armed "Free Burmans" under a Japanese officer had been intercepted by the Navy it was known that several hundreds of armed men, Japanese or Burmans, had landed successfully. In these circumstances there was very considerable danger that the demolition of the oil refineries might be interfered with. There were absolutely no reserves available to deal with this incursion but fortunately these forces did not show very much enterprise.

In these circumstances I ordered Major-General Cowan, who had just assumed command of 17 Indian Division, to clear the road and withdraw the 48 Brigade to Hlegu, the 16 Brigade at that place being brought back to cover Taukkyan cross roads. The action was necessitated as much by the situation at Pegu as by the fact that another enemy column stated to include tanks, which had also crossed the Pegu River, was proceeding west by a jungle track and had already passed through Paunggyi, north of Hlegu. It was obviously only a matter of hours before it would cut the Prome road north of Rangoon. The 63 Indian Infantry Brigade was at that time concentrated near Hlawga station but was still without its transport which, although the ships were then coming up the river, could not join it for 24 hours. Apart from 2 R.T.R., less one squadron, now withdrawn to Hlegu, one British battalion split up in detachments in Rangoon and Syriam, one squadron tanks and a company of 1 W. Yorks on the Prome road, there were no other troops of any value available.

108. *General Alexander arrives.* While still at Divisional H.Q. I heard that General Alexander had arrived, and I therefore suspended any action on my instructions until he had been able to visit Divisional H.Q. and judge the situation for himself.

It is necessary here to mention that on 22nd February, I received a telegram from A.B.D.A. Command stating that the War Cabinet had decided that, in view of the proposed large increase in the Army in Burma, Lieutenant-General Alexander should be appointed as Commander-in-Chief Burma, and that I should remain as C.G.S. after his arrival. I remained therefore in Burma till the end of April.

X. CONCLUSION

109. *Enemy Organisation and Methods.* Perhaps the most important characteristic of the Japanese soldier is his ability to live almost entirely on the country and to dispense with the enormous administrative organisation in rear of the fighting troops that is required by most armies.

He achieves this by being tough. He can live for five days on the rice he actually carries and he has been taught that he must reduce his expenditure of ammunition to that which he can carry. He uses any means of transport available – porters, civilians, bullock carts, boats, captured M.T., etc., but has little in the unit. His troops do not expect to be carried everywhere in M.T. The other main point is his insistence on the offensive spirit and the tactics of envelopment. Quite small forces will work round the rear of a much larger force and may succeed in defeating it entirely by bluff.

They are very thorough. There is no doubt that their officers have carefully studied the terrain of Burma and know far more about the jungle tracks than our own troops. They have arranged long ago for an intelligence service, for local guides, etc. They do not hesitate to fight in plain clothes or enemy uniform if it suits their purpose and, although they may deny any deliberate policy of committing atrocities, both officers and men often kill or maim prisoners or wounded after capture in a most brutal and coldblooded manner. They neglect enemy wounded completely – even more than they do their own.

Owing to the weakness of their administrative organisation, there is likely to be a considerable pause between the main phases of an operation. Furthermore if they lose the initiative they may well run short of either food or ammunition, or both. They are extremely careless as regards protective dispositions and in the presence of an enterprising enemy could be made to pay dearly. They do not like being attacked and when the day comes to take the offensive there is little doubt among our troops of their ability to defeat them.

In the jungle they make great use of whistle signals and battle cries, a method which our troops have tried to imitate. It is worth considering whether bugle calls would not also be valuable. They make great use of night for infiltration and to avoid being caught in the open by armoured fighting vehicles.

110. *Reasons for Loss of Rangoon.* The main reasons for the loss of Rangoon may be summed up as:-

(*a*) Reinforcement too late and in insufficient numbers.

(*b*) Inadequacy of defence preparations in practically every respect.

(*c*) Unsuitable organisation and training of our own forces.

(*d*) The superior numbers, preparations and training of the enemy.

The battle east of the River Sittang really settled the fate of Rangoon, but the enemy preferred to await reinforcements before pushing on. The decision that the 7 Australian Division could not be spared to go to Burma and the diversion at the last moment of the East African Brigade, a strong Brigade which had seen service, removed any prospect of retrieving the situation.

The inadequacy of the defence preparations in Burma has been sufficiently brought out by the narrative above. Without a sound foundation of this kind it is very difficult to make the best use of reinforcements thrown in at the last moment and throughout the campaign there has been the immediate menace of an administrative breakdown.

We had failed to secure the support of the local population or to arrest the leaders of disaffected elements. Owing to our failure to reinforce in time the enemy was nearly always a march ahead of us. It is easy to see that even one more infantry brigade received early in January would have sufficed to turn the scale in practically every battle from Kawkareik to Rangoon.

Throughout the operations the enemy was in superior numbers, usually about two to one on the actual battle front. Any idea that the Army in Burma during this period was driven back by inferior numbers is entirely incorrect.

111. *Training.* The lack of troops specially trained and equipped for jungle warfare, as compared with the specialist troops brought against them, or indeed troops sufficiently trained to take part in operations against an organised enemy in considerably superior numbers, was a very important factor.

112. *Burma Rifles.* Attempts had been made to turn the personnel of the Burma Rifles into regular soldiers of the standard pattern. Had they been suitably organised, trained and equipped as a frontier corps specially for jungle warfare, and placed under selected officers they might have been invaluable.

113. *Burma Frontier Force.* The Burma Frontier Force came under Army control for operations only at the commencement of the war. The Frontier Force had recently been expanded and was composed largely of good Indian material, but had few officers. It would have paid to have sent many of the good E.C.Os. available to the Frontier Force instead of to the Burma Rifles. The fire power of battalions was restricted by an insufficiency of mortars and automatics, which were not available in quantity until after the war with Japan had broken out, and units were then required to employ them in action before they had time to learn the efficient use of them. Owing to the fact that in peace there were no major frontier problems in Burma, the Burma Frontier Force were not ready or trained for serious war and units were further handicapped during action by the fact that they had an excess of baggage and transport, and that their peace time system of

administration was quite unsuitable for war. These factors affected the efficiency of the Burma Frontier Force and as a consequence it offered little resistance to the enemy.

114. *Jungle Warfare.* As regards the British and Indian Army units, the jungle has never, whether in India or Burma, been regarded as a "good training area." In the former this was understandable at a period when practically all the troops available were earmarked for Mid-East. In Burma it was incomprehensible. Jungle warfare was obviously inevitable if Burma were attacked and it is well-known to require a very high standard of training.

115. *Organisation and Equipment.* As regards organisation and equipment, most of the units in Burma, or which came to Burma from India, were on a mixed scale of M.T. and Pack. This I am now convinced was thoroughly unsound as units tended to get tied to roads and were unable to move across country with the same freedom as the Japanese. It introduced a road bound mentality among both officers and men. It has also provided the enemy with an admirable form of tactics, which consists in placing road blocks at suitable defiles behind our lines, so placed that they had to be cleared up before M.T. could pass.

In a country like Burma, or in any country without many roads and not normally passable to M.T., battalions should be organised entirely on a pack basis, and not with an unduly high scale of transport. All M.T. should be concentrated into a brigade unit which is tactically and administratively self-sufficient and can, if necessary, be sent to another part of the battlefield. Unless this is done, even late in the day, we shall continue to have units tied to roads and incapable of operating away from them. This organisation is equivalent to the regimental organisation which exists in foreign armies, for which it is essential we should devise some adequate substitute.

116. It is for consideration whether the demand for mechanisation and a high standard of equipment has not been overdone in recent years. For service in Europe or in the Middle East, it is no doubt justified though the Germans still retain horse transport in the infantry battalion. The Japanese have shown that a highly trained and disciplined army can achieve great things with a very light scale of equipment and no M.T. This was not only the case in the jungle and hills, but also on the plains east of Pegu and latterly both north and south of Prome. The secret, I believe, lies in the N.C.Os. of the Japanese Army, they are very highly trained, enforce very strict discipline and are given great privileges. Their soldiers are veterans and not raw recruits.

117. If all the Indian Army units did not show themselves to the best advantage in the campaign, it must be attributed to:-

(*a*) The presence of large numbers of recently joined and very young recruits in the ranks.

(*b*) A number of very recently joined officers who did not know their men and whose knowledge of Hindustani was hardly sufficient to get their confidence quickly.

(*c*) The effect of units being thrown into battle before they had time to collect themselves.

(*d*) The utterly strange conditions of warfare in the jungle.

(*e*) A distrust, often exaggerated, of units of the Burma Army.

As regards the latter many officers and men of all classes did well, and some units, but as a whole they were a source of serious weakness to the force of which they formed a large proportion throughout the operations.

118. *Achievements of the Army in Burma.* – There is no doubt, however, that although some units and some individuals may have failed, the Army in Burma, as a whole, fought extremely well. For many months they withstood the onslaught of superior numbers, with little reinforcement, no rest, and practically no hope of relief. During most of the time they have suffered heavily from enemy air attack and have received little or no support from our own air forces. They have had no canteens, few amenities and practically all lost their complete kit early in the campaign. The climatic conditions have been very trying. The fall of Singapore has undoubtedly had a depressing effect on morale. Discipline has naturally suffered to a considerable extent; this however has been largely due to the lack of any provost units to check straggling in the early stages.

Finally, it is fair to say that owing to the losses and hardships they had sustained, two brigades of the 17 Indian Division, i.e., about one-third the Imperial Forces that I handed over to General Alexander, were undoubtedly in no shape for a long and arduous campaign in the defence of Upper Burma, and I should like here to express my admiration for what they have achieved under his leadership. The position, however, was by no means hopeless. The remainder of the force available consisting of the Armoured Brigade, the weak 1 Burma Division (containing the 13 Indian Infantry Brigade and I and 2 Burma Brigades), the 63 Indian Infantry Brigade and three British battalions, had not been heavily engaged and there was also every reason to anticipate that the large Chinese forces now appearing in the field would give a good account of themselves.

Report by General the Honourable Sir Harold R.L.G. Alexander, K.C.B., C.S.I., D.S.O., M.C., on Operations in Burma from 5th March, 1942, to 20th May, 1942.

1. The following is a report on the operations of the Allied Forces in Burma from my arrival in that country on the 5th March, 1942, up to the 20th May, 1942, by which date the rear guard of the Imperial Forces had withdrawn into India.

2. I arrived by air at 12.00 hours on the 4th March at Dum Dum aerodrome Calcutta, where I met the Commander-in-Chief in India, General Sir Archibald Wavell, and there he gave me a resumé of the situation in Burma and a verbal directif to the following effect:-

"The retention of Rangoon was a matter of vital importance to our position in the Far East and every effort must be made to hold it. If, however, that was not possible the force must not be allowed to be cut off and destroyed but must be withdrawn from the Rangoon area for the defence of Upper Burma. This must be held as long as possible in order to safeguard the oil fields at Yenangyaung, keep contact with the Chinese and protect the construction of the road from Assam to Burma."

PART I. – OPERATIONS RESULTING IN THE LOSS OF RANGOON.

3. After this conference with the Commander-in-Chief I flew to Magwe, which I reached that evening. On the morning of the 5th March I flew to Rangoon, arriving at Army Headquarters at midday.

4.[3] *Situation at the Time of my Arrival.* On arrival at Army Headquarters I found that General Hutton was away at the front, and, in his absence, the situation was explained to me by the staff as follows:-

17 *Indian Division* were holding the area Pegu-Hlegu with – 48 Infantry Brigade and 7 Armoured Brigade in area Pegu; 16 Infantry Brigade – Hlegu.

Both these Infantry Brigades were very weak and disorganised as explained in General Hutton's Report.

63 Infantry Brigade, having just disembarked, was at Hlawga, sixteen miles north of Rangoon, but its transport was still on board ship.

1 *Burma Division* having handed over the defence of Southern Shan States to Chinese Sixth Army was located:-

13 Indian Infantry Brigade – Mawchi.
1 Burma Brigade – Pyu.
2 Burma Brigade – Nyaunglebin.

There was a gap of 40 miles between forward elements of 1 Burma Division and 17 Division.

There were Japanese forces in Waw and the neighbouring villages north and north-east of Pegu, and in addition Japanese columns had been infiltrating across the Sittang River between Pegu and Nyaunglebin under cover of darkness for some days. These had entered the Pegu Yomas, the jungle country north and north-west of Pegu.

5.[3] *Operations at Pegu.* In view of this situation, which looked, to say the least, serious, I set off at once for the Headquarters of 17 Division at Hlegu where I met General Hutton and Major-General Cowan, commanding 17 Division. The situation was here explained to me again but in more detail and General Hutton told me of the orders for the evacuation of Rangoon which he wished to issue but had held up pending my arrival. I was not satisfied that Rangoon could not be held but it appeared to me that the only course of action which could save the situation was to effect a junction between 1 Burma Division and 17 Division with the object of preventing any further Japanese infiltration into the Yomas.

I accordingly ordered 17 Division to carry out offensive operations against the Japanese at Waw and in the neighbouring villages with a view to relieving pressure on their immediate front, and at the same time I ordered 2 Infantry Brigade of 1 Burma Division to advance south from Nyaunglebin to join hands with 17 Division. The offensive carried out on 5th March by the 17 Division and part of the Armoured Brigade from Pegu was locally successful but during this operation the Japanese attacked from the wooded country bordering Pegu on the west and succeeded in capturing a part of the town. Considerable fighting took place there on 6th March but 17 Division were not successful in ejecting the Japanese. Meanwhile, the wider enemy encircling movement which had been in progress when I arrived had developed, and the road from Rangoon south-west of Pegu which had been under snipers' fire on 5th March was definitely cut on 6th March.

6. *Decision to withdraw from Rangoon.* Counter-attacks to open the road failed and I then ordered 63 Indian Infantry Brigade to be put at the disposal of the Commander 17 Division.

An attack on 6th March by this Infantry Brigade to open the road was not successful and the situation by noon on this day was as follows:-

The troops cut off in Pegu consisted of – 7 Hussars, 48 Indian Infantry Brigade, 1 W. Yorks, and 1 Cameronians.

[4] There was further confirmation that a force of 2,000 Japanese previously reported by Burma Frontier Force patrols had passed through Paunggyi about 30 miles north of Hlegu and was moving in a south-westerly direction.

[4] It was also confirmed about this time that a number of traitor Burmans with Japanese officers had landed at the mouth of the Rangoon River, threatening the Syriam refineries where there was only a small garrison.

In view of this situation I considered that the retention of Rangoon was quite impossible with the comparatively small forces at my disposal, dispersed as they were and with part of them already encircled.

I therefore decided that the right course of action was to order the destruction of the oil refineries at Syriam, the evacuation of Rangoon and the regrouping of my forces north of Rangoon in the Irrawaddy valley. The order to put the Denial Scheme into operation was issued at midnight on the 6th March.

7. *Force cut off and breaks out at Taukkyan.* On the morning of the 7th March, Army Headquarters, administrative units and troops not required to cover the demolitions in Rangoon area moved out of Rangoon on the Prome road. Near Taukkyan, twenty-one miles north of Rangoon at about 11.00 hours, the leading vehicles of Army Headquarters ran into an enemy road block and the column was held up. Attempts by the 1 Glosters, 2/13 F.F. Rifles and some tanks of the 7 Hussars throughout the day failed to clear the block. It must be remembered here that the force in Pegu was still cut off, all the efforts on the 6th March of the 63 Infantry Brigade to relieve it having been unsuccessful.

On the 7th March, however, the force in Pegu was ordered to cut its way out and this it eventually succeeded in doing with the loss of some of its transport. Meanwhile, 63 Infantry Brigade had concentrated near Hlegu and it was decided to use this brigade to attack the road block north of Taukkyan early on the 8th March, strongly supported by tanks and artillery.

This attack of 63 Infantry Brigade was unsuccessful in effecting an immediate clearance of the road block. The situation was very serious but such troops of 16 Indian Infantry Brigade as were available were collected from Hlegu, together with some tanks, and another attack was carried out later in the morning. This attack succeeded. The road block was found to be clear and, although there was a good deal of sniping which made it necessary to piquet the route with the 16 Infantry Brigade, the column moved north without further serious interference. That this was possible was partly due to the fact that the Japanese, in their eagerness to reach Rangoon, had passed further round our left flank and were actually entering the north-west outskirts of the town as our troops were moving north through the road block.

While the column, consisting of Army Headquarters, administrative units, etc., moved northwards from Taukkyan, the withdrawal of the remainder of 17 Division from Pegu and Hlegu continued. On the night of the 8th March, 17 Division (less a detachment of tanks and infantry which had been sent to keep open the road Taukkyan – Tharrawaddy) was concentrated in the Taukkyan area. It may be remarked here that intensive bombing attacks by the enemy could have done great damage, as the whole force was now concentrated in a comparatively small area.

That this did not take place was due to the temporary but complete ascendancy which had been established by the R.A.F. during recent Japanese attacks in which the enemy had sustained very severe losses. The few enemy bombers which did attempt to attack the Taukkyan area were kept at a great height by our light and heavy anti-aircraft artillery.

The move northwards from Taukkyan was commenced on the morning of 9th March.

My intention was to concentrate 17 Division in the area Thonze – Tharrawaddy – Letpadan and to hold the line Henzada – Sanywe Ferry – Thonze – Thonze Chaung.

The withdrawal from Taukkyan was without enemy interference and concentration in the new area was completed by evening of 11th March.

8. *Effect of the Loss of Rangoon.* The effect of the loss of Rangoon was very serious, since it is the only point of entry to Burma through which personnel and supplies can be moved in large numbers.

9. Rangoon was the base port for Burma and after the fall of that city the army was fighting facing its former base and with no L. of C. behind it. In the absence of a road to India the army was virtually cut off from outside assistance and could be supplied only with the very limited numbers of personnel and small quantities

of stores which could be brought in by air. Base and L. of C. installations and reserves of various commodities had already been moved north of Rangoon and this back loading had to continue throughout the withdrawal, which placed an enormous strain on the administrative machine and on the transportation agencies. Civil heavy repair installations in the Rangoon area which could not be moved were lost altogether and the maintenance of mechanical transport and equipment became a matter of great difficulty.

10. The destruction of the refineries, where the refining of all crude oil from the oil fields had been carried out, very much reduced the output of motor and aviation spirit and lubricating oils and rendered the Allied Forces in Burma dependent on such spirit as could be produced by improvised methods in the oil fields themselves, when reserve stocks had been consumed.

11. The loss of the Rangoon aerodromes with their efficient warning system had the most serious consequences for the R.A.F. and on the air situation in Burma. This will be touched on in more detail in a later paragraph.

12. Turning to the enemy side of the picture, the fall of Rangoon transferred to the Japanese nearly all the advantages in communications which had previously been held by the Imperial Forces. Instead of having to supply their army by difficult mountain roads the Japanese were now able, after effecting repairs to the port, to move very large forces by sea to Burma. In fact it is not too much to say that until such time as the road from Assam to Burma was completed the retention of Upper Burma by the allies was dependent on the amount of force which the Japanese decided to employ in that theatre. The task of the allies therefore was to impose the maximum delay on the enemy and make him expend resources which he might have employed elsewhere.

PART II. – REGROUPING OF FORCES CONSEQUENT ON THE FALL OF RANGOON.

13. A period of comparative quiet followed the withdrawal from Rangoon. Apparently, at this time the enemy was resting and refitting in the Rangoon area whilst his propaganda machine exploited to the full the fall of the city. This period of quiet was most welcome as my forces were badly in need of rest and reorganisation.

14. Having failed in my primary task of holding Rangoon, I now had to consider my secondary task which was the retention of Upper Burma. In order to achieve this it was necessary to regroup the forces.

15. *The Situation on the Irrawaddy Front.* At this stage the 17 Division was reforming in the area Thonze – Tharrawaddy – Letpadan and carrying out reconnaissances with a view to the selection of the most suitable ground on which to fight the enemy in the Irrawaddy valley. In view of the situation on the Toungoo front, a position around Prome and south of that town was finally chosen as offering the best ground for future operations.

16. *The Situation on the Toungoo Front, Arrival of the Chinese Fifth Army.* To divert attention from the Irrawaddy front, 1 Burma Division made on 11th March an attack to clear the villages of Shwegyin and Madouk. This operation, which was carried out by the 1 Burma Rifles and the 5/I Punjab Regiment, was successful, and on its completion 1 Burma Division, less 13 Infantry Brigade, was withdrawn to the area north of Kanyutkwin.

17. In reorganising my forces it was necessary to have more strength in the Irrawaddy valley. I therefore arranged for the Chinese Fifth Army to relieve the 1 Burma Division on the Toungoo front so that this Division could be brought across into the Irrawaddy valley, and concentrated there with the 17 Division. The date on which this could take place was dependent on the moves of the Chinese Fifth Army and it was not until the third week of March that the relief of the 1 Burma Division could be effected. Up to that time the 1 Burma Division, which had been covering the concentration of the Chinese, fought a delaying action back on Toungoo. It would have been possible, had the Chinese agreed, to have handed over to them a large area south of Toungoo. They were not however willing to go south of that place and it became necessary to give up this area or to abandon the concentration of the Imperial Forces in the Irrawaddy valley. This I could not afford to do.

18. During the same period, the 17 Division, in order to conform with the gradual withdrawal of the 1 Burma Division, commenced to move back towards the Prome area. To keep touch with events on the Toungoo front, columns from Frontier Force units were stationed in the Pegu Yomas to give warning and to prevent any Japanese infiltration through this area. Other light forces were also stationed west of the Irrawaddy to intercept enemy penetration on this bank of the River. Advanced detachments consisting of tanks and lorry-borne infantry were ordered to operate southwards along the Prome road towards Rangoon to delay and harass any Japanese forces moving north. The only engagement of any note which took place was an attack by the 1 Glosters supported by tanks against forces of Japanese and traitor Burmans at Letpadan on the 19th March. This attack was successful in capturing the town and inflicting losses on the enemy.

19. *Formation of a Corps Headquarters.* The concentration of the Imperial Forces now necessitated the formation of a Corps, especially as at this stage I was nominally in command of all Chinese forces operating in Burma. I therefore requested G.H.Q. India to supply me with a Corps Commander and a skeleton Corps Headquarters. The Corps Commander, in the person of Lieut.-General W.J. Slim, M.C., arrived on the 19th March and took over Command of the Corps (I Burcorps) but, owing to the limitations of air transport, a skeleton Corps Headquarters could not be provided from India and the staff and signals had to be found from Burma Army resources.

20. *Arrival of General Stilwell.* On the 12th March I went to Maymyo, now the centre of the Civil Government, which had been selected as the only suitable

location for my headquarters. On the 14th March General Stilwell of the American Army arrived and informed me that he had come to take over command of the Fifth and Sixth Chinese Armies. General Stilwell had only a small staff and no signal communications of his own, so that this arrangement did not appear very satisfactory. It was, however, the Generalissimo's order and I could not interfere, but I informed G.H.Q. India by telegram of this new development.

21. *My Visit to Chungking.* At this time I decided to go to Chungking for the purpose of paying my respects to the Generalissimo Chiang Kai-Shek, to explain to him the military situation in Burma, and to ensure that he was satisfied with the administrative arrangements which had been made for his troops. Accordingly I left Maymyo by air on the 24th March. I was warmly received by the Chinese and had several very satisfactory talks with the Generalissimo, at the last of which he expressed the wish for unity of command of the Imperial and Chinese Forces in Burma, and asked me to accept the command of all his troops in that country. On my return to Maymyo I informed General Stilwell of the Generalissimo's wishes and he readily agreed to serve under me as Supreme Commander in Burma. I should like to take this opportunity to add that General Stilwell and his American staff could not have been more loyal or more co-operative throughout the campaign. General Stilwell had my complete confidence. He was obviously liked and trusted by the Chinese, and he understood them and spoke their language.

22. *System of Command of the Chinese Armies.* Nevertheless, I must state here that the system of command of the Chinese forces in Burma was far from satisfactory. Nominally, I commanded all the Allied Forces. General Stilwell commanded the Chinese Fifth and Sixth Armies but he had to issue all his orders through a Chinese commander, General Lo Cho-Ying. There was, however, a system of liaison officers working under the Generalissimo and it appeared that no orders of a major nature issued by myself, by General Stilwell or by General Lo could be carried out unless they had the sanction of the Generalissimo, which had to be obtained through the latter's Liaison Mission, whose head was General Lin Wei at Lashio, and who in turn had a forward liaison officer in General Hou at Maymyo. Such an arrangement was obviously quite unsuitable for modern war since quick decisions for the employment of the Chinese forces were impossible to obtain and this, together with the almost total lack of knowledge of staff duties which existed in the Chinese forces, caused considerable delay in the execution of vital movements.

23. *Concentration of 1 Burcorps.* The move of 1 Burma Division, on relief by the 200 Chinese Division, to the Irrawaddy front commenced on the night of 21st–22nd March. Owing to the difficulties of communication between the Toungoo and Irrawaddy valleys, the bulk of the 1 Burma Division was despatched by rail and road via Pyinmana and Taungdwingyi. The 5 Burma Rifles proceeded by march route from Toungoo to Prome over the Yomas. On the 25th March the

newly formed 1 Burcorps issued orders for the concentration of the Corps in the area Allanmyo – Prome with 1 Burma Division in the area Dayindabo – Kyankpadaung – Allanmyo – Thayetmyo, 17 Division in area Wettigan – Prome – Shwedaung – Sinde, 7 Armoured Brigade in the area of Tamagauk in Corps reserve. The defence of the area was based on the two brigade groups in Allanmyo and Prome, the remainder of the force being mobile and prepared to act offensively. On the Irrawaddy the detachment of the Royal Marines, which had covered the demolitions at Syriam, found the crews for a river patrol.

24. *Operations resulting in the Loss of Toungoo.* On the Toungoo front the concentration of the Chinese Fifth Army was seriously delayed by the movement of the rear echelons of the Chinese Sixth Army and also by the disintegration of the railway system which was beginning to set in as a result of enemy bombing. On the 24th March, the situation on this front was as follows: - (For Chinese Order of Battle see Appendix "A").

All Imperial units had been withdrawn north of Toungoo en route to the Irrawaddy front.

The 200 Division was entrenched in and around Toungoo with the divisional cavalry unit holding the river line to the south. The Fifth Army Troops were in Pyawbwe with certain units forward under command of the 200 Division. The other divisions of the Fifth Army were:-

22 Division with leading regiment arriving at Pyinmana, rear formation at Lashio.

96 Division approaching the frontier.

On the 24th March, the Japanese made a surprise attack on the aerodrome north of Toungoo thus cutting off the 200 Division. The rear echelon of the 1 Burma Division, including the 23 Mountain Battery and Frontier Force Columns I and 4, were involved in the fighting for the aerodrome and put up a stout resistance. By the evening of the 26th March the whole of the Chinese 22 Division had been concentrated in the area Pyinmana – Yedashe and the leading troops of the 96 Division were approaching Pyinmana. On 28th March the 22 Division attacked south from Yedashe with the object of relieving the 200 Division at Toungoo but made little headway, and on the 1st April the 200 Division cut its way out from Toungoo, where it had been besieged for over a week, and passed through into reserve at Yezin, north of Pyinmana.

25. *The Japanese establish Air Superiority.* The air situation was, as has been previously mentioned, adversely affected by the loss of the Rangoon aerodrome. At this time there were in Burma only the following aerodromes fit for operational use:-

Magwe, Akyab, Lashio, and Loiwing (in China).

There were also the following landing grounds suitable only as A.L.Gs. or for fighters:-

Namsan, Heho, Mandalay, Meiktila, Piawbwe and Shwebo.

Toungoo aerodrome had by this time been rendered untenable by enemy bombing raids.

None of the above, with the exception of Loiwing, had an efficient warning system. This was partly due to lack of essential equipment and W/T personnel and partly to hills which acted as a screen to the approach of hostile aircraft.

So far as the air was concerned, the operational advantages were now with the enemy and this was soon demonstrated in the severe reverse which was sustained by the R.A.F. at Magwe on the 21st and 22nd March when a large number of aircraft, both fighters and bombers, were destroyed on the ground. This reverse forced the R.A.F. and the A.V.G. to withdraw from Magwe to Loiwing, 400 miles further north, and this reduced very much the effectiveness of the air force.

The supply of aircraft now became the ruling factor in the air situation in Burma. In view of the limited amount of aircraft available at this time, that is to say the end of March and the beginning of April, for the defence of India and Ceylon, it was decided that all R.A.F. units should be withdrawn from Burma, where it was uneconomical to retain aircraft in operational conditions which rendered high losses inevitable. However, an R.A.F. organisation known as "Burwing" was retained at Lashio and Loiwing and aircraft were flown over from India from time to time; but very little could be achieved in the circumstances prevailing.

That the decision to withdraw the R.A.F. to India was right there can be no doubt, but this decision left the Japanese with almost undisputed command of the air and this had a serious effect on the civil population and the working of the utility services and a somewhat lesser effect on the morale of the troops.

26. *Effect of Bombing on Public Utility Services.* At the end of March and the beginning of April, the Japanese commenced to make heavy bombing raids on centres of communication in Central and Upper Burma, raids being made on such places as Prome, Meiktila, Mandalay, Thazi, Pyinmana, Maymyo, Lashio and Taunggyi.

Except for the damage to house property, the material effect of these raids was not very great but the moral effect amongst the civil population was enormous. After a heavy raid on a town, the life of that community came practically to a standstill, the population moving into the jungle. From the military aspect, the effect on the working of the public utility services was most serious. Many railway employees and I.W.T. workers in the employment of the Irrawaddy Flotilla Company left their jobs. The Police force disintegrated, the power supply broke down and the Post and Telegraph service, to whom a tribute should be paid for the manner in which a large number of personnel stuck to their jobs, was affected to a lesser degree.

The effect of bombing on public utility workers was accentuated by the presence of their families, many of whom had not at this time been evacuated and it is a point for consideration in the future, that all workers in services on which military operations depend do better, when they know that their families have been removed to a place of safety.

PART III. – THE BATTLE FOR THE OILFIELDS.

27. *Operations South of Prome.* On the 26th March the Japanese commenced to operate against the positions held by 1 Burcorps in the Irrawaddy valley. Prome was bombed on the 26th March and three quarters of the town was burnt. On the 27th March four to five thousand Japanese and Burmese were reported to be on the west bank of the Irrawaddy opposite Tonbo. On the same day, at the request of the Generalissimo, I despatched from Chungking a telegram ordering offensive operations on the Irrawaddy front in order to relieve pressure on the Chinese Fifth Army, which at this time was heavily engaged. On the 28th March the Japanese advance guard on the east of the Irrawaddy attacked the 17 Division reconnaissance unit, the 1 Glosters, at Paungde and fighting continued throughout the day. Commander 1 Burcorps decided that this was a good opportunity for offensive action. Accordingly a force consisting of one armoured regiment and two infantry battalions attacked early on the 29th March and recaptured Paungde, but during the day a strong enemy force appeared at Padigon, six miles to the north. Another enemy force in considerable strength, after surprising and overcoming a commando unit on the west bank, crossed the river from Padaung and occupied Shwedaung establishing road blocks across the main road, thus cutting off the force at Paungde.

28. During the following 48 hours fierce fighting took place and, although the tactical situation was not unfavourable to the Imperial Forces, the familiar Japanese tactics of establishing road blocks in their rear forced the 17 Division to abandon their main object of destroying the enemy in the Paungde area in order to reopen their L. of C. This brought about the withdrawal of the 17 Division to the Prome area, which was completed by the evening of the 30th March. During this fighting the enemy was actively assisted by traitor Burmans and some Japanese were found to be wearing Burmese clothes. The commando unit referred to in paragraph 27 was surprised by Japanese soldiers who had disguised themselves in this manner.

29. *Withdrawal to the Dry Zone.* On the 30th March the Commander-in-Chief in India arrived by air in Burma and on the 1st April I accompanied him by air from Mandalay to Magwe, proceeding by road to Corps Headquarters at Allanmyo. At a conference which took place here on the afternoon of the 1st April the Commander-in-Chief agreed that, in view of the difficulties of the country and the fatigue of the troops in 17 Division, a withdrawal from Prome to the Allanmyo area should commence forthwith, and that this withdrawal might have to be continued even further north into the dry zone south of Taungdwingyi, where the country was more open and more suitable for the employment of tanks. On the evening of the 1st April the enemy attacked Prome and penetrated the defences held by the 63 Infantry Brigade securing the high ground south of the

town. The 17 Division was forced to withdraw on the 2nd April north and north-east of Prome. On the 3rd April the 17 Division moved back through 1 Burma Division, in position in the area Dayindabo – Pyalo, to the area Ywataung – Kyaukpadaung – Bwetkyichaung, the 48 Infantry Brigade and the 7 Armoured Brigade, less one regiment, moving during the night of the 3rd to 4th April to Satthwa. On the 3rd April 1 Burcorps issued an Operation Instruction covering the possibility of a withdrawal to the line Minhla – Taungdwingyi and the withdrawal from Prome, which was originally intended to stop at Allanmyo, was, in view of the tired state of the troops, continued to this line, which was reached by the night of the 4th-5th April except by the 2 Burma Brigade, moving up the west bank, which did not reach Minhla till the night of the 8th-9th April.

During this period the enemy air force was very active and there was a considerable amount of bombing and machine gunning in the forward area.

30. *Dispositions for the Defence of the Oilfields.* The dispositions of 1 Burcorps on the 9th April were on the general line Minhla, Migyaungye, Nyaungyatsan, Thadodan and Taungdwingyi. It will be noted that the stretch of front from Minhla to Taungdwingyi was over 40 miles and that in consequence there was no depth. With this in mind, I had on the 4th April requested General Tu Yu Ming, commanding Chinese Fifth Army, to send one Chinese regiment[5] to hold Taungdwingyi so as to enable 1 Burcorps to form a reserve. General Tu informed me that he had already ordered one battalion to Taungdwingyi. The fire power of the Chinese battalion was, however, not more than that of a company of Imperial troops. A regiment was therefore promised.

After further consideration I decided that at least one Chinese division was required to hold Taungdwingyi and accordingly I asked the Generalissimo, who arrived in Maymyo on the 6th April, to make a division available for this purpose. He promised that he would do so. In the event, however, only one Chinese battalion reached the Taungdwingyi area. The failure of the Chinese to supply a division for the defence of Taungdwingyi had the most serious consequences.

31. *Lack of Information.* I feel it is necessary to comment here on the lack of intelligence at my disposal. Owing to the hostility of the local population and to the total lack of air reconnaissance, information was most difficult to get. It appeared, however, from such identifications as were obtained that 1 Burcorps were opposed only by the Japanese 33 Division but that this Division was assisted by a considerable number of traitor Burmans. On the Chinese front only the Japanese 55 Division had been identified. The operations which took place about this time illustrate clearly the advantage which the initiative confers on a highly trained force which has the assistance of the local population in a country of great distances and poor communications. The successes which the Japanese gained cannot all be ascribed to their superior training and, at this time, superior morale.

32. *Destruction of the Oilfields.* On the 10th April it became apparent that enemy columns were moving north on tracks south-west of Taungdwingyi. On the

11th April a Corps striking force consisting of the 7 Armoured Brigade and the 48 Infantry Brigade moved south to attack the most easterly of these columns. Contact was established on the morning of the 12th April and by 0800 hours the 48 Infantry Brigade was being heavily pressed and bitter fighting took place in which the Corps striking force more than held its own. Another enemy column on the east bank of the Irrawaddy was attacked by the 1 Burma Brigade. Owing to the non-arrival of the Chinese division which had been promised for the defence of Taungdwingyi, the Commander 1 Burcorps now felt that he could not continue to hold Taungdwingyi and also cover the direct approach to the oilfields, and he represented this opinion to me. To have abandoned Taungdwingyi would have opened the right flank and rear of the Chinese Fifth Army, whose advanced troops were still south of Pyinmana, and it would also have uncovered the communications of the Imperial Forces through Mandalay.

On the 12th April therefore, I ordered 1 Burcorps to hold Taungdwingyi at all costs. This order was received at Headquarters 1 Burcorps on the morning of the 13th April and orders were then issued for the 48 Brigade and the 7 Hussars to come under command of the 17 Division and 7 Armoured Brigade less one regiment to come under command 1 Burma Division. Enemy pressure on the 1 Burma Division south of Magwe continued on the 13th and 14th and this caused a wide gap to be opened between the two Divisions. Moving across country the enemy pushed into this gap threatening the oilfields. Orders for the destruction of the Yenangyaung oilfields were issued on the night of the 14th April and the denial scheme was successfully carried out during the following 48 hours. It required two full daylights to complete the destruction ending with the blowing of the power house, which took place when the Japanese were already in the outskirts of Yenangyaung.

By the 16th April 1 Burma Division, less 2 Burma Brigade on the right bank of the Irrawaddy, had withdrawn to Kadaung Chaung, seventeen miles south of Yenangyaung. The 2 K.O.Y.L.I. who had been cut off in Myingun fought their way out and rejoined their Division.

33. *The Fight at Yenangyaung.* On the 17th April the enemy established road blocks north and south of the Pinchaung, immediately north of Yenangyaung, cutting off 1 Burma Division and some of the Corps Troops. The 2 Royal Tanks and Corps Troops fought their way out north but, by the time 1 Burma Division reached Yenangyaung on the night of the 17th April, the road blocks had been reestablished. After this action the greater number of the enemy dead were found to be clad in khaki uniforms and wearing felt hats of the type used by Gurkha and Burma Rifle units.

34. Meanwhile the 113 Regiment of the Chinese 38 Division had been moved from Mandalay to Kyaukpadaung and placed under command 1 Burcorps. On the morning of the 18th April this Regiment and the 2 Royal Tanks attacked the enemy road block north of the Pinchaung, but the attack went wide and failed to dislodge the enemy. An attack by 1 Burma Division failed to clear the block to the

south. On the evening of the 18th April information was received that an enemy column was moving north by Magwe. During this time the 17 Division and 7 Hussars holding Taungdwingyi and Natmauk were unmolested by the enemy.

35. On the 16th and 17th April, I visited Corps Headquarters and Headquarters of the Chinese Armies at Pyawbwe. At this time, and indeed previously, I impressed on General Stilwell the importance of Meiktila as a big centre of communications and I promised that, if possible, I would make the 7 Armoured Brigade, available for the defence of this place. Arrangements had already been put in hand to dump at Meiktila stocks of 87 octane spirit and lubricants and a dump of supplies had already been formed there since the 17 Division had, at this time, to be supplied through Meiktila and Pyawbwe.

At our meeting on the 17th April, General Stilwell discussed with me his plan for a counter attack south of Pyinmana and I promised to make the 7 Hussars available to assist the Chinese in this operation and orders were issued for them to be prepared to move to Pyawbwe. On the 18th April it became clear to me that the projected Chinese counter attack would not take place and, in view of the situation on the Irrawaddy front, and in the Shan States, I again visited General Stilwell's Headquarters at Pyawbwe on the 19th, having arranged to meet the Commander 1 Burcorps there. At this meeting, I stressed the importance of holding strongly the centres of communication from Chauk to Kyaukpadaung – Meiktila – Thazi. General Stilwell and I were in full agreement and it was arranged that the whole of the 38 Chinese Division should be placed under the command of 1 Burcorps.

36. We then discussed plans for offensive action. The deep penetration made by the Japanese 33 Division at Yenangyaung appeared to present a favourable opportunity for a counter stroke but, owing to the nature and extent of the country, this was beyond the capacity of 1 Burcorps alone, as considerable forces were required merely to find the enemy should he elect to move into the jungle. General Stilwell agreed to make available for a counter stroke the 200 Chinese Division and one regiment of the 22 Division in addition to the 38 Division, and arrangements were made to set in motion the moves of these formations towards Kyaukpadaung and Ywamun as soon as possible. Having made these arrangements I accompanied the Commander 1 Burcorps to his Headquarters between Meiktila and Kyaukpadaung. On arrival there I found that the attacks of the 113 Chinese Regiment and the 2 Royal Tanks had succeeded in clearing the northern bank of the Pinchaung but that 1 Burma Division had been unable to clear the Japanese from the south bank, 1 Burma Division were being attacked by an enemy column which had moved north from Magwe and columns sent out by the 17 Division from Taungdwingyi and Natmauk had not succeeded in relieving the pressure. I told the Corps Commander that 1 Burma Division must fight its way out and that, if necessary, it would have to abandon its wheeled transport. Commander 1 Burcorps issued orders to this effect on the evening of the 19th and by the morning of the 20th 1 Burma Division had succeeded in extricating

itself with the loss of a great part of its M.T. On the 21st April, 113 Chinese Regiment crossed the Pinchaung and entered the outskirts of Yenangyaung where it inflicted considerable casualties on the enemy.

37. *Operations on the Chinese Front.* At this point it is necessary to turn to the events on the Chinese front east of the Pegu Yomas. After the withdrawal of the Chinese 200 Division from Toungoo on the 1st April, the situation on the Fifth Army front was as follows:-

the 22 Division at Yedashe,
the 96 Division in the area Pyinmana,
the 200 Division in the area Yezin with Fifth Army Headquarters, at Pyawbwe.

The position of this army was not unsatisfactory as it was holding a comparatively narrow front in great depth. There was a lull in the fighting until the 7th April when the Japanese advanced from Toungoo and attacked the 22 Division in and about Yedashe. Heavy fighting followed and 22 Division suffered severe casualties until it was relieved by the 96 Division and was withdrawn north of Pyinmana on the 18th April.

38. The loss of Toungoo opened up to the enemy the road to Karenni and the Shan States via Mawchi. The Japanese were not slow to take advantage of this opportunity and, on the 5th April, began to develop pressure in this direction. At first the movement was comparatively slow but later, when enemy reinforcements arrived, the momentum rapidly increased especially as there was a failure on the part of the Chinese to carry out the demolitions which had been prepared. Unfortunately the two important bridges at Toungoo and Bawlake were not blown but the demolitions on the Toungoo – Mawchi road were gallantly blown by the Karen Levies after the Chinese had retreated. In these operations the Levies suffered considerable casualties. Karenni and the Shan States were held by the Chinese Sixth Army consisting of 55, 49 and the 93 Divisions. Owing to the great length of the front, the Sixth Army was much strung out and had only a small reserve in the Loilem area.

39. At the beginning of April, Karenni was held by one regiment of the 55 Division but, as a result of the Japanese threat to this front, the whole of the 55 Division concentrated to the south of Loikaw by the 18th April. On the 14th April Japanese tanks were reported in the Mawchi area and, on the 19th April, an engagement took place 20 miles south of Loikaw. On the 20th April a further Japanese attack was made seven miles north of Loikaw from the direction of Mongpai and, at the same time, the encounter south of Loikaw developed into a major battle. Some days prior to this it had been decided to evacuate Kengtung and some units of the 93 Division had already moved west on the Salween, but the great distances and lack of transport made the formation of a reserve by Chinese Sixth Army very difficult. The position in the Southern Shan States was now serious and it will be seen from later paragraphs in my despatch that it was the situation there which affected the whole of my future plans.

PART IV. – PLANS IN THE EVENT OF WITHDRAWAL NORTH OF MANDALAY.

40. *Initial Appreciation.* Towards the end of March it became necessary to consider future policy as regards the defence of Upper Burma in the event of the loss of Mandalay and, under my direction, an appreciation was prepared by my staff. The principal factors which influenced me at this time were:-

(*a*) The need to give the Chinese Armies every possible assistance with a view to keeping China in the war, and

(*b*) The gaining of time to allow India to build up her defences and to complete the roads from Assam to Burma and from India to China via the Hukawng Valley.

41. Accordingly the outline plan, which was drawn up as a result of this appreciation, contemplated the following dispositions in the event of the loss of Mandalay:-

(*a*) *The Chinese Sixth Army (in the Shan States)* – Troops east of the River Salween to withdraw on Puerh. Troops west of the River Salween to withdraw towards Hsipaw and Lashio.

(*b*) *Chinese Fifth Army* to withdraw astride the Mandalay – Lashio Road.

(*c*) *Imperial Forces* – In order to maintain touch with the Chinese, the 7 Armoured Brigade and one infantry brigade of the 17 Division to accompany the Chinese Fifth Army.

(*d*) The 17 Division, less one infantry brigade, to withdraw on the axis Mandalay – Shwebo – Katha covering the projected route to China via the Hukawng Valley.

(*e*) 1 Burma Division to cover the approaches to India through Kalewa.

The appreciation and plan were approved by the Commander-in-Chief in India during his visit to Burma on the 31st March and 1st April.

A draft directive, dated the 4th April, was isued to 1 Burcorps on the 6th April and this was subsequently confirmed in an Operation Instruction. Administrative arrangements were also put in hand to implement this plan.

42. *Rice Situation.* During the first half of April, however, it became apparent that, owing to the gradual loss of the rice producing areas in Burma, to the closing of rice mills and the difficulties of collecting sufficient grain, to the disintegration of the railways and the famine in Yunnan, it would be impossible to accumulate in Lashio or beyond, sufficient stocks of rice to feed the Chinese armies for more than a few weeks. Therefore, on the plan as it stood, a withdrawal north of Mandalay would probably mean the starvation of the Chinese armies unless supplies could be sent from China and this seemed highly improbable. I therefore decided to invite the Chinese to withdraw some of their forces via Shwebo should this become necessary, as there was a better chance of their obtaining rice in this area.

43. On the 18th April, Lieut.-General Hutton, who had been replaced as my Chief of Staff by Major-General Winterton at the beginning of the month, returned from a mission to General Headquarters, India. General Hutton had discussed with the Commander-in-Chief in India the question of Imperial Forces accompanying the Chinese in a withdrawal on China. He stated that the Commander-in-Chief was prepared to agree to a change in this part of the plan if I thought it desirable. Nevertheless, I was so impressed with the political considerations that I determined to give the Chinese the opportunity of accepting or refusing the assistance of British forces on the axis Mandalay – Lashio.

44. *Meeting with General Lin Wei.* Accordingly, I arranged for a meeting with the Generalissimo's principal liaison officer, General Lin Wei, at Maymyo on the 21st April. At this meeting I explained to General Lin Wei all the factors to be taken into consideration and I specifically offered the Chinese the 7 Armoured Brigade, which could only get their vehicles out of Burma by the Lashio road if we were forced to leave that country. General Lin Wei agreed:-

(*a*) That the bulk of the Chinese Fifth Army should withdraw north via Shwebo, and

(*b*) That it would be better that no Imperial Forces should withdraw towards Lashio and that the tanks should be employed for the battle of Mandalay on the most suitable ground, which was north of the Irrawaddy towards Shwebo.

On the 22nd April an outline of the new plan was sent by liaison officer to the Headquarters 1 Burcorps and, on the 23rd April, Operation Instruction No. 46, the contents of which had been agreed by General Stilwell's staff at Maymyo, was issued.

45. *Situation North of Yenangyaung.* – Before explaining in detail the new plan for a withdrawal north of Mandalay it is necessary to return to the situation of 1 Burcorps north of Yenangyaung. On the 20th April, the day following my agreement with General Stilwell to undertake offensive operations in this area, the dispositions of 1 Burcorps were as follows:-

17 Division holding Taungdwingyi – Natmauk.

7 Armoured Brigade under orders to move to the Meiktila area.

38 Chinese Division under command 1 Burcorps with -

113 Regiment and two battalions 112 Regiment area Yenangyaung.

114 Regiment under orders to move from Mandalay to Taungtha.

I Burma Division reorganising in the area of Mount Popa. This Division had lost, in the fighting at Yenangyaung, about 20 per cent. of its personnel, two Bofors, four 3.7 howitzers, four 25 pounders, most of its 3-in. mortars and nearly all its M.T. The Division was not in a fit condition to fight for some days.

Efforts were being made to organise as rapidly as possible the move of the 200 Chinese Division from the Meiktila – Thazi area to Kyaukpadaung and one regiment of the 22 Division to Natmauk. Owing, however, to the lack of transport and to the difficulty of co-ordinating plans with the Chinese Fifth Army, it appeared improbable that the force could be concentrated and ready for offensive action before the morning of the 22nd April at the earliest.

46. On the 21st April the seriousness of the situation in the Shan States brought about the abandonment of the projected offensive against the Japanese 33 Division in the Yenangyaung area. The 200 Chinese Division was ordered by General Stilwell to move to Kalaw and the 22 Chinese Division to concentrate in the Thazi area. In these circumstances it became a matter of supreme importance to hold securely the centres of communication south of Mandalay. Accordingly the following moves were ordered by 1 Burcorps:-

38 Chinese Division to concentrate at Kyaukpadaung.

I Burma Division to be prepared to move to Taungtha.

17 Division to withdraw from Taungdwingyi and later from Natmauk to positions north west and west of Meiktila at Mahlaing and Zayetkon.

7 Armoured Brigade to Meiktila under command of General Lo, who now took over command of the Chinese forces on the Pyawbwe front, General Tu having moved with the 200 Division to Kalaw.

47. *The New Plan.* – The plan contained in Operation Instruction No. 46 envisaged the following dispositions north of the Irrawaddy:-

West of the River Mu. – 1 Burcorps less the 7 Armoured Brigade with the 1 Burma Division astride the River Chindwin and a strong detachment covering the approach to Kalewa via the Myittha valley.

Between the River Mu and the Northern Reach of the Irrawaddy. – 38 Chinese Division and the 7 Armoured Brigade.

In and South of Mandalay and holding the Crossings over the River Myitnge. – 22, 28 and 96 Chinese Divisions.

It will be realised that a withdrawal from the Meiktila area would uncover the communications with Mandalay of any Chinese forces in the area Kalaw – Taunggyi and would prevent their withdrawal via Mandalay. The plan therefore was for all Chinese forces east of the railway Mandalay – Pyawbwe to move towards Lashio. The situation was very delicate at this time and it was impossible to issue a hard and fast plan for any further withdrawal since no decision could be made in the existing situation as to whether the 22, 28 and 96 Chinese Divisions would withdraw to the north or whether they would fall back on Lashio.

48. I must emphasise here that I had no intention of withdrawing north of the Irrawaddy unless forced to give up Kyaukpadaung and Meiktila and, for the defence of these areas, I had grouped my forces as follows:-

(*a*) Under command of General Lo (Chinese C.-in-C.). – 22 Division, 96 Division and the 7 Armoured Brigade (for the defence of the area Meiktila – Thazi – Pyawbwe).

(*b*) Under the command of Lieut.-General Slim, 1 Burcorps – 17 Division, 1 Burma Division, 38 Chinese Division.

28 Chinese Division (less one regiment not yet arrived) was preparing the defences of Mandalay.

I had to consider the dangerous bottleneck of Mandalay through which run the approaches to the Ava Bridge, the only bridge over the Irrawaddy. These approaches were very vulnerable to air attack. I was determined not to allow my forces to be pushed into the loop of the Irrawaddy below Mandalay and be forced to fight with this obstacle at their backs. In order to avoid this and also to avoid undue congestion in the approaches to the Ava Bridge, I had decided that the moment to order the withdrawal would be when my advanced forces had to leave the Meiktila area. I had also arranged earlier in the month for preparations to be put in hand for the construction of ferries over both the Irrawaddy and the Myitinge Rivers and of the approaches thereto in order to eliminate the bottle-neck as far as possible.

PART V. – THE JAPANESE BREAK-THROUGH IN THE SHAN STATES AND THE WITHDRAWAL OF THE ALLIED FORCES NORTH OF MANDALAY.

49. *Decision to withdraw North of Mandalay.* The situation in the Shan States which had become serious on the 20th April rapidly deteriorated. On the 21st April it was reported that the whole of the Chinese 55 Division had been scattered by the Japanese attack, and on the 22nd that the Japanese had captured Hopong and were advancing north towards Hsipaw and Lashio with armoured forces and motorised infantry. It was never possible to discover the exact strength of the Japanese thrust but of the weakness of the Chinese forces between them and Lashio there could be no doubt. A good deal of damage was done by panic in the rear areas, especially at Lashio, and I sent Brigadier Martin, my chief liaison officer with the Chinese forces, to attempt to restore order and confidence there, which he succeeded in doing. Under the orders of General Stilwell, 28 Chinese Division (less one regiment) was moved during this period from Mandalay to Hsipaw, but the disorganisation of the railways made this movement very slow. I therefore took steps to protect my rear by sending a detachment from the British Infantry Depot at Maymyo to hold the Gokteik Gorge on the Lashio Road. On 23rd and 24th April the Chinese 200 Division captured Taunggyi and advanced towards Hopong. On the 24th April I asked General Stilwell to come and see me at Maymyo. The situation, however, did not permit of his leaving his Headquarters and therefore on the morning of the 25th April, in company with my M.G., G.S., I went to General Stilwell's Headquarters at Kyaukse and I arranged to meet there General Slim, Commander 1 Burcorps. Here I learned that the enemy were putting heavy pressure on the Chinese 96 Division which was holding the front, that this Division was breaking up and that the Japanese were advancing from Pyinmana on Pyawbwe. One regiment in the Thazi area had been moved to the Shan States. In consequence, Meiktila was now devoid of

infantry. General Stilwell was not sanguine about the operations in the Shan States and I formed the impression that Chinese resistance on the Pyawbwe front was likely to collapse altogether very soon. I therefore issued orders for the plan of withdrawal north of Mandalay to be put into operation commencing on the night of the 25th/26th April. I also ordered 1 Burcorps to take over rear guard from the Chinese on the axis Meiktila – Mandalay and to cover the withdrawal of the Chinese 22 and 96 Divisions north of Meiktila. My decision was telephoned to Army Headquarters at 1300 hours and evacuation of units and installations remaining in Maymyo was begun.

50. *Decision to dispose Imperial Forces for Defence of India.* I now considered that the situation had clarified sufficiently for me to decide on the future role of the Imperial Forces. I was of the opinion that the capture of Lashio by the Japanese was only a question of time and that there would be nothing to stop them moving on Bhamo, thus turning my communications with Myitkyina. Subsequent events proved this opinion to be correct, but it was impossible for me to disengage any forces to send to Bhamo. I also thought that the condition of the Chinese armies precluded the possibility of being able to hold Mandalay and the Irrawaddy line for very long. In these circumstances, I decided that my main object was the defence of India, but I had two subsidiary objects:-

(*a*) to maintain touch with the Chinese, and

(*b*) to get as much as possible of the Imperial Force back to India so that it could be reorganised.

51. I issued to General Slim, Commander 1 Burcorps, on the 26th April, a D.O. letter embodying my plan which was to be implemented after the Mandalay – Irrawaddy line was given up. This was as follows:-

(*a*) for the defence of India two infantry brigades astride the Chindwin to delay the enemy as far south as possible, and

(*b*) a strong detachment in the Myittha Valley.

The above to be maintained eventually from Kalewa, as well as the detachment in (*c*) below.

(*c*) the remainder of the force to move via Ye-U on Kalewa leaving a detachment to cover this route.

(*d*) I determined to keep contact with the Chinese. I hoped to be able to keep the 38 Division which was fighting so well under the command of 1 Burcorps.

This plan was subsequently modified as will appear later.

52. The execution of the amended plan of withdrawal to the Mandalay – Irrawaddy line was most expeditiously put into effect by 1 Burcorps, the 17 Division, with the 7 Armoured Brigade under command taking over rear guard on the axis Meiktila – Mandalay. On the 26th April the 7 Armoured Brigade attacked and dispersed an enemy column eight miles south of Meiktila and the withdrawal of the rear parties of the 63 Infantry Brigade and 7 Armoured Brigade from this area

was delayed until midnight 26th/27th April in order to cover the 22 and 96 Chinese Divisions and the Fifth Army Troops, which had been ordered back from the Kalaw area.

On the 26th April I moved my Headquarters to Shwebo and preparations were put in hand for making the Ye-U-Kalewa road fit for M.T. as far as possible and for stocking the road with supplies and water. Major-General Wakely, Commander L. of C. Area, was placed in charge of all work on the road.

53. On the 27th April reliable information was received that a large Japanese force was in the Nagape area (west of Magwe) date uncertain, but probably between the 15th and 20th April, and that this force was moving north via Myittha Valley with the intention of cutting the Assam road at Kalemyo. In view of this information I visited Headquarters 1 Burcorps on 28th April and made there the following alterations to the plan for a further withdrawal when the Mandalay – Irrawaddy position had to be abandoned:-

The force moving up the Myittha Valley had already been increased to include the whole of the 2 Burma Brigade, which was on the right bank of the Irrawaddy. I confirmed this and in addition arranged for one infantry brigade of the 1 Burma Division to be sent by river to Kalewa and thence to Kalemyo. As a result of these alterations, the force astride the Chindwin would consist of one infantry brigade of the 1 Burma Division and one brigade of the 17 Division, leaving only the 17 Division, less one infantry brigade, 7 Armoured Brigade and Corps and Army Troops to withdraw via Ye-U on Kalewa.

The amended plan was confirmed in Operation Instruction No. 47 issued the following day.

54. *Events leading up to the Abandonment of the Mandalay – Irrawaddy Line.* At this time I was in close touch with General Stilwell and all plans were agreed with him. At a meeting at Shwebo, on the morning of the 29th April, General Stilwell informed me that the Chinese Fifth Army would, when Mandalay was given up, move to the north of Katha and that it would probably move thence to Bhamo. He was, however, uncertain on this point and was awaiting the Generalissimo's instructions. The capture of Lashio by the Japanese appeared imminent and this might force the withdrawal of the Chinese Fifth Army to India. General Stilwell also stated that exhaustion made it impossible for the Chinese 96 Division to take part in any fighting south of Mandalay and he therefore proposed to move this Division by train to Myitkyina as soon as possible. This left only the 22 Division to hold the crossings over the Myitnge River and therefore only a delaying action could be fought on this line. The 22 Division would have to continue its withdrawal up the left bank of the Irrawaddy eventually crossing by ferry at Singu. The weakness of the Chinese forces and the wide extent of the front made it clear to me that the Mandalay – Irrawaddy position could not be held for very long. General Stilwell asked that the 38 Division should revert to his command to cover the withdrawal to the north of the Fifth Army. I felt obliged to agree to this request.

55. India had already been asked to move supplies to Kalewa and, on the 29th April, Lieut.-Colonel Reynolds of the Q.M.G. Staff arrived by air at Shwebo. Lieut-Colonel Reynolds was given details of the latest plan and strengths and these he telegraphed to Delhi. It was known that the condition of the road Tamu – Kalewa would not permit of traffic once the rains began, and the movement of stores south of Tamu would have to be via the Rivers Yu and Chindwin. The maintenance capacity of this route was not known in any detail at Burma Army Headquarters and therefore it was not known what force could be maintained south of Tamu.

Lieut.-Colonel Reynolds left Shwebo by air on the 1st May. On the 3rd May I received a telegram from the Commander-in-Chief in India to the effect that, while supplies had been sent to Kalewa, it was not possible to maintain south of Tamu and that therefore I was to clear my force north of Tamu as rapidly as the tactical situation permitted.

56. At this time, it was estimated that the stocking of the road from Ye-U to Kalewa would take seven days and therefore I was anxious to hold on to the Mandalay – Irrawaddy position for this period. I felt, however, that the possibilities of doing so were slight and I urged my Administrative Staff to accelerate their arrangements as much as possible. The shortage of transport at the disposal of the army made it necessary to withdraw lorries from all possible sources including the 7 Armoured Brigade and 1 Burcorps. During the next few days drastic steps were taken in this respect, units being made to dump kit and stores which did not affect their immediate fighting value.

57. Meanwhile, the withdrawal to the Irrawaddy proceeded according to plan. The Japanese 55 Division followed up rapidly the rear guard in the axis Meiktila – Mandalay. On the evening of the 28th April, tanks with the rear party made contact with enemy motorised infantry south of Kyaukse. On the 29th April, 48 Infantry Brigade supported by tanks and artillery fought a most successful action all day in the Kyaukse area, inflicting about 500 casualties on the enemy with small loss to themselves. The enemy pressed strongly, ferrying up infantry in M.T. They failed, however, to make any progress.

58. By the evening of 28th April, 1 Burma Division had completed its crossing of the Irrawaddy at the Sameikkon Ferry between Myingyan and Myinmu, and by the evening of the 30th April the whole of the Imperial Force had withdrawn north of the Irrawaddy. The 17 Division, which had crossed the river at the Ava Bridge, was moving as rapidly as possible to its positions west of the River Mu. The 38 Chinese Division, which had crossed by ferry, had taken up its positions east of the River Mu. 1 Burma Division was moving to Monywa with the intention of embarking the 13 Infantry Brigade for Kalewa and the 1 Burma Brigade for the defence of the right bank of the Chindwin. The demolition of two bays of the Ava Bridge was, with the full agreement of the Chinese, successfully carried out at 23.50 hours on the 30th April.

59. Earlier on this day, a report had been received that the Japanese had occupied Lashio. This constituted a direct threat to Bhamo and Myitkyina as had been foreseen. A number of casualties and evacuees were on their way by river to Katha for evacuation by train to Myitkyina and thence by air to India. It was impossible for me to spare any forces and indeed, in view of the chaotic conditions of the railways, to move any forces to Northern Burma. I therefore issued by telegram to Colonel Upton, the Commander of the Northern Burma Sub-Area, instructions as to the policy to be adopted for the defence of and evacuation from Myitkyina, Bhamo and Katha.

60. Reports were also received on the 30th April that Japanese columns were at Hsipaw and Maymyo and I had to consider the possibility of a small enemy force moving through Mogok to the Irrawaddy at Thabeikkyin and Male. On the evening of the 30th April, therefore, I established observation posts on the east bank of the Irrawaddy and moved one squadron of tanks and one company of motorised infantry to the north of Shwebo.

61. *The Battle of Monywa.* At about 19.00 hours on the 30th April, a Japanese force attacked from the right bank of the Chindwin, subsequently crossing the river and occupying the town. There was in Monywa at this time only a detachment of about 150 men of 1 Glosters, finding guards, and at Alon, northwest of Monywa, there was the Headquarters of 1 Burcorps with a protective detachment and a Frontier Force column. The troops at Monywa, who were taken by surprise, put up a stout resistance, and the Commander 1 Burcorps put in an immediate counter-attack with the few troops at his disposal. Information of the attack on Monywa was received at Army Headquarters at 22.00 hours and orders were immediately issued for one squadron of tanks to move via Ondaw on Monywa, and during the night of 1st/2nd May the squadron of tanks which I had moved north of Shwebo for the protection of the left flank was also ordered to move on Monywa via Ye-U.

62. The situation created by the Japanese occupation of Monywa was serious since it cut off all the Imperial Forces west of the River Mu from the direct approach to Ye-U through Monywa and also prevented the move of any forces up or across the Chindwin. Further, there was no regular formation of Imperial Forces in position to oppose an enemy advance direct on Ye-U. The Commander 1 Burcorps at once ordered the 16 Infantry Brigade to move with all speed via Shwebo to cover the approaches to Ye-U from the south. The situation in Monywa, however, improved due to the prompt action of Commander 1 Burcorps and the courage and tenacity of the troops and by the morning of the 1st May the town was again temporarily in our hands.

63. Meanwhile, at 2045 hours on 30th April, orders were issued by 1 Burcorps for 1 Burma Division to advance on Monywa as quickly as possible. 63 Infantry Brigade was due to arrive by train at Chaungu early on 1st May and this Brigade and 48 Infantry Brigade at Myinmu were placed under command 1 Burma

Division. Later, however, 48 Infantry Brigade was ordered to move via Shwebo on Ye-U.

Orders were also issued, in pursuance of the original plan, for 13 Infantry Brigade to cross to the west bank of the River Chindwin but this move did not prove possible and had to be abandoned.

64. Early on 1st May the enemy crossed the River Chindwin south of Monywa and, assisted by local guides, attacked H.Q. 1 Burma Division, capturing a wireless set. This somewhat disorganised the chain of command. The enemy also reoccupied Monywa. During the day 1 Burma Division, with 63 Infantry Brigade and one squadron 2 R. Tanks under command, advanced to the south-east outskirts of Monywa with a view to attacking on the morning of 2nd May. One squadron 7 Hussars moved via Ye-U to the north of Alon.

65. My Headquarters, Headquarters 1 Burcorps and Headquarters 17 Division moved to Ye-U on 1st May. Before leaving Shwebo I had arranged for General Stilwell to meet me at Ye-U at 1800 hours that evening in order to co-ordinate plans for the withdrawal from the Mandalay – Irrawaddy position. At this meeting, at which Commander 1 Burcorps was present, General Stilwell agreed that a withdrawal could no longer be delayed and the code words to put this into effect were issued at 1845 hours. General Stilwell also agreed that the situation at Monywa demanded the withdrawal of 7 Armoured Brigade from its position in support of 38 Chinese Division east of the River Mu and orders were therefore issued for 7 Armoured Brigade to move forthwith on the axis Ye-U – Monywa. General Stilwell informed me that he intended to withdraw the Chinese Fifth Army to the Katha area but was uncertain of his further plans. Preparations were, however, in hand for a possible withdrawal to India.

I did not see General Stilwell again until his arrival at Dinjan at the end of May and, owing to the failure of his wireless, did not have any further communication with him.

66. On 2nd May, 7 Armoured Brigade, which had arrived south of Ye-U during the night of 1st/2nd May, attacked Monywa from the north assisted by improvised forces of infantry from 1 Glosters and F.F. Columns. 1 Burma Division attacking from the south-east cleared the outskirts of Monywa, but the attack was not pressed home since 1 Burma Division succeeded in moving round Monywa via Ettaw and in reaching the Ye-U road south of Budalin.

PART VI. – THE WITHDRAWAL TO INDIA.

67. *The Race for Kalewa.* – The operations had now developed into a race with the enemy for the possession of Kalewa. A warning was sent to General Wakely at Kalewa to establish local protection and to block the river approaches. As a result of this, a boom was constructed across the Chindwin to the south of Shwegyin and the detachment of Royal Marines, which had done such good work on the Irrawaddy, was despatched with Breda guns to cover this obstruction. G.H.Q. India were also requested to order air attacks on enemy craft moving up the

Chindwin. I learned later that such attacks were made on the 3rd or 4th May and I have no doubt that they imposed considerable delay on the enemy's advance up the river. There was also the possibility that the enemy might land at some point short of Kalewa and cut in on the Ye-U – Kalewa road. The most likely point for this to happen was at Maukkadaw from which place a Chaung gave easy access to the road at Pyingyaing. A detachment of the Bush Warfare School, reinforced by British infantry from the depot at Maymyo, was therefore sent to Maukkadaw. This detachment was later reinforced by two companies of Gurkhas. At this time I assumed that the 1 Indian Infantry Brigade was moving from Palel to Kalewa and I requested G.H.Q. India to hasten this movement, as I still had reason to believe that a Japanese force was advancing on Kalemyo via the Myittha Valley. I learned on 5th May that 1 Indian Infantry Bngade would not move into Burma, as it was not considered possible to maintain it in Kalewa, in addition to the troops from Burma that would also be in that area.

68. *Co-ordination with the Chinese Rear Guard.* – On the morning of the 3rd May, I received a visit at my Headquarters at Kaduma from General Li Jen Sun, commanding 38 Chinese Division. This Division was ordered to act as rear guard to the Chinese Fifth Army. General Sun felt that his task was difficult and he was anxious that the movements of his Division should be closely co-ordinated with those of 1 Burcorps. I had already issued orders about this but as a result of General Sun's visit I again impressed on the Commander 1 Burcorps that he must not withdraw from the Ye-U area until the Chinese 38 Division had passed to the north of Shwebo. In view of the excellent manner in which General Sun had always co-operated with the forces under my command I should have liked to take his Division with me to India but in the circumstances this was impossible.

69. *Description of Route.* – The problem now facing my force cannot be appreciated without some knowledge of the road conditions between Ye-U and Kalewa. This road was nothing more than a sandy track running from Ye-U via Kaduma, Pyingyaing and Thetkegyin to Shwegyin, eight miles south of Kalewa. It had been the intention to continue the road from Thetkegyin to a point opposite Kalewa but, owing to the difficulties of the last part of this route, which required a lot of rock blasting, this had not been possible and it was the lack of this last twelve miles of road, over which there was nothing more than a footpath, which caused the abandonment of the major portion of the M.T. and all tanks. The track from Ye-U passed through innumerable chaungs or nullahs, some of which were dry and sandy and some of which were wet. Between Pyingyaing and Thetkegyin there was a difficult hill section with many rickety bridges constructed only of brushwood or bamboo. Anyone seeing this track for the first time would find it difficult to imagine how a fully mechanised force could possibly move over it. The casualties to M.T. were heavy and the difficulties were much accentuated by the need to return empty lorries from Shwegyin in order to ferry back more troops and wounded. As the operations, progressed the road was organised into sections for two-way and one-way traffic and the work of the Field

Engineering units very much improved conditions in the later stages of the withdrawal to Shwegyin.

70. From Shwegyin all troops, motor vehicles and guns had to be transported to Kalewa by steamer. There were six steamers, the capacity of each being 600 to 700 men but only two lorries and two Jeeps. A special flat had to be constructed for taking vehicles, but owing to difficulties of embarkation from the beach at Shwegyin, full use could not be made of this method of transport. As a result of the low vehicle capacity of the ships, the transport problem, when units reached Kalewa, was acute. There was barely enough transport to carry essential unit equipment and ammunition and to evacuate the wounded. Fortunately the establishment of a system of staging camps stocked with supplies eliminated the necessity for units to carry rations. The track to a point opposite Kalewa was quite passable for infantry and pack animals and, in the early stages of the withdrawal, all refugees moved by this route, crossing the Chindwin to Kalewa in country boats.

71. As will have been seen from previous paragraphs, the withdrawal to Kalewa was forced on me before the stocking of the Ye-U road was finished. Nevertheless, the heroic efforts of the Administrative Staff and the drastic action which was taken to make transport available, enabled the distribution of stocks to be completed after the withdrawal had commenced. Supplies were back-loaded to the fullest possible extent and, although the force was placed on half rations on the 4th May, there was never any real shortage of supplies.

72. The road northwards from Kalemyo to Tamu was no more than a dirt track through the jungle and once the rains set in, which might take place at any time about the 15th May, this track would become impassable to M.T. I felt, therefore, that my operations were now as much a race with the weather as with the Japanese and as much a fight against nature as against the enemy.

   Nevertheless, I had other problems to consider. There was a large number of refugees on the road west of Ye-U and I was not prepared to abandon them either to the enemy or to possible molestation by the local population. There was also the problem of clearing from Shwegyin a large number of Army Troops and followers before the fighting formations, and I therefore ordered the Commander 1 Burcorps to delay at this stage the withdrawal of his rear guard. Fortunately, the enemy did not follow up closely on the road from Ye-U and, following a brush between the 7 Armoured Brigade and some enemy tanks north of Budalin on the 5th May, there was no further contact for some days.

73. On the 4th May, Commander 1 Burcorps proposed to withdraw one infantry brigade by the route Pyingyaing – Indaw – Pantha for the protection of his left flank.

   As this would reduce the shipping problem at Shwegyin I agreed to the proposal, and arranged for necessary supplies to be moved by steamer to Pantha.

A few days later, Commander 1 Burcorps also arranged that when the 48 Infantry Brigade, forming the rear guard, reached Shwegyin it would proceed thence by steamer to Sittaung. This plan eased the transport problem on the road from Kalewa to Tamu.

74. *The Fight at Shwegyin.* The threat of enemy air attack on river craft reduced the capacity of the steamer service between Shwegyin and Kalewa during the hours of daylight. The crews were nervous and guards were placed on all ships to prevent any attempt at voluntary evacuation. Fortunately, however, the steamer service was singularly free from air attack. Except for bombing raids on the boom on the 5th May, and at Shwegyin on the evening of 7th May, no air attacks of any importance took place.

On the morning of the 10th May an enemy force of approximately one battalion with mortars, attacked the covering force at Shwegyin. It subsequently transpired that this force had moved upstream in landing craft as soon as the detachment at Maukkadaw had withdrawn and had landed at Kywe just south of Shwegyin. There was fighting all day but, in spite of this, embarkation continued. During the late afternoon, the rear guard, the 48 Infantry Brigade, counter attacked, driving off the Japanese. Contact was then lost. Commander 1 Burcorps now decided that ferrying by steamer from Shwegyin was no longer practicable. There remained in Shwegyin at this time:-

Advance Headquarters 17 Division, 48 Infantry Brigade, 1/9 R. Jats, majority of the 7 Armoured Brigade, animal transport of 1 Burma and 17 Divisions.

Commander 1 Burcorps ordered all remaining guns, tanks and motor vehicles to be destroyed and personnel to move by the track to the ferry opposite Kalewa. The 48 Infantry Brigade, with under command 1/9 Jats and 2 D.W.R., finding guards on the ships, were embarked in steamers and proceeded upstream for Sittaung. The Headquarters 17 Division, 7 Armoured Brigade, the embarkation and administrative staff from Shwegyin and the animal transport were ferried across to Kalewa, which was at this time held by the 63 Infantry Brigade.

75. *The Transport Problem.* By the 9th May, staging camps on the route to Tamu had been established at Kalewa, Imbaung, Yezagyo, Khampat and Witok and the Army and Corps Troops were steadily marching from camp to camp as were the thousands of refugees which were now across the Chindwin.

Transport was the great problem. Fortunately the Commander 4 Corps who was now in command in Assam was able to place at my disposal a G.P.T. company which proved of inestimable value. I must also mention here the excellent work done by the 7 Armoured Brigade, whose high morale and great fighting capacity I have frequently stressed. During the withdrawal it was necessary to take from the 7 Armoured Brigade nearly all their vehicles for use in the general pool both east and west of the Chindwin, and after their tanks and remaining vehicles had been abandoned at Shwegyin, this Brigade continued to find drivers not only for the vehicles brought across the Chindwin but also to supplement the drivers of G.P.T. companies working north and south of Tamu. Six to seven hundred men were employed in this way. No praise is too high for the work done by this formation.

76. *Final Stages of the Withdrawal.* While the withdrawal of the main body had been in progress the 2 Burma Brigade was still moving up the Myittha Valley and on the 4th May orders had been issued by wireless for it to reach Kalemyo by the 14th May. The G.P.T. company placed at my disposal by the Commander of 4 Corps enabled this move to be accelerated and the Brigade was moved north by M.T. from Manipur River, crossing on the 13th May.

77. The withdrawal now continued without incident. Tactically, the principal anxiety of the Commander 1 Burcorps was that the enemy, moving up the Chindwin, which was parallel to the road Kalemyo – Tamu, might cut in and get astride his line of withdrawal. Even a small enemy force could have imposed a serious delay at this stage. Fortunately this threat did not develop.

78. On the 11th May, Lieut.-General N.M.S. Irwin, Commanding 4 Corps came to see me at my Headquarters near Tamu. I had already been informed that my army would withdraw through his covering force on the Lokchao River north of Tamu. I discussed with General Irwin his plans for the movement of my force to the Imphal area, which had received the approval of the Commander-in-Chief in India.

79. On the 14th May, Headquarters 1 Burcorps moved to Tamu and the next day I moved my Headquarters out of Burma to Kangpokpi, thirty miles north of Imphal. All troops of the Burma Army arriving in India now came under command of 4 Corps.

The withdrawal of 1 Burcorps, which was skilfully conducted, proceeded according to plan and by the 17th May all formations were successfully concentrated in the Tamu area.

At 1800 hours on the 20th May I placed the rear guard of 1 Burcorps under command of 4 Corps and my task came to an end.

PART VII – ADMINISTRATION

80. I have already mentioned the administrative situation as it was affected by the fall of Rangoon. The back loading of supplies and stores to Central and Upper Burma had been put in hand by General Hutton in January, and as a result reserves were available in the Mandalay area when Rangoon was lost. In the final stages of the evacuation, however, supplies and stores were, in view of the Japanese threat to the Rangoon – Mandalay railway, back loaded up the Irrawaddy Valley.

The results of back loading on this line with the railway ending at Prome were twofold:-

(*a*) A large number of locomotives and a good deal of rolling stock were inevitably lost.

(*b*) Supplies and stores had to be transferred to ships and flats on the Irrawaddy and considerable stocks were accumulated in the Prome area.

81. *Administrative Appreciation.* At the end of March a review of the stock situation in Burma was prepared by my administrative staff. The conclusions reached in this review were:-

(*a*) *Supplies.* The stocks of imported supplies together with present stocks plus future purchases of indigenous supplies were sufficient to feed the army for six months from 1st April. There was, however, the important proviso that the estimate must be reduced if:-

(i) Sources of indigenous supplies could not be held.

(ii) There was a further loss of stocks through enemy action.

The importance of this proviso was soon demonstrated. Large quantities of supplies were lost when the enemy captured Prome and there were further losses in the bombing and subsequent fires in Mandalay.

On the Toungoo front, the withdrawal to the north of that town surrendered to the Japanese some of the best rice growing areas in Burma. It will be seen that no great reliance could be placed on future purchases of indigenous supplies. The collection of these supplies became more and more difficult as the civil organisation disintegrated under enemy air attack.

(*b*) *Petrol and Oil.* Excellent work had been done by the administrative staff and the oilfield engineers in initiating the production of spirit and the manufacture of drums. Stocks held amounted to 1,000,000 gallons of petrol and 89,000 gallons of lubricants. By the 28th March production was at the rate of 1,100,000 gallons of spirit per month which was likely to rise to 1,600,000 gallons by the 16th April and 2,000,000 gallons by the first week in May. Requirements were estimated at 1,300,000 gallons a month. Provided the oilfields could be held the petrol and oil situation was satisfactory.

(*c*) *Medical.* There were sufficient stocks for six months except in the case of a few items which could be flown in.

(*d*) *Ammunition.* There was a serious shortage but sufficient of the more common types to last up to the rains when expenditure was likely to be on a reduced scale.

(*e*) *Ordnance Stores.* There was a shortage of clothing and equipment but there was a reasonable stock of small arms.

82. With no supplies coming into the country from outside, the administrative problem resolved itself into the back loading of supplies in conformity with the projected plan of operations. As the army withdrew to the north it was to a large extent carrying its base with it and in common with most adminstrative situations the problem was largely one of transportation.

83. *I.W.T.* On the Irrawaddy a system of short hauls had to be adopted, owing to the time required for the turn round of steamers, of which, owing to the lack of

crews there were too few in commission. The desertion of crews began soon after
the evacuation of Rangoon and it was accentuated by the bombing of Mandalay
and other places on the river and by the need to take some steamers into the forward area where they were more exposed to air attack. The tales spread by crews
returning from the front led to wholesale desertions. Some I.W.T. personnel
were flown in from India and, further to help the situation and to set an example,
I released twenty junior Staff Officers who volunteered for work on ships in any
capacity. The greatest credit is due to Mr. Morton of the Irrawaddy Flotilla
Company and his staff who, by their devotion to duty and cheerfulness, succeeded in keeping a large fleet of steamers at work right up to the end when, in
order that they should not fall into enemy hands, vessels were sunk at Mandalay
and Thabeikkyin and later at Sittaung.

84. The railway situation was very similar to that on the Irrawaddy in that the
dominating factor was the disintegration of the operating personnel. The desertions of railway operating personnel became so serious that in April I called in the
late Manager of the Burma Railways, Sir John Rowland, who was at this time at
Lashio in charge of the construction of the Yunman – Burma Railway. Sir John
Rowland undertook to do all in his power to keep the railway personnel at their
posts. The main plank in his platform was the evacuation of families of railway
workmen. In this, I am sure, he was right, but the strain of evacuating 10,000
women and children by train at a time when every wagon was required for the
movement of stores or military personnel was almost more than the administrative machine could bear. Nevertheless, although their capacity was reduced the
railways kept going as long as was humanly possible, due largely to the efforts of
Lieut.-Colonel C.P. Brewitt and his staff.

85. *Effect of Destruction of Oilfields.* On the 16th April, the oilfields were destroyed.
This at once set a limit to the length of the campaign. The collection and distribution of rice alone was dependent almost entirely on motor transport and
without rice the armies could not be fed. The stocks of petrol held in the middle
of April were estimated to be sufficient for two months, but they were widely
distributed and the shortage of P.O.L. was felt before the Imperial Forces
reached India.

   It is interesting to note that the effect of the destruction of the oilfields was
never fully appreciated by the Chinese who proposed to send more troops into
Burma after the destruction had taken place.

86. *Medical.* The problem of evacuating to India the sick and wounded was a
source of constant anxiety. After the loss of Rangoon, casualties were evacuated
by air from Shwebo and later from Myitkyina. During April, however, when such
evacuation was easy, sufficient aircraft were not available with the result that
there was an accumulation of sick and wounded in the hospitals in Burma.

   When the withdrawal north of Mandalay commenced, I decided that the sick
and wounded must be evacuated at all costs. Consequently, hospital equipment
and medical stores were abandoned in order to save the patients.

At the end of April when the Japanese captured Lashio a considerable number of sick and wounded were on the Irrawaddy en route to Myitkyina. It was impossible to make any change in this plan but I understand that the majority of these men reached India safely.

The remainder of the sick and wounded were evacuated to India by motor transport. There can be no doubt that many of the wounded travelling in lorries over the bumpy tracks to Shwegyin and Tamu endured great suffering. It was better, however, that they should endure this rather than be left behind and the fact that 2,300 men were evacuated in this way, with very little transport available, is evidence of the efficiency and tireless devotion of the Medical Directorate.

87. *Changes of Plan.* As will have been seen from preceding paragraphs, changes of plan were almost inevitable in the circumstances prevailing. That I should have been able to change a plan, for which administrative arrangements had already been made, was, under the difficult transport conditions prevailing, a high tribute to the staff.

88. *Administration of the Chinese Armies.* This Report would not be complete without some account of the administration of the Chinese armies operating in Burma.

The Chinese have no administrative services as understood in a modern army. Until the arrival of the Chinese Expeditionary Force in Burma the Chinese had never operated outside their own country where they depend for rations upon local purchase and for transport upon local requisitions of vehicles and animals. Casualties are handed over to voluntary organisations or left in the villages to be cared for by the inhabitants. These facts were not fully realised until the arrival of the Chinese Armies in Burma and this resulted in the administration of the Chinese forces being unsatisfactory throughout the campaign. The position was aggravated by the serious shortage of administrative units available in the Army in Burma. These were inadequate at the outbreak of war and the position grew worse when reinforcements arrived without services due to shipping difficulties. As a result, the administrative organisation which could be placed at the disposal of the Chinese was inadequate.

The gap was to some extent filled by the Staff of the Chinese Liaison Mission who though not intended for this purpose, acted as administrative staff officers to the formations to which they were attached.

The big problem was the provision of supplies, more particularly rice. The collection and distribution of rice down to Chinese divisions was my responsibility and this task absorbed no less than 300 lorries in the Shan States alone. Forward of the divisional dumps, distribution was a Chinese responsibility. It will be appreciated that demands on the transport and petrol at my disposal were considerable.

The lack of administration was particularly noticeable on the medical side. The Chinese arrived with no medical stores or units. Later certain voluntary organisations such as Dr. Seagrave's Medical Mission appeared and a Burma Army C.C.S. and one staging section together with medical stores were made available by me for the Chinese armies. A certain number of Chinese sick and wounded were also admitted to British hospitals.

The gratitude of the Chinese for the attention given to their wounded in these hospitals was most marked. Nevertheless, the medical organisation was quite inadequate to deal with the large numbers of Chinese casualties incurred in the later stages of the campaign.

The ordnance situation was also unsatisfactory in that reserves of ammunition, clothing and equipment were practically non-existent. Here I was unable to help as the types of stores required were not common to both armies.

On the other hand, in the later stages of the campaign I was able to make available to the Chinese a considerable quantity of engineer stores and explosives.

To sum up, the administration of the Chinese forces worked reasonably well only so long as operations were not too fluid.

PART VIII. MISCELLANEOUS.

89. Commandos and Levies.

(*a*) *Commandos.* In Burma, the Bush Warfare School, so called for purposes of deception, trained selected officers and other ranks to form the nucleus of guerrilla units in China where they came under control of 204 Mission. Training was given in demolitions in order to fit the personnel for operations on the enemy's lines of communication.

Three commandos consisting entirely of British personnel were already operating in the Southern Shan States when I arrived and they remained there working in co-operation with the Chinese. These commandos undertook one or two operations on the Thai frontier but circumstances were such as to prevent their being any real threat to the enemy's lines of communication. I was therefore anxious to move these commandos to the Irrawaddy front but owing to the difficulties of collecting them from their scattered and dispersed positions I was unable to achieve this.

At the beginning of April, Colonel Wingate, who had had considerable experience in raising and organising units for deep penetration in Abyssinia, arrived at Maymyo. In order to form such units in Burma, Colonel Wingate required British personnel of high morale. Since the army was at this time cut off from India, the only source of supply was the already depleted British battalions. Moreover, the success of deep penetration units depends to a large extent on their operating in a friendly country. This condition did not exist south and east of the Irrawaddy. Colonel Wingate therefore returned to India in order to raise deep penetration units there for possible operations later in the Chin country.

(*b*) *Levies.* The proposal to form Levies was first made in January when the army was still in Moulmein. Later, Mr. (now Lieut.-Colonel) Stevenson of the Burma Frontier Service who had been organising Levies in the Northern Shan States was deputed to do the same work in the Southern Shan States and Karenni and he was finally made responsible for all Levies in Burma.

Karen Levies were formed in the Mawchi area and were reinforced by a number of Karens specially released from the Burma Rifles. I have already mentioned the excellent work carried out by these Levies. To organise Levies in the Chin Hills I selected Lieut.-Colonel Haswell of the Burma Rifles but he had barely sufficient time to complete his organisation before the army withdrew from Burma. The Chin Levy Organisation has now been taken over by India and I see no reason why it should not have considerable success.

90. *Refugees.* The refugee problem in Burma was of a special character. Of the 14 million inhabitants of this country about one million were Indians and it was they who provided the reliable business element and who staffed most of the public utility undertakings. In these circumstances, the Indians were not popular with the Burmese and they realised that they depended for their security on the British "Raj." When this failed they felt they must get out or be murdered. In this they were probably right.

The Indian exodus from Burma had a two-fold result. It created a big refugee problem and, at the same time, it robbed the country of the very people who should have kept going the civil organisation.

The principal effect on military operations was the strain placed on the transport agencies, which were themselves beginning to break down. The strain was most severely felt in the period immediately following the fall of Rangoon when it was still hoped that the situation might be stabilised some distance south of Mandalay.

To my mind there can be no doubt that the needs of an army must come before those of refugees but, in Burma, the position was not straightforward since failure to evacuate the refugees would have caused a breakdown in all the utility services. Everything possible was therefore done by my staff in allotting transportation facilities to refugees. The exodus of the Indian population made labour, both skilled and unskilled, almost impossible to obtain. This was a hard blow in view of the shortage of technical units and the complete lack of military labour.

The civil organisation in charge of refugee evacuation in Burma did remarkably well and I should like particularly to mention Mr. Vorley, who was in charge of the evacuation from the Mandalay area, and Mr. Hughes, I.C.S., my Chief Civil Adviser. In the withdrawal to India, the feeding arrangements for the thousands of refugees who came out through Kalewa and Tamu worked extremely well and very few demands were made on the army for rations. The refugees themselves were no bother and the majority of them, more particularly the women, displayed a courage and heroism under most trying conditions which were worthy of the best traditions of India.

91. *Indigenous Units.* I cannot close my report without making some mention of the behaviour of the indigenous units. Political considerations arising out of the separation of Burma from India brought about the enlistment of Burmese into the Burma Army. Prior to this, only Karens, Chins and Kachins had been enlisted. That this former policy was right was amply demonstrated by the

fighting in Burma. The Burmese proved thoroughly unreliable and deserted wholesale and thus they began the disintegration which later affected all indigenous units except the Signals. As the campaign progressed, the Karens and Kachins also began to desert. This, I think, was largely because they felt they were being cut off from their families. This feeling affected the Karens first since many had their homes in Lower Burma. The Chins on the other hand, did not desert to the same extent, which is almost certainly due to the fact that the final withdrawal was through their country.

As a result of the distrust and suspicion engendered by desertions, often in the face of the enemy, only two battalions of the Burma Rifles remained in the Burma Division at the end of the campaign. One of these was composed of Chins and the other was wholly Indian.

I must pay a tribute to the Burma Army Signals which had a large proportion of Karens and some Burmese personnel. This unit did magnificent work and was completely reliable.

PART IX – CONCLUSIONS.

92. It may be thought that after 3 years of war it is a little late still to be learning lessons from our enemies. The old proverb, however, should be a safeguard against this feeling, and after an unsuccessful campaign one must of necessity examine the causes of failure.

I do not propose further to comment on the events which led up to the loss of Rangoon since it was already too late to save that city when I arrived in Burma. I have stated earlier and I wish to emphasise again that in the absence of a road to India the loss of Rangoon virtually decided the issue of the campaign. Thereafter my task was to impose on the enemy the maximum delay possible with the means remaining at my disposal.

93. *Training and Equipment.* From what I had learned of the nature of the fighting since the beginning of the campaign and from my personal experience of the operations in Burma, I was impressed by the apparent ease with which the Japanese were able to outflank our forces by moving through thick jungle country, whereas our troops were tied to the roads.

The reason for this was that the Japanese were organised, equipped and trained for the type of country over which they fought whereas our troops were not. The Japanese also had the help of local guides and the assistance of many friends amongst the local population. In fact they had all the advantages which accrue from having a plan and from preparations made over a long period in time of peace.

The Imperial Forces were almost completely mechanised down to unit transport which made movement off the few roads almost impossible.

As the campaign progressed units supplemented their motor transport by the local purchase and requisition of bullock carts. This form of transport, however, is too slow and cumbersome for tactical use in the jungle where pack transport or porters are really required. The technique of jungle fighting, as understood by the Japanese, was virtually non-existent in my force. Success in this type of fighting depends largely on the ability of parties to find their way through the jungle and to keep touch with one another. It demands a knowledge, of all types of signalling by visual and by sound and also requires a high scale of low powered wireless sets with infantry battalions. It demands also training to eliminate the sense of loneliness which so often saps the morale of those who are not used to it.

Quite apart from jungle fighting, however, the infantry were not sufficiently well trained in modern tactics which require above all else the ability to manoeuvre in small parties under the fire of their own weapons. Towards the end of the campaign, however, some formations had learned how to take the Japanese on at their own game.

There had been no training with tanks prior to the arrival of the 7 Armoured Brigade and it was not unnatural therefore that the armoured units did not receive the support from the infantry which they needed. The infantry, on the other hand, came more and more to rely on the tanks to get them out of a tight corner.

The country on the whole was unsuitable for the employment of armoured fighting vehicles. In the thick jungle country they were necessarily confined to the roads and tracks and even in the open country of the dry zone the small bunds surrounding paddy fields caused the tanks to slow down in order to avoid breaking their suspension. Nevertheless, the tanks did invaluable work and the reliability of the American M3 or "Honey" was quite remarkable.

94. *Power of the Offensive*. It did not need the Burma campaign to prove the power of the offensive under modern conditions, more particularly in its effect on the civil population. Burma was singularly dependent on her poor communications particularly railways and I.W.T. As has been explained at some length these soon began to break down and I wish to draw attention once again to the vulnerability in this respect of eastern countries where the ignorance and gullibility of the population renders them even more susceptible to the lying tongue of rumour than their western brothers.

This campaign was fought by comparatively small forces over a very large area and therefore militarily the offensive, coupled with air superiority and the help of the local population, enabled the Japanese to concentrate superior forces at the decisive point, since the defence had necessarily to be more dispersed.

The right method of defence was, I am convinced, to hold defended localities well stocked with reserves of supplies and ammunition covering approaches and centres of communication and to have behind these defended localities hard-hitting mobile forces available to counter-attack the enemy should he attempt to surround the defence. When this method was tried in the battle south of Prome it was already too late, for by that time supplies were too scarce to be risked in any large quantity in the forward area and the fear of being cut off was already too deeply implanted in the minds of the soldiers.

95. *Morale.* Properly to appreciate the achievements of the Burma Army, it is necessary to know something of its experiences before my arrival. At the battle of the Sittang the 17 Division was cut off and had to swim the river. The equivalent of a brigade was lost and the remainder arrived on the west bank practically naked, with no equipment and with only some of their personal weapons. It is a high tribute to the Commanders in this formation that the Division was reformed and re-equipped and with the addition of the 63 Infantry Brigade fought gallantly for another three months before withdrawing into India. The 1 Burma Division suffered constantly from the disintegration of its indigenous units but it in turn reorganised to include battalions brought in from outside, and remained a fighting formation to the end. This clearly illustrates the influence which a few really good Commanders can exercise.

Practically every formation in these two Divisions had at one time or another been surrounded by the enemy and had fought its way out. This had a cumulative effect. Further, the 17 Division fought for five months without rest and practically without reinforcement and for only one period of three days did it have another formation between it and the enemy. This was a big strain.

The loss of air superiority also had a moral effect out of all proportion to the damage done by enemy air attacks.

One of the biggest factors which influenced morale was the sense of being cut off from the outside world. This had an influence on the soldier which I did not appreciate until the closing stages of the campaign for, when the troops knew that they were no longer cut off from outside assistance, they fought with renewed vigour and gallantry.

The value of long training as a formation and the confidence resulting therefrom was well exemplified by the 7 Armoured Brigade which retained its cheerful outlook and fighting capacity throughout.

96. *Air.* I have already commented at some length on the air situation and I do not propose to say more except to record once again that the lack of aircraft in India, as in Malaya, was one of the causes of failure.

97. *Unity of Command.* There was no real unity of command of the Allied Forces in Burma, although I had been nominally appointed the Commander of the Chinese Armies. Consequently full use could not be made of the forces available and I feel most strongly that, allied as we are to different nations, unity of command must be achieved in each separate theatre of war.

Appendix "A"
ORDER OF BATTLE – CHINESE ARMIES IN BURMA
Chinese Fifth Army
  22 Division }
  96 Division } Employed on Toungoo front South of Mandalay.
  200 Division }

Chinese Sixth Army

55 Division	Loilem – Loikaw – Karenni }
49 Division	Mongpan area } Southern Shan States.
93 Division	Kengtung area }

Chinese 66 Army

38 Division	Originally allotted for defence of Mandalay, but subsequently placed under command 1 Burcorps.
28 Division	Relieved 38 Division at Mandalay, subsequently moved back to Hsipaw. (two regiments only)

Note

1. *War Office footnote* – The Commonwealth Government at that time considered that diversion of their Force would have exposed Australia to great risk at a time when the Japanese were advancing Southwards rapidly and when the invasion of Java was imminent.
2. Note the small number of rifles available.
3. See General Hutton's Report, Section IX.
4. See General Hutton's Report, paras. 104, 106 and 107.
5. A Chinese division was organised on the basis of three regiments each consisting of three battalions.

2

GENERAL SIR ARCHIBALD P. WAVELL'S DESPATCH ON OPERATIONS IN THE EASTERN THEATRE, BASED ON INDIA, MARCH 1942 TO 31 DECEMBER 1942

The War Office, September, 1946
The following Despatch was submitted to the Secretary of State for War on September 27th 1943, by FIELD-MARSHAL The VISCOUNT WAVELL, G.C.B., C.M.G., M.C., A.D.C., Commander-in-Chief, India.

1. This despatch deals with the arrangements for the defence of India against Japanese invasion, which became a serious threat after the fall of Rangoon early in March 1942, and with the preparations later in 1942 to undertake an offensive to recapture Burma. There was little fighting during the period, but the story of the events and of the measures taken is not without interest.

SITUATION IN MARCH 1942.

2. When Rangoon fell, in March 1942, it was obvious that the whole of Burma might be occupied by the Japanese and that India itself and Ceylon lay under imminent threat of invasion.

The forces available for defence at this time were dangerously weak. The Eastern Fleet had only one modernised battleship immediately available and the fleet as a whole was in no position to dispute with the Japanese fleet command of the Bay of Bengal or of the waters round Ceylon. There were only one British and six Indian divisions available for the defence of the whole of India and Ceylon, apart from forces for defence of the N.W. Frontier and for internal security, both of which were well below the strength estimated as necessary for these commitments. No single one of these divisions was complete in ancillary troops or fully equipped or adequately trained. Three of them had two brigades only.

The number of A.A. guns (heavy or light) to defend Calcutta, (India's largest city), her most important war industries and other vital points, which were or were soon likely to be within effective bombing range, was less than 150, against an estimated total requirement of some 1,500.

The Air Force available for the commitments of defending India and Ceylon and of supporting the army in Burma was similarly inadequate, as was the number of airfields. For the defence of Calcutta one fighter squadron was available with eight serviceable Mohawks. Fifty Hurricanes were delivered to Ceylon in March, and the three fighter squadrons allotted to the defence of the island were equipped during March, just in time to meet the enemy air raids in April.

The remaining air force available (two fighter squadrons and one light bomber squadron) was allotted to Upper Burma, where the greater part of it was destroyed by enemy attack at Magwe on the 21st and 22nd March. The remnants were withdrawn to India to re-form for its defence.

The airfields in Eastern India were quite inadequate and the warning system was only in a rudimentary stage.

3. On the 7th March, just before the fall of Rangoon, I cabled to the Chiefs of Staff a short appreciation. I expressed grave doubts of my ability to hold Burma, and anticipated a subsequent attack by the Japanese on N.E. India. I considered at this time that an undue proportion of our very inadequate land and air resources in the East was being allocated to the defence of Ceylon. In particular the diversion to Ceylon of a brigade of the 70 British Division, the only British division available in India, caused me concern. Ceylon already had two Indian Brigades and two brigades of local troops; two Australian brigades were being lent to its defence and an East African brigade was on its way there. My view was that if we lost command of the sea and air around Ceylon an additional brigade would be of no avail to secure the naval bases at Trincomalee or Colombo, which the Japanese could destroy without landing, in the same manner as at Pearl Harbour or Manila, whereas a complete British division in North-East India would have been a most valuable reserve and would have done something to restore shaken public morale.

The War Cabinet ruled, however, that the defence of the naval bases in Ceylon must have priority, and confirmed the diversion thither of the 16th Brigade of the 70th division.

4. The War Cabinet took immediate steps to reinforce India, ordering the 5th and 2nd British Divisions there. The 5th Division arrived in May and the 2nd Division in June. They also arranged to send such aircraft as could be spared; but the position in the Middle East was tense at the time and it was not easy to meet our requirements. In a telegram sent on the 27th March I estimated our air requirements as-

9 Fighter squadrons for the defence of Bengal.
3 Fighter squadrons for Madras and the east coast ports.
6 Fighter squadrons for Ceylon.
4 Fighter/Reconnaissance squadrons for support of the army in Burma.
4 Fighter/Bomber squadrons for support of the army in Burma.
11 Light Bomber squadrons.
4 Medium Bomber squadrons.
2 Heavy Bomber squadrons.
7 General Reconnaissance squadrons.
4 Flying-boat squadrons.

6 T.B. squadrons.

4 B.T. squadrons.

a total of 64 squadrons.

Our actual strength at the time was:-

1 Fighter squadron (Mohawks) at Calcutta.

1 Fighter squadron (Audax)[1] at Dinjan.

1 Fighter squadron (Hurricanes) at Akyab.

3 Fighter squadrons (Hurricanes) in Ceylon,

1 Light Bomber squadron (Blenheims) in Ceylon.

1 G.R. squadron (Hudsons) at Calcutta.

2 Flying-boat squadrons (Catalinas) in Ceylon.

There was, on paper, a Light Bomber Squadron at Calcutta, but it had no serviceable aircraft.

There were also four Army Co-operation squadrons in India with obsolete types of aircraft suitable only for North-West Frontier.

Reinforcements of fighter and bomber aircraft in considerable numbers were on their way at this date, but our operational strength could not be materially increased before the middle of April.

There were some American heavy bombers in India which could assist in the defence of India in emergency, but they were birds of passage, intended for use in China and not under my control. I could not reckon on them in any plan of defence.

Thus the only portion of my command which had any scale of air protection at all was Ceylon.

JAPANESE NAVAL RAID.

5. It was, as it turned out, fortunate that such defence as was available was mainly in Ceylon, since a Japanese naval raid into Indian waters took place in the early days of April, in the course of which Colombo was attacked by carrier-borne air-craft on the 5th April and Trincomalee on the 9th April. Our defending fighters inflicted considerable losses on the enemy aircraft, which did little damage on land; but they suffered some losses themselves; and the Blenheim squadron, which was sent to attack the Japanese aircraft-carriers, was practically destroyed without accomplishing anything. Had the attack been renewed it would have been difficult to meet. Though little damage had been caused on land, two 8-inch cruisers, Dorsetshire and Cornwall, and aircraft-carrier (Hermes) and some smaller naval vessels had been sunk by Japanese aircraft in the waters around Ceylon.

In the Bay of Bengal Japanese light forces and aircraft, sank just on 100,000 tons of merchant shipping, dropped a few bombs on Vizagapatam – the first on Indian soil, and caused a panic there and elsewhere on the Eastern Coasts of India, which, in the absence of naval and air forces, were practically defenceless.

This was India's most dangerous hour; our Eastern fleet was powerless to pro-tect Ceylon or Eastern India; our air strength was negligible; and it was becoming increasingly obvious that our small tired force in Burma was unlikely to be able to hold the enemy, while the absence of communications between Assam and Upper Burma made it impossible to reinforce it.

Fortunately the enemy naval force withdrew, and no Japanese surface warships have since appeared in Indian waters. It is conceivable that the Japanese raid was made with the object of securing Indian rejection of the proposals brought out by the Cripps Mission, which were then under discussion at Delhi.

6. On the 13th and 14th April I met Commander-in-Chief, Eastern Fleet, at Bombay and discussed with him the defence of India. He confirmed that with his present force he could do nothing to prevent the invasion of Southern India or Ceylon, and could not send naval forces into the Bay of Bengal to protect shipping or the east coast of India. He also informed me that practically the whole of the Eastern Fleet would be engaged in operations against Madagascar and would not be available in Indian waters.

An appreciation from the Chiefs of Staff in London was received on the 23rd April. It confirmed my general appreciation of the danger to India, *i.e.*, that an invasion of N.E. India by sea, land and air was the most probable threat, while an attack on Ceylon was possible; it recognised the powerlessness of the Eastern Fleet to offer effective opposition; accepted that the land forces in India were inadequate by at least one Armoured Division, one Army Tank Brigade and four infantry divisions, which deficiencies could not be met till late in 1942; and gave the air squadrons required as 66 (there were in India at this time 15 operational squadrons, rising to a total of 25 by the end of June).

The telegram ended with the conclusion:-

"If Japanese press boldly westwards without pause for consolidation and are not deterred by offensive activities or threats by Eastern fleet or American fleet, nor by rapid reinforcement of our air forces in N.E. India, our Indian Empire is in grave danger."

7. May and June seemed likely to be the critical months for India. It was, therefore, disturbing to me to find that at the end of April the Eastern Fleet, instead of being strengthened, was likely to be further reduced for operations in the Mediterranean to provision Malta, that two brigades of the 5th British Division, on its way to reinforce India, were being diverted for the capture of Madagascar, to which also was being sent an East African brigade which I had been led to expect for Ceylon; and that the Australian Government was demanding the return to Australia of the two brigades in Ceylon.

I protested with some vigour, but the Minister of Defence, who had to look at the whole picture, decided that the attempt to relieve Malta must be made; that Madagascar should be occupied to secure the sea route to the Middle East and India; and that it was necessary for political reasons to release the Australian brigades.

Events proved his judgment correct; and the danger to India never developed. Great efforts were made to build up our air force; and during the summer two

British divisions (2nd and 5th) gradually arrived. By July, when the monsoon broke, the critical period for India had passed.

DEFENCE OF NORTH-EAST FRONTIER OF INDIA.

8. Meanwhile, as described in my despatch dated the 14th July, 1942, the troops in Burma, under General Sir Harold Alexander, were being driven northwards; and after the Japanese break-through to Lashio in the latter part of April and the consequent collapse of Chinese resistance in N.E. Burma, I had to order the withdrawal of the Burma Army across the Indian frontier into Assam. This was completed by the 20th May.

The situation of Eastern Army (Lt.-General Sir Charles Broad) which was responsible for the defence of N.E. India was by this time as follows:-

IV Corps (Lt.-General N.M.S. Irwin) was responsible for the defence of Assam. The Burma Army (17 Indian Division and 1 Burma Division) passed under his command on arrival in India; apart from them he had only one brigade (1st Indian Infantry Brigade), which had been moved from the N.W. Frontier into Manipur State and was astride the Palel – Tamu road; and one battalion of the 49th Indian Infantry Brigade.

XV Corps (Lt.-General Sir Noel Beresford-Peirse) was responsible for the defence of Bengal against seaborne invasion or an advance up the Arakan Coast. It comprised 14 and 26 Indian Divisions, both incomplete, and certain troops which formed the garrison of Calcutta.

70 British Division (less one brigade group in Ceylon) was at Ranchi with the rôle of meeting any seaborne expedition which landed on the Orissa coast; it also constituted the only reserve available for Assam or Bengal.

Thus IV Corps had some 500 miles of frontier to guard with little except the tired and disorganised Burma Army; while the XV Corps with two incomplete and partially trained divisions had to secure some 400 to 500 miles of land frontier and sea-coast. The 70 Division (two brigades only) was responsible for another 200 to 300 miles of the coast-line besides acting as general reserve. There was, until the arrival of the 5th British Division at Bombay, which was not completed till the 20th May, no other reserve available in India.

9. Certain auxiliary forces were formed to assist in the defence of N.E. India. On the frontiers of Assam and Bengal local levies were raised amongst the hillmen of the Lushai, Chin and Naga hills; this force, which amounted to some 2,500 men, was known as "V" Force. It was of doubtful fighting value but would have been of value to watch hill tracks, collect information and to harry the enemy's line of communications had he advanced into the hills. A force was also organised to man river boats to patrol the great waterways that intersect Eastern Bengal. It was known as the Sundarbans Flotilla.

THE TRANSPORTATION PROBLEM.

10. Apart from the small number of troops available, the defence of N.E. India was complicated by the poverty of the communications from the rest of India into

Assam and Eastern Bengal. Assam is cut off from the rest of India by the great Brahmaputra river which is unbridged throughout its length. Its level fluctuates during the year by as much as 25 feet and its course sometimes by several miles. The railway system east of the Brahmaputra was a single track metre gauge with no modern train control system and very limited resources in locomotives and rolling stock. The system was served by wagon ferries at two places over the Brahmaputra capable of dealing only with a very limited number of wagons per day. There is no all-weather road from India to the west bank of the Brahmaputra, while the only west to east road in Assam was the second class single width road which ran from Gauhati ferry to the North-East; so that the deficiencies of the railway could not be replaced by road transport; indeed, all vehicles had to be transported to Assam by rail. Nor could river transport solve the problem. Many steamers had been sent earlier in the war to the rivers of Iraq, and the river system merely led to the railway system on the east bank, which was the limiting transportation factor.

On the Bengal front, communications were no better. The delta of the Ganges is unbridged; and the railway, which terminated a short distance beyond Chittagong, is single line, metre-gauge. Some small use could, however, be made of sea transport.

11. I have already in my Burma despatch of the 14th July, 1942, given some account of the endeavours to construct a road from Assam to Burma. At the same time (about February, 1942) the construction of an adequate railhead and advanced base at Manipur Road station on the Bengal and Assam railway was undertaken. At the time this was a wayside halt in the heart of dense jungle at the spot where the road to Imphal takes off. It was unfortunately intensely malarial. Here a railhead had to be laid out in a short time, to handle 1,000 tons of stores a day, eventually rising to 2,000 tons, while depot areas had to be made to hold a reserve of 30 days for a force of three divisions, together with a generous complement of non-divisional troops and labour.

Much other work had to be done to improve the communications in Assam. A new railhead and advanced base was made at Ledo; an additional river port was made at Doinaigon on the Brahmaputra north of Jorhat, and the railway was extended to meet it; many additional crossing places were made on the railway and the control system improved; the ferry capacity over the Brahmaputra at Gauhati ferry was greatly increased; and other improvements to the railway, road and telegraph system carried out.

12. The transportation problem would have been an extremely difficult one in any event. It was further complicated in 1942 by the following events. There was an exceptionally heavy monsoon which caused extensive flooding and interruption of railway communications north of the Brahmaputra and elsewhere; and also resulted in continual landslides on the road to Imphal, which was the sole line of communications to a large part of the force. This was followed by the worst malaria epidemic which India had known for many years; there was a

particularly high incidence amongst lorry drivers and transportation personnel, which had a cumulative effect in worsening the situation. Finally, from August onward, the rebellion organised by Congress after the breakdown of the Gripps negotiations in April was directed especially against our communications to N.E. India.

The Japanese raid into the Bay of Bengal (see paragraph 5) in April caused for some time the practical closing of the Bay of Bengal and the eastern ports to shipping and threw extra strain on the railways. The port of Chittagong was closed altogether and much of the port equipment was removed in May, when a Japanese attack on Chittagong seemed probable.

13. The transportation and other difficulties enumerated above naturally had a considerable effect on the efficiency of the troops. Those in Manipur, who were dependent on the Imphal road for supply, had to subsist on less than full rations for a considerable portion of the summer, and the resultant malnutrition increased their susceptibility to malaria and other disease. It was impossible also, owing to the breaking of the road, to provide satisfactory medical accommodation and equipment or to evacuate the sick to better conditions. This again increased the sick rate. Many of the troops had been through the exhausting Burma campaign and should have been relieved and rested had the reliefs or transport facilities been available. In October, November and December, when conditions began to improve, some 20,000 sick had to be evacuated from Eastern Army area. This was in addition to some 15,000 who had been evacuated before the rains, when the army returned from Burma.

The disturbances caused by Congress in August threw a fresh strain on the army, which had to be used for internal security instead of its legitimate work of training and equipping for the dry weather season. The equivalent of 58 battalions had to be employed; of these 24 belonged to the Field Army and the equivalent of 7 were formed from Reinforcement Camps and Training Centres; the remainder were battalions already allotted to internal security duties. The employment of units from Reinforcement Camps and Training Centres resulted in delay to the flow of reinforcements to formations on the Eastern Frontier which were already seriously below strength owing to the high incidence of malaria.

I should like to pay a tribute to the admirable spirit and discipline shown by the troops engaged on the unpleasant task of restoring order during these troubles. The civil services, armed and unarmed, worked in close co-operation with the military forces in dealing with disorders. The work of the police, who were often isolated, was generally admirable, and their steadfastness greatly lightened the burden thrown on the troops.

REFUGEE PROBLEM.

14. Besides the troops evacuated from Burma, India had to deal with some 400,000 civilian refugees from Burma in varying states of distress. Some came by sea from Akyab, before it fell into Japanese hands; large numbers came through

Imphal; and others by the Hukawng valley route to Ledo. The arrangements to feed and transport these numbers presented a very serious problem, while from the security aspect it was necessary to set up some organisation to try and prevent the infiltration of enemy agents. The arrangements for the reception of refugees were placed by the Indian Government under Major-General E. Wood, who received invaluable assistance from the organisation controlled by the Indian Tea Association. The Imphal route, by which the majority of the 180,000 refugees entered Assam, was comparatively easy; but the route up to the Hukawng valley from Myitkyina by Maingkwan and Shingbwiyang to Ledo was from Shingbwi-yang onwards only a difficult mountain track with several rivers to cross. After the rains began, mud and swollen rivers made this route practically impassable from end of May onwards, and a number of the refugees were marooned at Shingbwi-yang for the monsoon period, having to be fed by air; while some perished in the attempt to get through. Other parties who attempted to reach Ledo from Fort Hertz via the Chaukan pass were only rescued with considerable difficulty.

CHINESE FORCES IN INDIA.

15. When the Japanese broke through to Lashio in April part of the Chinese forces in Burma were cut off from return to China. Part of these sought to reach India. One Division, 38th, which had been operating with the British forces, reached Imphal in good order about 6,000 strong. Part of the remainder of the Chinese Fifth Army eventually got through to India by the Ledo route; others made their way north-east into the Kachin country north-east of Myitkyina and returned to China by mountain tracks, though only after considerable losses from starvation and disease.

General Stilwell himself, the American Chief of Staff to the Generalissimo, had been cut off in Burma and had to make his way on foot to Assam.

16. I decided to place all Chinese troops that had reached India in a camp at Ramgarh that had previously been an Italian Prisoner-of-War camp. Here they would be re-equipped and trained by the United States forces.

Towards the end of September I received through the American staff a request from the Generalissimo that additional troops should be flown from China into India to make up the force at Ramgarh to a complete corps of two divisions, which, after equipment and training, would operate from India into Burma. I accepted this proposal after approval by His Excellency the Viceroy and His Majesty's Government. The troops were flown in during October, November and December, and by the end of the year the numbers of the Chinese force at Ramgarh amounted to approximately 30,000.

MILITARY SITUATION DURING SUMMER.

17. By the end of June immediate anxiety for the safety of India had lessened. The 5th and 2nd British Divisions were arriving, though neither was yet complete, much anti-aircraft artillery and other units had reached India, and the air strength was gradually increasing. The Eastern Fleet was still incapable of disputing

command of Indian waters with a Japanese fleet; but the enemy had shown no signs of mounting an expedition against India, and the monsoon weather made this improbable for some months. India therefore had a breathing space to re-organise, train and prepare.

The 23rd Indian Division was gradually formed in Manipur, and the 1 Burma Division, which was now renamed 39th Indian Division, was withdrawn to Shillong to refit and reorganise. The two Indian armoured divisions which were being formed began to receive some equipment. A force was sent to Ceylon at the end of June to replace the two Australian brigades which were withdrawn.

18. Meanwhile, however, events in other theatres affected India's preparations. The operations to capture Madagascar had delayed the arrival of reinforcements and equipment, but had removed a potential menace to India's line of communications with the United Kingdom.

The reverse suffered in the Western Desert in June and the close approach of Rommel's army to the Nile delta caused the diversion of units and equipment, especially aircraft and tanks, from India to the Middle East. Though India was still far from secure, the danger to Egypt was obviously far more threatening; and on the 30th June I cabled to General Auchinleck offering any assistance that India could afford. He asked for an anti-tank regiment, which I sent, together with 100 carriers and other aid.

A danger more nearly affecting India arose from the German advance towards the Caucasus, which threatened Persia and Iraq and the Persian Gulf. A large proportion of the garrison had been moved across to Egypt to meet the threat to the Delta, and it seemed to me that the only way to reinforce Persia in time to halt a German advance through the Caucasus, should the Russians fail to hold the Caucasus – as at one time seemed possible – would be to send troops from India, weak though her defences were. I therefore offered to make available one or both of the two newly arrived British divisions (2nd and 5th) and an armoured brigade. Eventually the 7th Armoured Brigade and 5th Division were despatched to Iraq. They left India in September.

MEETING IN CAIRO.

19. Early in August I received a summons to meet the Prime Minister and C.I.G.S. in Cairo, where the whole position in the Middle East was to be discussed. I also accompanied them to Moscow for conversations with the Soviet Government and General Staff.

So far as India was concerned, the main outcome of these discussions was the decision to relieve the Middle East Command of responsibility for Persia and Iraq, so as to enable it to concentrate on the defeat of Rommel's army and the removal of danger from the Nile Delta. The command of Persia and Iraq, which secured the western frontier of India, had already passed during the war from Middle East to India and then back again. It was now suggested that they should again be placed under the C.-in-C., India. I was willing to accept this additional responsibility, provided that the R.A.F. allotted to these countries was under the control of the A.O.C.-in-C., India. Difficulties arose about this, and it was decided to create a separate Command, P.A.I.C., directly under the War Cabinet. It was decided that India should retain the 2nd British Division which had been provisionally held in readiness to reinforce Persia and Iraq.

EXPANSION OF THE AIR FORCE.

20. As has already been indicated, the air strength in India in March was almost negligible. To build it up, much more was, of course, required than the supply of air squadrons or aircraft. A programme to construct over 200 airfields had to be undertaken, which threw a heavy strain on the material resources of India (such as cement), on the transportation system by rail and road, on the engineer personnel and supply of labour. In March there had been only some 30 to 40 airfields suitable for operation, even in fair weather; by the end of November the number was approximately 150. A large programme of signal construction was also necessary; repair and salvage organisations had to be brought into being; schools for training had to be arranged, and many other establishments formed. Nothing but a rudimentary warning system existed in Eastern India, and much work was required before it was even reasonably effective.

No details of the expansion need be given. By the end of 1942 there were 29 squadrons operational and another 20 forming, in addition to 2 squadrons of transport aircraft and 1 P.R.U. squadron. This was much short of the minimum force considered necessary for the security of India, but a great improvement on the defencelessness of March. Balloon barrages were established at Calcutta and Jamshedpur.

The Indian Air Force took part in the expansion, and is being raised from 4 squadrons equipped with obsolete machines to 10 squadrons with modern aircraft.

21. Air operations during the monsoon from June to October were naturally on a small scale; but were notable for the skill and determination with which crews operated in bad weather. Targets on the Burma coasts, in the Chindwin valley and on Akyab Island were attacked with success; and a constant reconnaissance of the Bay of Bengal, over enemy aerodromes in Burma and of the Port of Rangoon was maintained as far as possible. Air information was, however, severely restricted not only by the weather but by shortage of long-range aircraft. During this period the enemy air force was almost completely inactive.

EVENTS DURING MONSOON FROM JUNE TO OCTOBER.

22. On the eastern front of India there was little military activity during the monsoon period. Some good patrol work in difficult conditions was carried out in the Chindwin valley by troops of the 23rd Division and local levies. The rains were exceptionally heavy, and all northern Burma and Assam are highly malarial during the rainy season. It seemed at one time that the enemy intended to move from the Chindwin and Myitta valleys into the Chin Hills, which were held only by local levies whom we could not support in the absence of communications.

The Chins became alarmed by Japanese threats and depressed by shortage of food, and there was a danger that they might come to terms with the enemy. The danger was averted by vigorous bombing of the enemy and the dropping of supplies to the Chins.

I had determined in June to re-occupy Fort Hertz (Putao) in the extreme north of Burma, in order to protect the landing ground there and to raise and support Kachin levies to operate between Myitkyina and Fort Hertz. There was no road from India to Fort Hertz, and a detachment could only be flown in by air. It was September before this was possible and it had to be preceded by a small detachment dropped by parachute to prepare the landing ground.

INTERNAL SITUATION.

23. Reference has already been made to the disturbances organised by Congress in August and their effect (see paragraph 13). Internal trouble of a different kind necessitated the use of troops and the declaration of martial law in part of Sind north of Hyderabad. A fanatical sect of Moslems known as the Hurs had long terrorised a considerable district through which the main line from the port of Karachi runs. On the 16th May, 1942, a gang of Hurs derailed the mail train from Karachi and then attacked it. It was impossible to tolerate such dangerous lawlessness on one of the principal lines of communication in India. Since the police and civil authorities were unable to deal with the situation, a military force was sent and martial law declared. Major-General R. Richardson, M.C. was appointed Military Administrator. Under his able direction the situation soon improved, but so deep-seated was the terrorism of the Hurs, and so difficult the country, which contains large areas of marsh and of desert, that the troops were still employed at the end of the year.

A company of a Parachute battalion was employed for some time in operations to round up bands of Hurs, probably the first use of parachutists in civil disturbances.

Recruiting was not affected by any internal trouble, and some 60,000 recruits continued to be enlisted each month.

24. In July a small expedition to Datta Khel in Waziristan became necessary to deal with tribal disturbances inspired by the notorious Fakir of Ipi. The operations were short and successful. On the whole the situation on the N.W. Frontier during 1942 was noticeably stable.

REORGANISATION OF COMMANDS.

25. During the period covered by this review it became necessary to reorganise the system of Military Commands in India. Three Armies were constituted to deal with the threats of invasion of N.W., N.E. and Southern India, while a Central Command was created in order to relieve the Army Commanders of large areas with internal security problems only, and of a considerable amount of responsibility for administration and training. Lt.-General N.M.S. Irwin took

over command of the Eastern Army, Lt.-General Sir Noel Beresford-Peirse that of the Southern Army, and Lt.-General H.B.D. Willcox the Central Command.

OCEAN BASES.

26. When Japan entered the war, and especially after the loss of Singapore, the Navy felt the need of additional bases in the Indian Ocean. Bases were selected at Addu Atoll in the Maldive Islands, Diego Garcia in the Chagos Archipelago, Seychelles and Mauritius. India was made responsible for the garrison of these and also of Cocos Island and Rodriguez (East of Mauritius). The defences of Addu Atoll were originally designed on a considerable scale, but were later reduced. Scrub typhus and malaria caused a very high sick rate in the garrison and labour units working on the airfield and defences; but this showed signs of improvement by the end of the year as a result of jungle clearance.

After the occupation of Madagascar I suggested that Mauritius, Rodriguez and Seychelles could better be garrisoned from E. Africa. This was accepted and on the 1st September these places passed to the E. African Command. I returned the Mauritian garrison from Diego Garcia to Mauritius during September and replaced it by Indian troops.

PREPARATIONS FOR OFFENSIVE.

27. Even before we had been driven out of Upper Burma, I had in April issued instructions for the re-conquest of the whole of Burma to be planned. An estimate was to be made of the troops required, of the measures for their main-tenance, and of the special training and equipment necessary; airfields and the maintenance arrangements for a large air force were to be planned, since air superiority was the first requisite for operations against Burma by land or sea.

Planning has continued ever since, and has shown the difficulties of the prob-lem and the extensive preparations required. There is no connection by rail or road between India and Burma, and the country through which routes must be made to support an invasion is extremely unfavourable – high hills, dense jungles and fever-ridden valleys, with no local supplies available and a very limited popu-lation to provide labour. Moreover, the rivers and mountain ranges all run from north to south. Communications in this direction, therefore, that is with the grain of the country, are comparatively easy; whereas movement from west to east, against the grain, is very difficult. Any advance that we make from Assam or from the coast will thus have great natural obstacles to overcome, whereas the enemy based on Rangoon and the south can operate up and down the valleys with much greater freedom. The poor communications to N.E. India, from which the advance must be made, have already been described.

Nor are the approaches for a sea-borne expedition more favourable. Down the whole of the west coast of Burma runs the steep jungle clad range of the Arakan Yoma, passable only by a few bridle paths. The south coast, from Point Negrais to the south of the Rangoon river, is the delta of the Irrawaddy, a tangled wilder-ness of mangrove swamps and creeks, impassable for any but an amphibian force in small boats and extremely difficult even for it. Further east, the Gulf of

Martaban is shallow with extensive mud flats which preclude a landing anywhere north of Moulmein. A land advance from Moulmein on Rangoon, which must be the objective of any expedition against South Burma, has to cover more than 100 miles and to cross several large rivers, while exposed to flank attack from Thailand.

The climate practically restricts operations to a period of less than six months, from November to the middle of May, since in the S.W. monsoon the rainfall is so heavy as to render most roads impassable and to restrict all flying operations; and the stormy winds make landing on the west coast impracticable. Finally, the whole of Upper Burma and most of Lower Burma are intensely malarial.

28. Early in June I considered that definite plans for the recapture of Burma could be put in train; and I cabled home outline plans of operations. I said that I proposed to operate in a series of small columns against the line of the river Chindwin from Kalewa to Homalin, with possible separate advances from Ledo and Fort Hertz against Myitkyina. I would then push on to the line Kalewa – Katha – Myitkyina; and exploit any success towards Shwebo, Bhamo and the line of the Irrawaddy.

I pointed out the difficulties due to the poverty of communications both in Assam and in Upper Burma, the unhealthy climate, and lack of trained troops. I asked especially for the strengthening of the Air Force at my disposal. At the same time I instructed G.O.C.-in-C. Eastern Army to undertake a limited offensive, as outlined above, into Upper Burma, with October 1st as date for commencement; and to push troops from Chittagong towards the Burma border, and to improve communications with a view to an advance into Arakan later on. Meanwhile I continued to plan a seaborne expedition against Lower Burma, with an original target date of November 1st.

29. The succeeding months were a period of frustration so far as plans for an offensive into Burma were concerned. The heavy monsoon, the severe incidence of malaria, and the Congress disturbances of August and September delayed the preparations in Assam for the advance into Upper Burma and interfered with the training of the troops; while the continuance of operations in Madagascar deprived India of troops, ships and landing craft which were necessary for the preparation of the sea-borne expedition. On the 3rd July I had to report that I could see no prospect of mounting an expedition against Lower Burma before January, 1943; and early in September the G.O.C.-in-C., Eastern Army, informed me that he would be unable to begin operations from Assam before the 1st March, 1943.

In a cable of the 18th July, the Chiefs of Staff had stated the conditions in which a full-scale expedition against Burma might be launched in the winter 1942–43; they were most unlikely to be fulfilled. Also, after detailed discussion with G.O.C.-in-C., Eastern Army, I had to accept his view that an advance into Upper Burma could not begin before the 1st March.

It was obvious therefore that I had to content myself with only very limited objectives for the winter of 1942–43; and I accordingly issued instructions in the middle of September, 1942, defining the object of operations during this period as:-

(*a*) To develop communications and establish ourselves in a favourable position for reconquering Burma and reopening the Burma Road at the first opportunity.

(*b*) To bring the Japanese to battle with the purpose of using up their strength, particularly in the air.

I said that my intentions were:-

(*a*) To capture Akyab and to reoccupy Upper Arakan.

(*b*) To strengthen our position in the Chin Hills.

(*c*) To occupy Kalewa and Sittaung, and thence to raid the Japanese L. of C.

(*d*) To make such administrative preparations as would allow of the rapid advance of a force towards Upper or Lower Burma should opportunity offer during the campaigning season of 1942–43.

30. On the 18th and 19th October I discussed with General Stilwell, the American Chief of Staff to Marshal Chiang Kai-Shek, Chinese co-operation in an offensive into Burma. He produced a plan drawn up by the Generalissimo for the reconquest of Burma which was generally on the same lines on which we were already working, i.e., an advance by land forces into Upper Burma and a sea-borne expedition against Lower Burma. He proposed that a large Chinese force should advance from Yunnan into North-East Burma at the same time as the Chinese Corps being assembled at Ramgarh in India (see paras. 15 and 16) advanced from Ledo on Myitkyina and a British force from Manipur towards Mandalay. We agreed that these plans were generally suitable, but that the date by which they could be put into execution could not yet be definitely fixed.

OPERATION FOR CAPTURE OF AKYAB.

31. Early in autumn I set on foot preparations for a sea-borne expedition to re-capture Akyab. It was at first intended to be carried out at the beginning of December, but neither the shipping, troops or necessary air force could be made available for various reasons, principally the prolongation of operations in Madagascar. By the middle of November I was forced to abandon hope of being able to mount a seaborne expedition against Akyab, and decided that the only chance of capturing it was by an advance from Chittagong down the Arakan coast to secure the Mayu Peninsula, whence an attack on Akyab could be launched from short range. This plan had the disadvantage that it made surprise most unlikely, and Arakan was a most unfavourable theatre, into which I should certainly not have made a deep land advance on any scale had sea transport been available. I also realised that the troops available had had little opportunity of training in jungle warfare. I hoped, however, that, if the advance in Arakan could proceed rapidly, it would be difficult for the Japanese to reinforce in time; and considered it was

better to take the risks involved than to remain inactive on this front during the winter.

Instructions for this operation were issued to G.O.C.-in-C., Eastern Army, on the 19th November, 1942. The progress and results will be described in a subsequent despatch. By the end of the year 14th Indian Division had crossed the Burmese frontier and had occupied Maungdaw and Buthidaung, from which the Japanese withdrew without fighting. The division was preparing to push on down to Foul Point at the southern end of the Mayu Peninsula, from whence it was intended to launch an assault on Akyab. Unfortunately, rain had already delayed the progress of the division.

NORTHERN BURMA OPERATIONS.

32. I had a conference with General Stilwell on the 17th December at which plans for Upper Burma in the early part of 1943 were discussed. General Stilwell was anxious, in spite of the administrative difficulties, to secure as much of northern Burma as possible, in order to cover the construction of a road from Ledo by Myitkyina to Paoshan to join the Burma Road, and also to secure the airfield at Myitkyina. The construction of the Ledo – Myitkyina road had now been undertaken by the Americans. It was agreed that all preparations should be continued with the object of an advance into Upper Burma from Yunnan (Chinese force), Ledo (Chinese Corps from Ramgarh) and Manipur (British IV Corps), to begin on the 1st March if the progress of road-making and administrative situation permitted.

33. On IV Corps front, 23rd Indian Division had advanced two brigades into the Tamu area in the Kabaw valley, while 17th Indian Division moved forward towards the Chin hills down a new road which was being constructed towards Tiddim. There was some patrol incidents in the Kabaw and Chindwin valleys but no major action.

In northern Burma Kachin levies based on Sumprabum did some excellent work in harassing Japanese forces north of Myitkyina. In the Hukawng valley a small force of Japanese and rebel Burmans advanced to Shingbwiyang in October but withdrew after bombing attacks by the United States Air Force.

OPERATIONS OF THE R.I.N.

34. The main work of the Royal Indian Navy in the period under review has been convoy duty. Several Japanese submarines were known to be operating in the Indian Ocean, but no ship in convoy was lost. A number routed independently were sunk, chiefly in the vicinity of the Mozambique Channel, but generally speaking enemy submarines were not numerous. Ships of the R.I.N. made a number of depth charge attacks on possible submarines, but no sinkings were claimed.

On the 11th November H.M.I.S. *Bengal*, commanded by Lieutenant Wilson, while on passage from Australia to India convoying the Dutch tanker *Ondina*, encountered two Japanese armed merchant cruisers south of Cocos Island.

Though the enemy was greatly superior in strength, H.M.I.S. *Bengal* closed at once and fought a most spirited action at close range, sinking the larger of the enemy ships. The Dutch tanker gallantly supported *Bengal.* This action reflected the greatest credit on the commanders and crews of *Bengal* and *Ondina.*

Launches of the R.I.N. and of the Burma navy operated from Chittagong in support of the army's advance in Arakan.

AIR OPERATIONS, OCTOBER-DECEMBER.

35. With the improvement of the weather after the monsoon, a systematic air offensive was begun against the enemy airfields and communications in Burma, to the extent that our resources allowed. Attacks were made both by day and night and had undoubtedly very considerable effect. The air force also provided direct support for the Army in Arakan and Assam; defended by fighters Calcutta, Chittagong and other vulnerable points; protected shipping in the Bay of Bengal; carried out visual and photographic reconnaissance; and dropped large quantities of supplies in the Chin hills for the local troops, at Sumprabum for the Kachin levies and for the garrison of Fort Hertz.

The Japanese air force showed only sporadic activity. Between the 25th and 28th October the enemy made a series of heavy raids on airfields in the Dinjan area which the Americans had lately taken over. One of these caused considerable damage, since the warning system proved ineffective. In December, the enemy attacked our forward airfields in the Fenny and Chittagong areas and the docks at Chittagong; he caused little damage. At the end of the year he made a series of small attacks by night on Calcutta. These did little damage but caused an exodus of labour.

SUMMARY.

36. From the above it can be seen that the Indian Command had a full and eventful year in 1942. It had been rudely awakened from a somewhat detached interest in the war by the shock of Japan's aggression and the wholly unexpected disasters in Malaya and then Burma. When the danger approached closely, both the armed forces and the nation were unprepared to meet invasion. Ever since the beginning of the war India had sent troops abroad almost as quickly as they could be trained, and had kept in India, except for the minimum necessary for the defence of the N.W. Frontier and internal security, only new formations under training, with incomplete equipment. In 1942 a considerable proportion of these half-trained formations had been sent to Malaya or Burma in the hope of holding up the enemy. So that in March, 1942, India had not a single fully-trained division. The Air Force, as shown, was similarly ineffective and the Eastern Fleet was unable to control Indian waters. So India stood in greater peril of invasion than for some hundreds of years.

That India was able six months later to pass from a defensive to an offensive basis may be counted something of an achievement, especially in view of the administrative difficulties and internal troubles that were encountered. Prompt assistance was sent from the United Kingdom, and as many troops and air squadrons as could be reasonably spared from our commitments elsewhere were allotted to India.

ACKNOWLEDGEMENTS.

37. I should like to place on record my appreciation of the invaluable assistance and wise advice given me by His Excellency the Viceroy and Governor-General, the Marquess of Linlithgow, K.T., P.C., G.C.S.I., G.C.I.E., O.B.E., D.L., T.D.

38. I am greatly indebted to His Excellency Colonel Sir John Herbert, G.C.I.E., Governor of Bengal, and His Excellency Sir Andrew Clow, K.C.S.I., C.I.E., Governor of Assam, and to the civil officers of those Provinces; also to His Excellency Sir Reginald Dorman-Smith, G.B.E., Governor of Burma, and his officers, and to Vice-Admiral Sir Geoffrey Layton, K.C.B., D.S.O., Commander-in-Chief, Ceylon.

39. I have received most valuable co-operation from Admiral Sir J.F. Somerville, K.C.B., K.B.E., D.S.O., Commander-in-Chief, Eastern Fleet, and Rear-Admiral A.F.E. Palliser, C.B., D.S.C., Flag Liaison Officer, Eastern Fleet, in connection with problems affecting the Royal Navy; and from Vice-Admiral Sir H. Fitzherbert, K.C.I.E., C.B., C.M.G., Flag Officer Commanding, Royal Indian Navy.

40. I have been in daily touch with Air Chief Marshal Sir R.E.C. Peirse, K.C.B., D.S.O., A.F.C., on Air Force questions, and have formed a very high opinion of his abilities and character. Under his direction the co-operation of the Air Force with Army and Navy has been outstanding. I wish also to mention the services of the following R.A.F. officers: A.V.M. W.H. Stevenson and Air-Commodore T.M. Williams.

41. I am very grateful to General Sir Alan F. Hartley, K.C.S.I., C.B., D.S.O., my Deputy, who has given me most loyal support and assistance; his great experience of India and the Indian Army has been invaluable.

42. The work of my Chief of General Staff, Lieutenant-General E.L. Morris, C.B., O.B.E., M.C., has been of a very high order. He got through an immense amount of work without fuss or friction; and his sympathetic but firm personality promoted smooth and efficient working in the complex Indian military machine, which had not been geared to a major war on its immediate borders and required considerable working up.

43. I was ably assisted both by the Civilian Staff, C. MacI. G. Ogilvie, Esq., C.S.I., C.B.E., I.C.S., as Secretary, and his successor, C.M. Trivedi, Esq., C.S.I., C.I.E., O.B.E., I.C.S, who took his place when the original Defence Department was divided into Defence and War Departments, and E.T. Coates, Esq., C.S.I., C.I.E., I.C.S., my Financial Adviser, and by the Principal Staff Officers (Lieutenant-General W.H.G. Baker, C.B., D.S.O., O.B.E., Adjutant-General, Lieutenant-General W.G.H. Vickers, C.B., O.B.E., Quarter-Master General, and Lieutenant-General Sir C.A. Bird, K.C.I.E., C.B., D.S.O., Master General of

the Ordnance). I wish to record the services of these officers and also of my Engineer-in-Chief, Major-General R.L. Bond, C.B.E., D.S.O., M.C., who directed the very large programme of airfield construction and other work; and of my Director of Medical Services, Major-General A.C. Campbell Monro, C.B., I.M.S., who effected a great improvement in the medical services in difficult conditions.

44. Command of the Eastern Army, which was responsible for the defence of the threatened frontier of India, was exercised first by Lieut.-General Sir C.N.F. Broad, K.C.B., D.S.O., and after August 1942 by Lieut.-General N.M.S. Irwin, C.B., D.S.O., M.C.; both these officers carried out a most difficult task of command and administration with ability and energy.

Note
1. The Audax was not designed as a fighter and had been obsolete as an Army Co-Operation machine before the war; its maximum speed was 150 m.p.h.

3

FIELD MARSHAL VISCOUNT WAVELL'S DESPATCH ON OPERATIONS IN THE INDIA COMMAND, 1 JANUARY 1943 TO 20 JUNE 1943

The War Office, March, 1948.
PREFACE BY THE WAR OFFICE.

SINCE the conclusion of hostilities with Japan, certain Japanese documents, handed over to the Headquarters of the 12th Army in Burma after the Japanese surrender have been examined. It has been established from these documents, that the Japanese plan of operations in Burma for the winter 1942–43, was to make an offensive into India against the oilfield at Tinsukia via the Hukawng Valley, and with another force to capture Imphal and then Dimapur, in order to cut off any Allied Troops in the Tinsukia area and to occupy Northern Assam. A Japanese document gives as the reasons why these plans were not put into effect, first the Allied offensive in Arakan and secondly the penetration of Brigadier Wingate's 77th Brigade into Northern Burma. By Japanese admissions, Field Marshal Viscount Wavell's operations, described in this Despatch, accomplished their main purpose, which was by offensive action to keep the Japanese forces engaged and thereby prevent an offensive into India at a time when India was unprepared.

The following Despatch was submitted to the Secretary of State for War on 27th June, 1944, by FIELD-MARSHAL VISCOUNT WAVELL, G.C.B., C.M.G., M.C., A.D.C., Commander-in-Chief, India.

1. This despatch deals with the operations and general situation in the India Command from January 1st to June 20th, 1943, the date on which I ceased to be Commander-in-Chief in India. It includes an account of the fighting in Arakan and in Upper Burma during the first half of 1943, and of the planning and preparations which took place during the same period for the campaigning season of 1943–44.

PLANS FOR FIRST HALF OF 1943.

2. The objectives I had laid down for the Winter of 1942–43 were the capture of Akyab in Arakan; the strengthening of our position in the Chin Hills (*i.e.*, about Tiddim and Fort White), and the establishment of forces on the Chindwin river between Kalewa and Sittaung, whence the Japanese lines of communication

further east were to be raided, and preparations were to be made for a further advance into Upper Burma should opportunity offer.

These British operations were to be combined as closely as possible with operations by Chinese troops directed by General Stilwell (who held the post of Chief of Staff to the Generalissimo, Marshal Chiang Kai-shek). These aimed at occupying North-East Burma as far as an approximate line Myitkyina – Bhamo – Lashio, with the object of covering the construction of a road from Ledo into China, which was being made by American engineers. A Chinese force from Ledo, with American direction but under my control, was to advance on Myitkyina to join hands with a Chinese force from Yunnan, which General Stilwell informed me would advance in strength on March 1st, 1943 I had a conference with General Stilwell on December 10th, at which I undertook to do all I could towards assisting a Chinese Advance from Yunnan, and reoccupying Upper Burma in the spring of 1943; but I emphasized the seriousness of the administrative problem, our limited resources, and the unlikelihood of any rapid progress owing to road-making difficulties, both from Ledo towards Myitkyina and eastwards from the Imphal plain towards the Chindwin.

The troops, actually available in India at the beginning of 1943 and the state of their training and equipment are shown in Appendix A.

OPERATIONS IN ARAKAN.

3. The operations in Arakan had only a limited objective, the capture of the air-fields on Akyab island at the end of the Mayu peninsula. There is no practicable land route out of Arakan into Burma proper, from which it is separated by a range of steep, jungle-clad hills with no roads. Arakan itself is extremely difficult campaigning country with poor communications, much thick jungle and steep hills, and a wet and unhealthy climate. In the First Burmese War more than one hundred years previously it had been the scene of a British expedition, in which the force had been almost entirely destroyed by disease.

The capture of Akyab had been originally planned as a seaborne expedition, for which the 6th British Brigade of the 2nd Division had been specially trained and was to form a landing force with the 29th British Brigade, which had taken part in the Madagascar operations. The rôle of the 14th Indian Division in this plan was a purely diversionary advance from Chittagong. Unfortunately, I was not provided with the necessary resources for the landing operations.[1] The 29th Brigade and their landing crews suffered from malaria in Madagascar and had to be sent to South Africa to recuperate. It became apparent that neither naval escorts, transports, landing craft, nor air forces to cover the landing would be available in sufficient numbers during the winter of 1942–43 to undertake the sea-borne expedition against Akyab; which had every prospect of success, if it could have been carried out at the end of 1942 or beginning of 1943, since the Japanese garrison was small and there were few defences on the island.

4. I was unwilling, however, to give up the attempt to capture Akyab, and considered that it might be possible by a rapid advance down the Arakan coast by the

14th Indian Division to reach the southern end of the Mayu peninsula (Foul Point) and thence launch a short range assault in the few landing craft available and in local vessels, by the 6th Brigade and part of the 14th Division. Speed in the advance was essential so as to reach Akyab before the Japanese could reinforce the island or strengthen the defences.

There were, however, serious obstacles to a rapid advance in the nature of the country and the communications. There were no road communications other than those we could make as we advanced, which entailed the bridging of numerous creeks. The forward echelons had to be organised on a pack transport basis, which caused difficulties in a formation which had been trained on a mechanised basis. Sea communications were hampered by the nature of the coast line, which offered no landing facilities except within the Naf and Mayu rivers; they could only be used as their mouths were secured by our advance. Supply by air was out of the question, owing to our lack of transport aircraft.

5. At the beginning of the campaign the enemy held Maungdaw and Buthidaung with a force estimated at two battalions with eight guns. The initial advance of the 14th Division was delayed by the weather and administrative difficulties. The leading Brigade, the 123rd Indian Infantry Brigade, was about to attack the enemy positions, in the middle of December, 1942, when the enemy withdrew, and we occupied Maungdaw on December 16th and Buthidaung on December 17th. The 14th Division followed up on a two-brigade front; the 47th Indian Infantry Brigade moving down the coast towards Foul Point, and the 123rd Brigade east of the Mayu river towards Rathedaung. By December 27th, the 47th Brigade had reached Indin, and a patrol actually rounded Foul Point and reached Magyichaung; by the same date the 123rd Brigade arrived opposite Rathedaung and a patrol reported it clear of the enemy, though this cannot have been correct. At this time it appeared that the Japanese did not intend to hold the Mayu peninsula. If the troops had been able to push on at once, the whole peninsula might have been secured.

6. There now occurred an unfortunate delay of some ten days, due to administrative difficulties. It may be that the urgency of the situation was not fully realised and that troops should have been pushed forward in spite of all difficulties to take advantage of the situation. But the brigades were operating at the end of a very tenuous line of communications of over 150 miles from railhead, and the weather was unfavourable, heavy rain making the road impassable.

When the advance was resumed on January 6th, the enemy had constructed strong defences in the Donbaik –Laungchaung area and at Rathedaung. The 47th Brigade attacked the Donbaik position on January 18th and 19th. The attack failed, mainly owing to the difficulty of locating enemy machine-guns and mortars in the jungle.

The 47th Brigade was now relieved by the 55th Indian Infantry Brigade, and preparations were made for a fresh assault with the aid of tanks. This was made on February 1st and failed, two of the six tanks used being ditched and two knocked out by anti-tank fire. An attack on Rathedaung by 123rd Brigade on February 3rd also failed after some initial success. The 55th Brigade attacked Donbaik again on February 17th and again failed. It was now relieved by the 71st Brigade of the 26th Indian Division. The intervals between the attacks were due entirely to difficulties of communications which made reinforcement and supply very slow. The long stretch of hastily constructed road was continually interrupted by rain; and supply by sea was hampered by the lack of vessels of suitable size and draught to enter the river and use the anchorages at Cox's Bazaar and Maungdaw; it even proved necessary to withdraw vessels of the R.I.N. from minesweeping and patrol duties, to remove their guns, and use them as cargo ships.

7. By this time it became obvious that the Japanese had been reinforced and had probably the whole of one division on the Arakan front. Strong defences had now been made on Akyab island I discussed the situation with General Irwin, commanding the Eastern Army. It seemed improbable that the Mayu peninsula could be cleared in time to deliver the assault on Akyab before monsoon conditions, which appear about the middle of March, made landing hazardous, and it was obvious that the enemy had by now made full preparations to defend all landing places. General Irwin recommended that we should prepare defensive positions and give up the attempt to clear the Mayu peninsula. I refused to accept this recommendation and to take up a defensive attitude without first obtaining a marked success over the enemy, so that the troops should be confident of their ability to beat the Japanese. I directed General Irwin to use the 6th Brigade (British) of four battalions, which had been held at Chittagong in readiness for the attack on Akyab, to assault the Donbaik position in conjunction with the 71st Indian Brigade. My intention was that the attack should be delivered in great strength and depth with the object of swamping the Japanese positions.

8. Meanwhile the Japanese began a counter offensive, directed in the first instance against our eastern flank on the Kaladan river. Two small columns had moved into the Kaladan valley at the time of our advance on Rathedaung. One column, consisting of a battalion of Indian infantry from the 123rd Brigade, moved from the Mayu valley by a track across the hills into the Kaladan valley; the other, consisting of two companies of Tripura Rifles (State Forces), came down the valley from the north. Our forces had occupied Kyauktaw by the time of the Japanese attack. The enemy appears partly to have come up the Kaladan river from Akyab and partly to have infiltrated through the hills from Pakokku on the Irrawaddy. They employed their usual enveloping tactics against communications and forced the battalion of the 123rd Brigade to withdraw westward across the hills with some loss, and the Tripura Rifles to retreat northwards up the valley. The enemy followed up this success by crossing the hills and attacking the communications of 123rd Brigade opposite Rathedaung. After some heavy fighting, the 123rd Brigade, which had been closely engaged for three months, was relieved by the 55th Brigade and withdrew to Buthidaung.

9. The attack of the 6th Brigade on the Donbaik position took place on March 18th and failed. The troops succeeded in advancing some distance into the enemy defences, but were unable to deal with the enemy's underground strong points, which remained in action behind our forward troops; while the enemy guns, mortars and machine-guns, concealed in the jungle, carried on firing on our troops which had penetrated the line quite regardless of their own troops which were still holding out. Our forward troops were eventually all killed or compelled to withdraw. The attack was made with great dash and determination but was not carried out in the strength or depth that I had considered necessary to overrun the enemy position. The losses of the attacking troops were heavy, especially in officers.

10. Meanwhile the 55th Brigade opposite Rathedaung was attacked in flank and rear and cut off from Buthidaung on March 17th. By a counter-attack and with the assistance of 71st Brigade it succeeded in extricating itself from a dangerous position but lost some equipment and a considerable number of animals. East of the Mayu river we were now forced back to a position covering Buthidaung. The enemy then began similar infiltration tactics against our troops west of the Mayu range, and at Indin on April 5th overran the headquarters of the 6th Brigade. There was heavy fighting here, and severe casualties were inflicted on the enemy in counter-attacks; but by the middle of April we had withdrawn on this flank to positions covering Maungdaw.

11. By the end of March, the 26th Division had taken over the greater part of the front, most of the 14th Division being withdrawn further north to rest. Some of the troops were tired and many units were weak through battle casualties and disease; reinforcements took some time to settle down to the abnormal conditions of jungle fighting. But in view of our command of the air I still hoped we could regain the initiative. I accordingly issued the instructions to Eastern Army which are given in Appendix B. They were to the effect that positions to cover the Maungdaw – Buthidaung road, the Maungdaw air-field and the mouth of the Naf river were to be held for the monsoon period in as great depth as possible, and that we were meanwhile to regain the initiative by offensive action on both sides of the Mayu river.

12. Shortly afterwards, in the middle of April, I was summoned to the United Kingdom to discuss plans for the winter of 1943–44 (see paragraph 46 below). During the first three months of 1943 I had visited the Eastern front on a number of occasions and had kept in close personal touch with Commanders and operations. During the remainder of the period under review, I was in the United Kingdom or U.S.A. and in touch only by long-range telegraph reports.

13. We failed to regain the initiative, and in fact lost our positions at Maungdaw and Buthidaung. Japanese forces continued their infiltration tactics through the thick jungle along the spine of the Mayu ridge; and by early May established themselves with a strength of at least two battalions on the road between

Maungdaw and Buthidaung and destroyed a bridge. All attempts to dislodge them failed, so that it was necessary, on May 7th, to withdraw the force from Buthidaung by the Ngakyedauk Pass to the west of the Mayu ridge south of Bawli Bazaar. The movement was carried out without interference by the enemy; but a quantity of transport which could not be removed had to be destroyed.

14. The enemy continued to infiltrate against our communications; and it was finally decided to take up positions further north, abandoning Maungdaw, although it had been developed as an advanced base since its capture in December, and its loss involved the destruction of considerable quantities of stores. An attempt might have been made to hold and maintain it by means of the Naf river; but in view of the tired state of the troops and their lack of jungle training the attempt was not judged advisable. By the start of the monsoon, our forces in Arakan were back approximately in the positions from which the advance had begun five months earlier. The enemy, who was also obviously suffering from maintenance difficulties, withdrew to the Maungdaw – Buthidaung line which he had held at the beginning of operations. This ended active operations in Arakan except for small patrol enterprises.

On May 20th I decided to replace Lieut.-General N.M.S. Irwin, Commander of the Eastern Army who had been for some time suffering from ill-health, by General Sir George Giffard.

15. The result of these Arakan operations was undoubtedly disappointing. But they must be viewed in their proper perspective. They were represented in some quarters as an "invasion of Burma". Actually, as already stated, they had one objective only, Akyab island, and I should not have committed troops deeply into the unhealthy Arakan jungles had I had available the naval and air forces, landing craft and transports for a seaborne assault on the island.[1] When it became obvious that these would not be forthcoming, I took the risk, sooner than keep my troops standing idle, of trying to reach Akyab by an overland advance. I was well aware of the difficulties and dangers, and that the troops I was employing were not fully trained or equipped; they had been organised and trained up to the autumn for the defence of Bengal.

16. When these operations were initiated, I had been informed by General Stilwell that the Chinese Armies in Yunnan would advance into Upper Burma in force early in 1943, and I had intended that the IV Corps from Assam should advance in co-operation with them. I had therefore reason to suppose that the Japanese in Upper Burma would he fully occupied and unlikely to move reinforcements to Arakan. Actually, the Chinese made no move; and the IV Corps, owing to administrative difficulties was unable to be as active as I had hoped. The Japanese were therefore able to reinforce Akyab and Arakan from Upper Burma.

17. That Japanese defences, skilfully prepared and concealed, and held to the last, are difficult to overcome without considerable superiority of numbers and equipment and good training has been abundantly shown in the fighting in New

Guinea and elsewhere in the S.W. Pacific, and in the actions which have taken place this spring on the Burma frontier. We had never the necessary superiority in these respects to assault positions such as Donbaik and Rathedaung; and our tactics were not always appropriate, owing to inexperience. The enemy counter-offensive was skilfully planned and executed; and their mobility and infiltration tactics in the jungle are undoubtedly difficult to counter. It was not possible to feed by air troops which had been cut off from their base by these tactics, owing to the lack of transport aeroplanes.

18. In the initial advance the troops of the 14th Division fought boldly and well. It was only in the latter stages of the fighting, after several months continuous engagement in an unhealthy climate and under the discouragement of failure that there was any deterioration in the endurance and fighting capacity of the troops.

19. Strategically, we failed to reach Akyab and finished in the same positions from which we had started, but the capture of Akyab by an overland expedition was always in the nature of a gamble. We suffered some 2,500 battle casualties and probably inflicted at least as heavy losses on the enemy. The greatest gain from the campaign was experience of the enemy's methods and of our own defects in training and organisation. The serious loss was in prestige and morale.

On balance I shall certainly never regret that I ordered the campaign to take place in spite of lack of resources.

SUPPORT BY R.I.N. AND R.A.F.

20. Launches and coastal craft of the Royal Indian Navy played a considerable part in these operations, both along the coast and in the Naf and Mayu rivers, and showed much enterprise in a number of small actions, of which the following are examples. On January 27th a launch on patrol in the Mayu river rammed and sank a large launch full of enemy troops, at least fifty of whom were killed. On the night of February 21st–22nd Coastal craft landed a raiding party at Myebon, about sixty miles south-east of Akyab, which inflicted casualties, destroyed stores, and re-embarked without loss. On February 26th motor launches on patrol north of Ramree Island intercepted two Japanese motor launches, sank one and damaged the other, inflicting at least 50 casualties on the enemy.

21. The R.A.F. gave invaluable aid to the Army during these operations, both by attacks on enemy positions in close support and by attacks on other targets in forward areas, such as boats on the rivers or transport on the tracks and roads. The action of the R.A.F. is described in greater detail in paragraphs 32 to 36.

OPERATIONS IN NORTHERN BURMA.

22. My intention had been that during the winter the IV Corps (17th and 23rd Indian Divisions) should advance into Burma and establish itself on the Chindwin river between Kalewa and Sittaung. The only strategical objective of these operations was to assist the advance of the Chinese forces into Northern Burma (see paragraph 2 above) by engaging as many enemy troops as possible.

There were two possible routes leading towards the objective from the Imphal plain in Manipur over the high range into Burma. The road from Imphal by Palel to Tamu (in the Kabaw valley) had been constructed in 1942, from Palel to Tamu it was a single-way mountain road liable to frequent interruption in the rains; the distance from Imphal to Palel is 28 miles; and from Palel to Tamu 36 miles. The other possible route was from Imphal by Bishenpur to Tiddim (145 miles), thence to Fort White and down into the Kabaw valley at Kalemyo; this route had certain obvious advantages in the approach to Kalemyo, since it was screened by hills to the east until close to Kalemyo, whereas an advance to Kalemyo from Tamu was exposed throughout to enemy attacks from across the Chindwin. General Irwin favoured the development of the Tiddim route and placed most of our limited road-making resources on it. A visit to the front early in February convinced me that our resources were quite insufficient to develop the lengthy Tiddim route in time, and that it was in fact unlikely that it could ever be made into a serviceable line of communication owing to the engineering difficulties. It seemed likely that the monsoon would find us with no reliable road into Burma at all. I therefore ordered the diversion of our road-making effort to the improvement of the Tamu road, which was at least known to be practicable.

23. The lack of transport, of road-making material and of other administrative resources, which are referred to elsewhere in this despatch, made it necessary to postpone operations against Kalewa and Sittaung. When it was found that the Chinese troops in Yunnan had no intention of making a move, the strategical basis of our advance disappeared; and in the end operations in the Kabaw Valley were confined to strong offensive patrols.

OPERATIONS OF 77TH INDIAN INFANTRY BRIGADE.
(WINGATE'S FORCE.)

24. Early in 1942, while operations in Burma were still being conducted, I had asked for the services of Lieut.-Colonel O.C. Wingate, D.S.O., who had served under my command in Palestine in 1938 and in Abyssinia in 1941, to organise guerilla activity in Burma. He arrived too late to effect anything in Burma; but on the withdrawal from Burma in May 1942 he put before me a proposal to train a brigade for long-range penetration behind the enemy lines. The brigade was to have a special organisation and was to be independent of the normal lines of communication and to be supplied from the air. I approved Colonel Wingate's proposals, and placed him in command of a Brigade formed of the 13th Battalion of the King's Regiment, the 3/2nd Gurkha Rifles, 142nd Commando Company and 2nd Battalion of Burma Rifles. These were not picked units in any way, but were the only ones easily available at the time. The formation was known as 77th Indian Infantry Brigade and began jungle training in the Central Provinces in July 1942. Its original rôle in the reconquest of Burma was to penetrate into Central Burma at a time when both Upper and Lower Burma were being attacked by large forces. When our restricted resources permitted only a very limited advance in Upper Burma, I considered whether I should employ the Brigade at all

during the winter of 1942–43. With a view, however, to giving the maximum possible assistance to the Chinese advance which was due to take place on March 1st (see paragraph 2 above), I decided to use the Brigade in Upper Burma to cut the enemy line of communication to Myitkyina and if possible also to Bhamo and Lashio. It was accordingly moved to Imphal early in 1943. At the beginning of February I learnt from General Stilwell that the Chinese in Yunnan had no intention of advancing. The operations of the 77th Brigade would thus have no support and no strategical purpose. I had therefore to decide whether it was wise to employ the Brigade at all. I went to Imphal and had a long discussion with Brigadier Wingate on the evening of February 6th, as a result of which I decided to let the operation continue, in order to gain experience of the working of these columns. I inspected the Brigade, which was organised into seven columns, on February 7th; and it began its move next day. Each column was self-contained with pack transport, and had machine-guns and mortars. There was no artillery, and supply was by local purchase and air.

25. The directive given to the Brigade was to enter Burma through the front held by the 4th Corps; to cut the main North and South railway line between Mandalay and Myitkyina; to harass the enemy in the Shwebo area; and then, if circumstances were favourable, to cross the Irrawaddy and cut the railway line Maymyo – Lashio.

To assist the main body to cross the River Chindwin (about Tonhe) and reach the railway some 150 miles distant without opposition, two of its Gurkha columns were sent to cross the river 50 miles to the South, and to co-operate with movements by the 23rd Division in that area, who were to simulate an attack on the enemy position at Kalewa. These two columns were to cross the river three days before the main body of the Brigade, and then, after moving south to attract the attention of the enemy, to move quickly to the east, cross the river Irrawaddy at Tagaung, and await the arrival of the main force in the mountains around Mongmit. Supply dropping for these columns during this period was to be by day so as to attract attention; otherwise the normal practice was to drop supplies by night.

So far as can be judged the deception was successful; at any rate the main body had crossed the Chindwin without opposition by the 18th February, and succeeded in reaching the railway unopposed.

Two columns fell out of the enterprise at an early stage. One of the two southerly columns was trapped in an ambush, broke up and returned to Assam in small parties; and one column of the main body, in a brush with some enemy, became scattered, lost much equipment and was cut off from the other columns; as this column had shown poor fighting qualities its commander decided to march it back to the Chindwin.

26. The main body reached the railway and successfully carried out a series of demolitions; four bridges were destroyed, the side of a gorge blasted to bring

down thousands of tons of rock on the line, and the track was cut in 70 other places.

I had given Brigadier Wingate a free hand to decide whether after cutting the railway he returned to Assam or crossed the Irrawaddy and raided further east. As one of the main objects of the expedition was to gain experience, he eventually decided to cross the Irrawaddy, largely in order to ascertain whether the equipment and methods of river crossing evolved during training were practical. The crossing of the Irrawaddy by the various widely separated columns was accomplished between March 9th and 18th.

27. Across the Irrawaddy the Brigade began to encounter difficulties. It was hot, water was not easy to find, and the health of men and animals began to suffer. There were more Japanese in the area than had been expected, and many M.T. tracks which gave the enemy mobility, hence it became difficult to arrange supply dropping. Eventually the operations against the Mandalay – Lashio railway were abandoned, and it was decided to recross the Irrawaddy and return to India. An attempt to cross the Irrawaddy at Inywa (south of Katha) was discovered by the enemy, and failed. The order was therefore given for the force to break up into Dispersal Groups – a manoeuvre which had been practised during training – and to cross the river on a very wide front and return to India independently. This was successfully done, most Groups reached the Chindwin in the area occupied by the 23rd Division near Sittaung; one column crossed it as far north as Tamanthi and went thence to Kohima; one marched due north and won out by Fort Hertz, one went east to Paoshan, was hospitably received by the Chinese Army and flown back to India by the Americans. The majority of the force had returned by the first week in June. The Brigade had spent four months inside territory occupied by the Japanese.

28. The enterprise had no strategic value, and about one-third of the force which entered Burma was lost. But the experience gained of operations of this type, in supply dropping from the air, and in jungle warfare and Japanese methods, was invaluable. The enemy was obviously surprised and at a loss, and found no effective means to counter the harassment of our columns. The operations showed the necessity for a very high standard of training and physical fitness in troops employed on such expeditions. In general, Brigadier Wingate's theories and leadership were fully vindicated. A detailed and frank account of the enterprise is given in his printed report of the operations. As soon as the expedition started, I had issued orders for the formation of another brigade (in Indian Infantry Brigade) on similar lines.

OPERATIONS IN N.E. BURMA.

29. Early in 1942 the construction of a road from Ledo (in North-East Assam) towards Myitkyina in Upper Burma had been begun. Work had been interrupted by the evacuation of Burma and by the monsoon; but had been resumed in November. In December the Americans took over the construction, with the

intention of eventually driving a supply route through to China. By June 20 road-head had crossed the Paungsa Pass, 46 miles from Ledo. The nature of the country and the climate made the work extremely difficult. To protect the construction, the Americans employed a part of the Chinese troops who had been trained in India under American supervision (see paragraphs 15 and 16 of my Despatch on operations in the Eastern Theatre based in India, Mar.–Dec. 1942).[2]

30. I mentioned in my last Despatch[2] (paragraph 22) the reoccupation of Fort Hertz in the extreme north of Burma to support the operations of the Kachin Levies towards Myitkyina. These levies, under Lieut.-Colonel Gamble, did most valuable work in harassing the Japanese forces in the Myitkyina area during the early part of 1943; so much so that they stung the enemy into retaliation. Early in March a considerable Japanese force advanced on Sumprabum, temporarily dispersed the levies, and seemed to threaten Fort Hertz. There was a moment when it was represented to me that only a brigade could save Fort Hertz. There was no brigade available; the only means of communication with Fort Hertz were by air; and very few transport aircraft were available. I had one additional company flown in to Fort Hertz. The Japanese did not advance beyond Sumprabum and the levies soon recovered their morale.

OPERATIONS OF R.I.N.

31. Apart from the assistance given by small craft in the Arakan operations (see paragraphs 6 and 20 above), there is little to record of the operations, of the Royal Indian Navy, which carried on its normal escort and patrol duties. There was no enemy naval activity in the Indian theatre during the period.

AIR OPERATIONS.

32. During the period under review the R.A.F. continued to expand in numbers and began to receive more modern aeroplanes and equipment. In 1943 it can be said to have passed definitely from the defensive to the offensive. We were still, however, much below our requirements, and our aircraft were deficient in range and performance, and included many obsolete or obsolescent types. The operational strength of the R.A.F. by June 1943 was-

18 Fighter squadrons,
2 Squadrons long-range bombers,
2 Squadrons medium bombers,
11 Squadrons light bombers,
2 Squadrons torpedo bombers,
6 Squadrons Flying-boats,
2 Squadrons Transport aircraft,
2 General Recce. Squadrons,
1 Photographic Recce. Squadron,
1 Coastal Fighter Squadron,
1 Night Fighter Squadron.

The Fighter Squadrons were equipped with Hurricanes and Mohawks; the heavy bombers were Liberators, the medium bombers Wellingtons, and the light bombers Blenheims and Vengeances. The torpedo bombers were Beauforts, the flying-boats Catalinas, and the transport aircraft Hudsons and Dakotas. There were also a few Spitfires and Hurricanes used for photographic reconnaissance. The General Reconnaissance Squadrons were equipped with Hudsons whilst the Coastal Fighter Squadron and the Night Fighter Squadron were both equipped with Beaufighters.

The strength of the 10th American Air Force also increased and by June it had available approximately 60 fighters (Kittyhawks), 50 heavy bombers (Liberators) and 70 medium bombers (Mitchells). Working in close co-operation, the R.A.F. and U.S.A.A.F. together established air superiority over the Japanese air forces operating from Burma.

33. The objects of the Air Force operations during the period under review were:-

(*a*) To establish and maintain air superiority in Burma;

(*b*) To support the operations of the Army;

(*c*) To disrupt enemy communications in Burma;

(*d*) To defend India against air attack; and

(*e*) To supply from the air, forces which could not be supplied by normal means.

The first object was attained by attacks by day and night on enemy-occupied airfields and air installations and bases and by taking every opportunity to engage the enemy in the air.

Direct support of the Army was centred on the Arakan operations where the main fighting took place. The nature of the country, mainly dense jungle, made location of the enemy forward troops usually impossible; and though considerable success was achieved on occasions by bombing on targets indicated by artillery fire or pin-point methods, greater effect was obtained by attack on objectives in the immediate rear of the enemy's forward troops, *i.e.*, sampans and small boats on the waterways, bullock carts and other vehicles on the roads, or the forward movement of troops. These attacks were carried out chiefly by low-flying fighters.

Attacks on communications in Burma were made on railways (marshalling yards, bridges, rolling stock), on road-bridges and transport, on river craft, on depots and similar objectives. In general, the R.A.F. bombers attacked the short-range targets up to 250 miles from our forward airfields, while the Americans with their larger range and bigger armament attacked the more distant objectives. All bombing by U.S. aircraft and by R.A F. light bombers was carried out by day, night bombing being carried out by R.A.F. medium and heavy bombers. Hurricanes with long-range tanks were also used for attacks on transportation.

The defence of India against air attack requires little mention. In December 1942, as recorded in my last despatch,[2] the enemy made a series of small raids on the Calcutta area. In response to my request for night fighters, a flight of

Beaufighters arrived in Calcutta on January 14, 1943. On January 15th three enemy aircraft attempted to raid Calcutta and were all three shot down by a single Beaufighter. Four enemy aircraft made a raid on January 19th, of which two were certainly destroyed and one probably. There were no further attacks west of the Brahmaputra.

34. Apart from attacks on India, the enemy air force made occasional raids on our forward airfields and attacks on our troops or bases in Arakan. These attacks had little success; and generally the enemy's air activity was surprisingly small. Our constant attacks on his airfields forced him to keep his main air forces outside range of our bomber effort; his practice was to fly in a force of bombers from Thailand or Malaya, carry out one or two raids and then fly back again to distant bases. His bomber raids were always escorted by fighters; these fighters were a match or more than a match for our Hurricanes, unless they could gain an effective height before the approach of the enemy; and it became obvious that re-equipment with Spitfires of at least some of our fighter squadrons was required.

35. Supply dropping was carried out to maintain the 77th Brigade (see paragraphs 24 to 28), also to our forward troops in the Chin Hills and in the extreme north-east of Burma between Fort Hertz and Sumprabum, where our levies were operating. 300 tons of supplies were dropped on 77th Brigade and nearly 1,500 tons on other forces. Operations were over jungle country in difficult conditions, but not a single aircraft was lost.

36. The R.A.F. from North-East India also carried out regular sea reconnaissance over the Bay of Bengal, while aircraft from Southern India and Ceylon patrolled convoy routes and shipping lanes.

Photographic reconnaissance was carried out regularly over Burma; while long-range aircraft also made photographic reconnaissance flights over Sumatra, the Nicobar Islands, Andaman Islands and the west coast of Thailand.

ADMINISTRATIVE EFFORT.

37. These operations by land and air on India's north-eastern frontier, though on a comparatively small scale, required a very considerable administrative effort to support them. The difficulties of the lines of communication to Bengal and Assam were stated in paragraphs 10 to 13 of my last despatch.[2] Work on the improvement, both of the railways and on Inland Water Transport routes, has been continuous, but has not always been able to keep pace with the increasing demands. In particular, the narrow gauge railway to North-East India had during the first half of 1943 to meet the following demands, which competed with each other:-

(*a*) Supply of troops of IV Corps in Manipur to enable them to advance into Burma;

(*b*) Supply of American and Chinese troops in Ledo area and for Ledo road construction, (*c*) Supplies to be transported by air route into China;

(*d*) Materials and labour for construction of airfields in north-east Assam;

(*e*) Supplies for civil population of Assam.

The first of the above demands involved the building up of depots and stores along 350 miles of road; materials for a very large programme of road construction (see paragraph 22); the making of additional hospitals and other administrative establishments; as well as the daily maintenance of nearly 100,000 men, at distances up to over 200 miles from railhead.

The continual increase of American and Chinese forces employed on the Ledo road in the extreme north-eastern corner of Assam threw an additional strain on the transportation system. In February, after the visit of General Arnold to Chungking (see paragraph 43), the Americans suddenly decided to double the monthly tonnage target of air-borne supplies to China, from 10,000 to 20,000 tons. Though it did not prove possible, during the period under review, to reach the higher figure, plans had to provide for the delivery of this additional quantity of supplies at air-head, and for large increase of petrol, oil and other supplies for the extra aircraft required on the Chinese route. Further, the Americans demanded as a matter of urgent necessity the construction of more air-fields in Assam, which involved the transport of large quantities of materials and the diversion of engineering resources and labour from other important projects.

Besides all these military needs, the civil population of Assam had to be kept supplied by the same tenuous line of rail. If the priorities between all these conflicting requirements had remained constant, the task would have been difficult enough; but it was continually being complicated by the introduction into the programme of some fresh project of prior urgency; which often meant the removal of the limited resources in labour, machinery, etc., from one site to another. The fact that the requirements and views of the British, Americans, Indians and Chinese were involved and did not always coincide still further complicated the problem and introduced the danger of international friction. The wonder was not that projects were seldom completed by the target date but that so much got done.

38. I gave orders for a through road from India to Assam to be constructed, in order to assist the supply problem and to avoid the necessity of all wheeled vehicles being sent to Assam by rail instead of under their own power. This Assam access road ran through Bihar and north Bengal, but progress in construction was slow due to lack of resources.

MEDICAL.

39. The medical situation continued to require constant enlargement of hospitals in the operational area and strained India's inadequate resources to the utmost. Malaria remained the chief problem. During the Arakan operations casualties from malaria were extremely heavy, and the sick rate in Assam was also high. Weekly admissions to hospital in Eastern Army reached 10,000 in June, of which over half were due to malaria.

A Medical Mission from the United Kingdom visited India to investigate our shortage of medical personnel, and made valuable recommendations.

FOOD SUPPLIES.

40. By the end of 1942 the supply of food grains in India was obviously short of her needs, and we had great difficulty in obtaining foodstuffs for the Armed forces. I was compelled to draw the attention of the Government of India to the dangers of the food situation; and in January had to make a reduction in the flour ration of the Army.

CEYLON AND OCEAN BASES
(ADDU ATOLL, DIEGO GARCIA, COCOS ISLANDS).

41. These continued to remain the responsibility of Commander-in-Chief, India, but there is little to record of them during the period. The enemy made no attack or threat against any of them. There were some changes in the garrison of Ceylon, the 16th British Brigade of the 70th Division (see paragraph 8 of my previous Despatch)[2] being moved from Ceylon to rejoin its Division.

Ceylon was a valuable training ground for jungle warfare. At Addu Atoll A.A. guns were installed and airfields developed, the health situation was much improved.

INTERNAL SITUATION.

42. The internal situation in India during the first half of 1943 was quiet. The operations in Sind against the Hurs, undertaken to guard vital railway communications and restore public order and confidence (see paragraph 23 of my last despatch),[2] ended on June 1st, when martial law was removed. The head of the sect, the Pir Pagaro, was tried and executed.

The situation on the North-West Frontier of India gave no trouble during the period. Recruiting continued at a generally satisfactory rate, but it became obvious that the Indian Army had reached its expansion limit on a voluntary basis; the intake was now only sufficient to maintain the existing strength. The intake of Indian officers for the Army and the R.A.F. was disappointing both in quantity and quality.

PLANNING FOR FUTURE OPERATIONS.

43. In January I received information that Field-Marshal Sir John Dill, General Arnold, commanding the American air forces, and General Somervell, head of the American Service of Supply, would visit India after the Allied Conference at Casablanca to discuss plans for the recapture of Burma. They arrived at the end of January, and General Stilwell came also from China. Discussions were held on February 2nd and 3rd at Delhi. I had given orders some time previously for the preparation of a plan to recapture Burma during the cold weather of 1943–44, and the draft of this plan, which had been completed just before the arrival of the party, formed the basis of our discussions. As a result of these I submitted to the Chiefs of Staff an outline plan which may be summarised as follows.

The plan provided for an offensive in three phases:-

Phase 1. – To begin in November 1943, consisted in an advance by 10 Chinese divisions from Western Yunnan towards Myitkyina, Bhamo, Lashio, and eventually Mandalay; by the Chinese troops which had been trained at Ramgarh, from Ledo on Myitkyina; and by 3 British divisions from Manipur on Pakokku and Mandalay.

Phase 2. – Was to take place in December 1943, and was to consist of simultaneous seaborne assaults on the Western coast of Lower Burma, and landings were to be made on Ramree island, Taungup, Sandaway, Gwa, and Bassein, with the main object of securing airfields, also of advancing from Taungup on Prome; during this phase the British and Chinese advance in Upper Burma would be continued.

Phase 3. – Was to take place in January 1944, and was to consist of a direct seaborne and airborne assault on Rangoon, while the operations in Phases 1 and 2 continued.

Field-Marshal Dill and General Arnold then went to Chungking to discuss the plan with the Generalissimo, and I took General Somervell for a short tour of the Eastern Front. We met again in Calcutta and confirmed the outline plan.

44. The plan was admittedly a bold and hazardous one; but it was the only one which offered, to my mind, a chance of recapturing Burma in one campaigning season, between two monsoons; and this was what I had been instructed to do The plan did not commend itself to my A.O.C.-in-C., Air Chief Marshal Sir Richard Peirse, nor to Admiral Sir James Somerville, Commander-in-Chief, Eastern Fleet, who had been unable to be present at the discussions with the Americans but who visited Delhi later in February. Their objections were mainly that the cover by air forces would be insufficient; and that the direct assault on Rangoon would be impracticable if the enemy installed a heavy scale of defences in the Rangoon river. My comment was that I thought that by the winter of 1943-44 the Japanese air strength might have been considerably reduced, and that while I agreed that an assault up the Rangoon river would be extremely hazardous if the Japanese had installed a heavy scale of defence, there was at present no sign that they had done so or intended to do so.

I never received from the Chiefs of Staff or War Cabinet either approval or condemnation of the plan; but the resources required to implement it were obviously not forthcoming. I had stated our requirements at 182,000 tons per month beginning in March if the plan was to be prepared and executed in the winter 1943–44. The shipping programmes for March and April provided less than half of this.

45. Meanwhile in the middle of February I had ordered my planning staff to prepare plans for operations against Sumatra and Java, so as to have available alternative plans, if the Combined Chiefs of Staff decided against the scheme for

the reconquest of Burma. Plans for the capture of the Andaman Islands and for the invasion of Northern Sumatra were also examined.

46. I had intended to visit Australia in May to see the progress of the war against the Japanese in South-West Pacific, to learn what I could from their tactical methods and training, and to discuss the co-ordination of operations from India with those in South-West Pacific. I proposed then to suggest a visit to London in June to settle plans for the winter. When, however, I put this programme to the C.I.G.S. early in April, I was instructed to proceed forthwith to U.K. without visiting Australia, to discuss future plans for the war against Japan. I left India on April 18th and arrived in London on April 22nd.

47. The War Cabinet did not favour the plan I had proposed and which the Americans had accepted. It was decided to discuss operations from India against Japan at a conference in Washington to which I accompanied the Prime Minister and Chiefs of Staff, with the A.O.C.-in-C., India, and the Commander in Chief, Eastern Fleet.

The discussions in Washington did not result in any new proposals for action from India in 1943–44. It was decided that-

(*a*) First priority should be given to developing the air route to China to a capacity of 10,000 tons a month;

(*b*) There should be land and air operations into Upper Burma from Ledo and Imphal, combined with a Chinese advance from Yunnan.

(*c*) Akyab and Ramree Islands should be captured by amphibious operations.

In fact, the only difference from my plan for 1942–43 (see paragraph 2) was the addition of Ramree Island to the objectives.

48. On the instructions of the Prime Minister I returned to London from Washington for further discussions. In June, His Majesty the King was graciously pleased to appoint me to be Viceroy of India, and on June 20th I was succeeded as Commander-in-Chief in India by General Sir Claude Auchinleck.

GENERAL REMARKS.

49. This despatch marks the end of my active military career. During the present war, in just under four years, from September, 1939 to June, 1943, I have directed some fourteen campaigns; in the Western Desert of North Africa, in British Somaliland, in Eritrea, in Italian Somaliland, in Abyssinia, in Greece, in Crete, in Iraq, in Syria, in Iran, in Malaya, in the Dutch East Indies, in Burma, in Arakan. Some have been successful, others have failed.

I should like to express my admiration for the general strategy of the War Cabinet and for the bold and imaginative use made of our limited resources during these first four years, of war. I have always been placed during these years at the far end of the Supply line, and have always been short of troops and equipment and air forces for the tasks I have had to undertake; but I have always been conscious that everything possible was being done to support me, that my lack of resources was due to a general shortage, that my difficulties were sympathetically understood and that I was being given all possible help and encouragement. For this I am most grateful.

50. I regret to have one exception to make. During the operations recorded in this despatch I received neither encouragement nor help nor understanding of the difficulties, only criticism for the failure of a bold attempt to engage the enemy with inadequate resources, in hazardous circumstances.

That my plans were not unsound is, I think, shown by the fact that the plans adopted by the South-East Asia Command for the winter 1943-44 have been practically the same as those I laid down for the previous winter; and that the Long Range Penetration Groups which were initiated by Major-General Wingate under my direction have been adopted and extended as a result of the experience I originated. That I had considerable difficulties to encounter is shown by the fact that in spite of greatly increased resources and another year's training and experience, progress in Burma in the campaigning season of 1943-44 has been little, if any, greater than in the corresponding period of 1942-43.

A glance at a map will give some idea of the distances involved in operations from India, and therefore of the magnitude of the administrative problem.

THE SOLDIER.

51. In this my last despatch I should like to pay a tribute to the British soldier. He has shown himself in this war, as in all others, the finest all-round fighting man in the world. He has won so many victories that he never doubts of victory; he has suffered so many disasters and defeats on his way to victory that defeat seldom depresses him. He has adapted himself to desert and to jungle, to open plains and to mountains, to new foes, new conditions, new weapons with the same courage and humorous endurance of difficulties and dangers which he has always shown. His staying power is a sure guarantee of final success.

Whatever the qualities of the soldier, the value of an army depends in the end on the leadership of the regimental officer, and in the British Army this still remains worthy of the men they lead. Whatever method may be adopted in the future to officer the British Army, it must ensure the same standard of leadership and the same close relations with the soldier.

My experience is that our staff system and system of command is too cumbrous and over elaborated, and needs revision. We have lost the merit of simplicity in our system of command, in our tactics and in our equipment, by always trying to provide for every possible contingency.

52. Next to the British, I have had most to do with the Indian soldier, and owe much to him. In this war he has shown in addition to his proved fighting qualities a remarkable ability to adapt himself to the complexities of modern war and to learn new weapons and new methods.

53. I have had the honour to have had placed under my command during this war troops of many other nationalities: Australian, New Zealand, South African,

American, French, Polish, Czech, Greek, Dutch, Sudanese, East African, West African, Burmese, Chinese. To them all I tender my gratitude and respect.

<h2 style="text-align:center">ACKNOWLEDGMENTS .</h2>

54. During the two years I have been Commander-in-Chief in India, I have been most fortunate in having the support and advice of a great and wise man, His Excellency the Viceroy and Governor-General, the Marquess of Linlithgow. I offer him my grateful thanks.

55. During the period under review, the Commander of the Eastern Army Lieutenant-General N.M.S. Irwin, C.B., D.S.O., M.C., held a most difficult post, with heavy and extended responsibilities both for command and administration. In spite of frequent ill-health, he carried out his task with great energy and devotion to duty.

56. I am indebted to the Commander-in-Chief, Eastern Fleet, Admiral Sir James F. Somerville, K.C B., K.B.E., D.S.O., for his ready help in all matters which were within his resources; these did not unfortunately allow of the Eastern Fleet supporting the operations in Arakan.

57. Air-Chief-Marshal Sir Richard E.C. Peirse, K.C.B., D.S.O., A.F.C., has always given me the closest possible support of the Air Force, and has helped me in every possible way. We have worked closely together for nearly 2½ years, and I shall greatly value the association.

58. I have acknowledged the services of my principal assistants and staff in paragraphs 41 to 43 of my last despatch.[2] They continued to give me most able and loyal support during the period under review.

59. A list of recommendations for honours and awards has already been submitted and approved.

APPENDIX "A."
SKELETON ORDER OF BATTLE
FORCES OF THE FIELD ARMY, INDIA COMMAND, JANUARY, 1943.

EASTERN ARMY.
  Army Troops.
    1 Hybad. L. (Div. Recce Regt).   Ranchi.
    12 F.F.R. (M.G. Bn.).   Calcutta.
  88 *Ind. Inf. Bde.*
    5 Jat   }
    14 F.F.R.   } Comilla – Chittagong Area.
    1/16 Punjab   }
  14 *Ind Div*
    129 Fd. Regt.   }
    130 Fd. Regt.   } Arakan.
    23 Mtn. Regt.   }

```
    44 L.A.A Regt.              }
     9 Jat (M.G. Bn.)           }  Arakan.
 47 Ind. Inf. Bde³
     1 Innisks.                 }
     1 Rajput                   } Arakan.
     5/8 Punjab                 }
 55 Ind. Inf. Bde³
     2/1 Punjab                 }
     8 Raj. Rif.                } Chittagong Area.
     1 Dogra                    }
123 Ind. Inf. Bde³
    10 LF.                      }
     8 Baluch.                  } Arakan.
     1/15 Punjab                }
 26 Ind. Div.                   }
    160 Fd. Regt.               }
     3 Ind Fd. Regt.            }
  4 Ind. Inf. Bde.              }
     6 Sikh                     }
     8/8 Punjab                 }
     3/9 G.R.                   }
 36 Ind. Inf. Bde.              } Calcutta Area.
     1 N. Staffs                }
     8 F.F. Rif.                }
     5/16 Punjab                }
 71 Ind. Inf. Bde³              }
     1 Lincolns                 }
     7/15 Punjab                }
     9/15 Punjab                }
 39 Ind. Lt. Div.
    24 Ind. Mtn. Regt.          Shillong.
    27 Ind. Mtn. Regt.          Ambala.
    24 A.A./A. Tk. Regt.        Calcutta.
     2 D.W.R. – Div. Sp. Bn.    }
     1 Sikh – Bde. Recce Bn.    } Ranchi.
     2 F.F. Rif. – Bde. Recce Bn.  }
106 Ind. Inf. Bde.
     2 Rajput                   }
     1 Jat                      } Shillong.
     1/8 G.R.                   (Tempy. With 16 Ind. Inf. Bde.)
113 Ind. Inf. Bde.
     2 K.O.Y.L.I.               }
     5/1 Punjab                 } Shillong.
     1 R. Garhwal Rif.          }
```

16 *Ind. Inf. Bde*[3]
  2/8 Punjab   Risalpur (joined in Feb.).
  7 Jat   } Digboi.
  7/14 Punjab   }
109 *Ind. Inf. Bde*[3]
  9 Rajput   Chin Hills.
Nepalese
  Kali Bahadur   } Area Imphal – Palel. Dets Manipur
  Shere   } Road. Shungann and Ledo.

4 CORPS   ASSAM
  17 *Ind. Lt Div*   }
  21 Ind. Mtn. Regt.   }
  29 Ind. Mtn. Regt.   }
  129 Fd. Regt.   }
  82 A.A./A. Tk. Regt.   }
  1 W. Yorks – Div. Sp. Bn.   }
  4 F.F.R. – Bde. Recce Bn.   }
  7 Baluch – Bde. Recce Bn.   }
  48 *Ind Inf. Bde.*   }
  1/4 GR   }
  2/5 R G.R.   } Imphal Area.
  1/7 G.R.   }
  63 *Ind. Inf. Bde.*   }
  1 Glosters   }
  1/3 G.R.   }
  1/10 G.R.   }
  23 *Ind Dtv.*[3]   }
  28 Ind. Mtn. Regt.   }
  158 Fd. Regt.   }
  2 Ind. A /Tk. Regt.   }
  28 L.A.A. Regt.   }
  1 *Ind. Inf. Bde.*   }
  1 Seaforth   } Imphal Area.
  1 Assam R.   }
  1 Patiala Inf.   }
  37 *Ind. Inf. Bde.*   }
  3/3 G.R.   }
  3/5 R.G.R.   }
  3/10 G.R.   }
  49 *Ind. Inf. Bde.*   }
  4 Maharattas   }
  5 Raj. Rif.   }
  6 Maharattas   }

77 *Ind. Inf. Bde. (Independent)*.
13 Kings }
3/2 G.R. }
2 Bunf. } Manipur Road.
142 Coy. }

FIELD ARMY UNITS IN INDIA OUTSIDE THE WAR ZONES, JANUARY, 1943.

15th IND. CORPS	Ranchi Area	Corps units short of vehicles, and training incomplete.
70 *Div.*	Ranchi Area	Training incomplete; artillery short of signal equipment and vehicles.
50 *Ind. Tank Bde.*	Ranchi Area	Deficient of tracked carriers and certain types of small arms.
16 *Inf. Bde.*	Detached from 70 Div. in Ceylon.	Units much under strength, and short of equipment; animals unfit.
33RD IND. CORPS	Madras Area	Incompletely trained Corps units.
19 *Ind. Div.*	Madras Area	Below strength in leaders and personnel. Three months further training required to become fully efficient.
25 *Ind. Div*	Salem-Trichinopoly-Kolar Gold Field.	Recently completed to full equipment and in process of training with it.
GENERAL RESERVE.		
32 Ind. Armd. Div.	Dhond Area (near Poona)	Subject to provision of necessary equipment, was expected to be ready for war by June, 1943.
43 Ind. Armd. Div.	Secunderabad	Concentrating and in an early stage of training.
251 Ind. Tank Bde.	Dhond Area	Unready for war. Many units newly raised or reorganised.
254 Ind. Tank Bde.	Dhond Area	Short of equipment and training.
2 Div.	Bombay-Ahmednagar Area.	Under training in Combined Operations.
7 Ind. Div.	Chindwara (C.P.)	In process of jungle training; 30 per cent. very young and raw soldiers; short of some of its artillery.
50 Ind. Parachute Bde.	Campbellpore (N.W.F.P.)	Forming.
CEYLON ARMY COMMAND		
20 Ind. Div.	Mayugama	
34 Ind. Div.	Kandy	
21 E. African Bde.	Anuradhapura	Adv. Bde. of 11th E. African Div. arriving.
99 Ind. Inf. Bde.	Trincomalee Fortress	

APPENDIX "B."
G.H.Q. OPERATION INSTRUCTION No. 19.

To
G.O.C.-in-C., Eastern Army.
1. Since there is now no possibility of capturing Akyab before the monsoon, His Excellency the Commander-in-Chief directs that the object of operations before the rains in that area will be to regain the initiative and inflict a severe defeat on

the enemy. To this end offensive operations will be initiated on both sides of the Mayu River.

2. At the same time you should consider, and prepare – so far as this can be done without weakening your offensive action – positions to be held during the monsoon period.

3. Your positions must cover the Maungdaw–Buthidaung road, Maungdaw air-field and the mouth of the Naf River, with as much depth as possible in front of them. If possible, the Indin landing strip and the Yezogyaung–Apaukwa track should be covered. The latter offers the shortest route to the Kaladan Valley, which may be of considerable importance in operations after the monsoon.

4. The forces under your command in the Mayu area have advantages over the enemy of numerical preponderance, better equipment and the support of superior air forces. If these advantages are skilfully used, it should be possible to take successful offensive action and achieve your object. The enemy's over-confidence engendered by recent successes may lead him to expose himself to an effective counter-stroke; particularly East of the River Mayu.

5. You will, in conjunction with A.O.C., Bengal, draw up joint plans to implement the above policy. An appreciation and copies of Directives issued to the Naval and Air Force Commanders are attached.

(Sd.) A.W.S. MALLABY,
Major-General,
for *Chief of the General Staff.*

New Delhi, 1*st April*, 1943.

———

Copy to G.O.C.-in-C., Eastern Army; Lieut.-Commander R.D. Franks, O.B.E., R.N., C.O., Mayu Force; A.O.C., Bengal; D.M.O.

———

Dated 1*st April*, 1943.

AIR HEADQUARTERS (INDIA) OPERATION INSTRUCTION No. 1. (Issued in conjunction with G.H.Q. Operation Instruction No. 19, dated 1st April, 1943.) This instruction relates to the air action to be taken between now and the end of the monsoon.

Object.
2. The object of these operations for which you are jointly responsible in conjunction with G.O.C.-in-C., Eastern Army, is to inflict a defeat upon the Japanese land forces and secure before the rains and hold until next dry season a position in Arakan which has been indicated to G.O.C.-in-C.

3. Accordingly, the policy for the employment of the air forces under your command must be directed to gaining and maintaining a favourable air situation best calculated to assist the military object.

Air Operations: Bengal Command.

4. The air action to be undertaken by the air forces under your command should be considered as being in two phases, *viz.:-*

1*st Phase:* – from now until the monsoon breaks.

2*nd Phase:* – during the monsoon.

1*st Phase.*

5. To keep the Japanese air forces on the defensive and maintain air superiority over the area of our land operations.

(*a*) *Fighter Operations.* – Offensive operations in strength are to be undertaken primarily in forward areas. In this connection the operation of fighter aircraft from Maungdaw and establishment of an effective warning system will be important.

(*b*) Bomber and long-range fighter attacks are to be carried out against enemy occupied air-fields as a primary task.

(*c*) Attacks against opportunity targets and enemy communications leading towards the theatre of operations, particularly river communications north of Akyab, are to be undertaken as a secondary task.

2*nd Phase.*

6. (*a*) You are to endeavour to maintain forward fighter offensive policy, to ensure the continuance of local air superiority, and to protect our coastal shipping southwards from Chittagong.

(*b*) Attacks against enemy occupied air-fields are to be continued when opportunity offers and with the same priority attacks against lines of communication and shipping in the enemy forward areas.

7. Subject to the above you are to conserve your air effort during this phase, and to build up reserves in order to operate with maximum force in support of sea and land operations immediately after the monsoon.

8. Copies of Directives issued to the Naval and Army Commanders are attached.

(Sd.) G.B.A. BAKER,
Air Vice-Marshal,
Senior Air Staff Officer.

To
A.O.C., Bengal.

———————

Copies to G.O.C.-in-C., Eastern Army (5 copies); Lieut.-Commander R.D. Franks. O.B.E., R.N.

———————

Office of F.L.O. (India), New Delhi.

OPERATIONAL INSTRUCTION – MAYU FORCE.

Forces.

1. Your command consists of the two Burma M.Ls. and two L.C.S. at present in the Mayu River. Your immediate Naval Superior is the Naval Officer in Charge, Chittagong.

Object.

2. Your object is to assist by all means in your power the military operations.

Method.

3. In determining the method by which you render such assistance you are constantly to keep in mind the needs of the Commander, 14 Division. The following courses are, amongst others, to be considered:-

(*a*) Maintain attack by night patrols, on the enemy's river L. of C., both in forward areas and south of Rathedaung. Our air forces will endeavour to force the enemy to operate these L. of C. by night.

(*b*) Attack enemy armed craft in the Mayu River.

(*c*) Harass the enemy forces on the river banks.

(*d*) Increase the mobility of our land forces by carrying troops or towing sampans.

You are to bear in mind that your repair facilities are limited and that it will not be possible to provide you with reinforcements before the end of the monsoon.

Administration.

4. For administration and maintenance you are to be guided by paragraphs 4 to 9 inclusive of the instruction, dated 19th March, 1943, left with you by S.O. Force "Z."

Enclosures.

5. Copies of the instructions issued to the Army and Air Force Commanders are attached.

(Sd.) A.F.E. PALLISER,
Rear-Admiral,
for *Commander-in-Chief, Eastern Fleet.*

To
Lieut.-Commander R.D. Franks, O.B.E., R.N. (C.O. Mayu Force).
Copies to N.O.I.C., Chittagong; G.O.G.-in- C., Eastern Army; A.O.C., Bengal Command.

Notes

1. The landings in North Africa and later in Sicily (November, 1942–July, 1943) took higher priority and there were insufficient resources for both operations. (Note by the War Office)
2. Published as a Supplement to The London Gazette on the 18th September, 1946.
3. Mixed Tpt. – Animal and M.T.

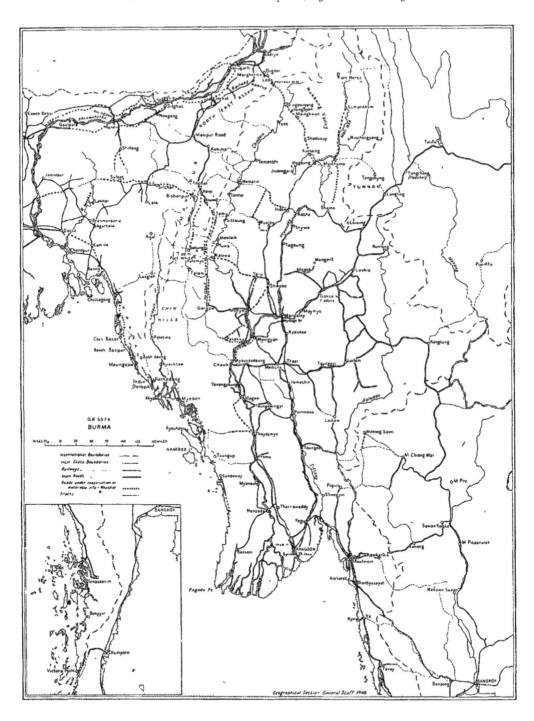

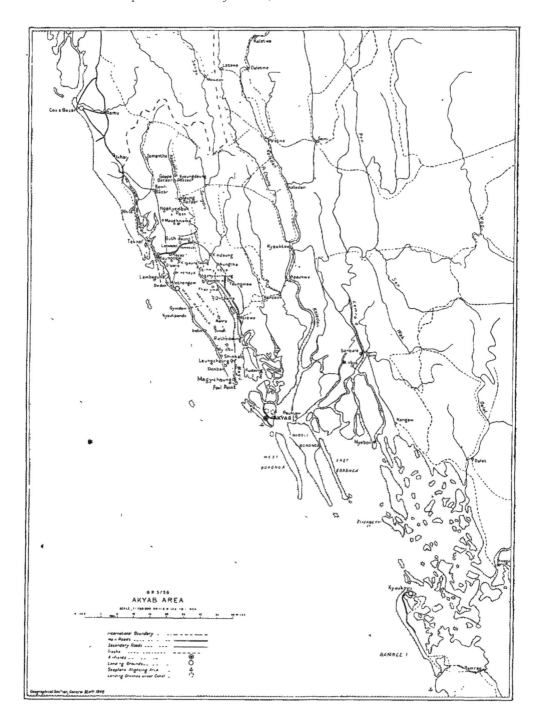

SOUTH-EAST ASIA

Equatorial Scale 1 30,000,000

4
FIELD MARSHAL SIR CLAUDE J.E. AUCHINLECK'S DESPATCH ON OPERATIONS IN THE INDO-BURMA THEATRE BASED ON INDIA, 21 JUNE 1943 TO 15 NOVEMBER 1943

The War Office, March, 1948.
The following Despatch was submitted to the Secretary of State for War on the 22nd November, 1945, by FIELD MARSHAL SIR CLAUDE J.E. AUCHINLECK, G.C.B., G.C.I.E., C.S.I., D.S.O., O.B.E., A.D.C., Commander-in-Chief, India.

INTRODUCTION.

This Despatch covers the period between my appointment as Commander-in-Chief of the India Command on the 20th June, 1943, in succession to Field Marshal Viscount Wavell and the 15th November, 1943, the date on which I handed over responsibility for the conduct of operations against the Japanese in the Indo-Burma Theatre to Admiral Lord Louis Mountbatten on his appointment as Supreme Allied Commander of the newly created South East Asia Command.

In his Despatch covering the operations in the India Command from January to June, 1943, Field Marshal Viscount Wavell describes how he planned to capture Akyab and establish our forces on the line of the Chindwin River between Kalewa and Sittaung with the Eastern Army under General Irwin. He goes on to show how the Eastern Army failed in its objects owing to lack of resources, the inexperience of the troops engaged, and the fact that the Japanese were able to bring up substantial reinforcements. At the beginning of the monsoon our forces in Arakan and the Japanese forces opposing them were generally speaking back in the positions they had held at the start of the operations.

As Field Marshal Wavell says, the greatest gain from the campaign was experience; the serious loss was prestige and morale. It became my most urgent task to rectify defects in training and equipment, and to restore the morale and prestige of the Army which had no doubt suffered a severe shock, so much so that commanders and men were apt to place the need to protect themselves against the Japanese before the need to seek him out and destroy him. There had been neither time nor opportunity to give the troops that specialised training in fighting in the jungle in which the Japanese were adept, having trained their troops to this end before they entered the war. The disastrous campaigns in Malaya and

Burma had invested the Japanese Army with a reputation for skill and invincibility, far removed from reality, and this had to be destroyed before the offensive spirit could be fully re-established throughout our own Army.

Internally India had remained quiet after the disturbances of August, 1942. The Congress Party, which had been responsible for this outbreak, was made powerless for the time being by the internment of its leaders and by other measures, and unrest subsided. There were, however, other causes giving rise to anxiety. Various factors, including the unfavourable course of the war against Japan, had shaken public confidence and caused a sharp rise in the prices of food, cloth and other basic commodities towards the end of 1942. The impracticability of setting up any satisfactory system of rationing of essential articles in a country so administratively undeveloped as India led to widespread hoarding, and an economic crisis ensued. This persisted throughout the period covered by this Despatch, hampering the war effort, embarrassing the internal administration and giving rise to famine conditions in Bengal and parts of Southern India.

Nevertheless in spite of an almost unrelieved tale of failure in the Indian Theatre, the turn in Allied fortunes in Europe and Africa at the end of 1942 and the entirely changed aspect of the war against Germany by the commencement of the period of this Despatch had a tonic effect on India. No less heartening had been the Allied recovery in the South West Pacific, where the Japanese were being driven back, had lost heavily in aircraft and shipping and were clearly finding it difficult to maintain and protect the widely dispersed commitments they had undertaken.

These events had not failed to have their effect on our fighting forces; they were reflected in their high morale and general desire to get at the enemy. Many difficulties, however, had hindered the development of our resources and communications in India and particularly in the north-east. Delays in the provision of stores and materials, shortage of labour, limited transportation capacity, natural obstacles to constructional work due to the forests and climate in Assam and Burma, and disease – all had handicapped progress. During the winter and spring of 1942–43 a succession of major projects had in fact accumulated and competed for the limited engineer and transport resources available, and though progress was made, completion forecasts were seldom realised. At the onset of the monsoon in June, 1943, much still remained to be done of what had been planned in the previous year. Such then was the situation in June, 1943.

Part I of this Despatch deals with plans that have been prepared and examined during the period.

Part II describes such operations as have taken place on land, sea and in the air. For various reasons which were unavoidable, those on land and sea were insignificant. In the air, however, there were operations on an important scale throughout the period.

Part III contains an account of progress in organisation, training and administration, both in regard to land forces and those preparing for amphibious operations, also in regard to the air forces and the building up of their widespread ground organisations. So much effort was expended in these directions during the period; and the range of activities was so wide, that I have in this part of the Despatch gone into considerable detail. The importance of building a firm foundation on which to base future operations was so great as to justify the inclusion of a full record of the work done. The new South East Asia Command was to depend almost entirely on India as its base for the prosecution of future operations against the Japanese.

PART I – PLANS FOR FUTURE OPERATIONS.
1. *The Basis of Planning during the Period June – November* 1943.
Coincident with my appointment as Commander-in-Chief in India, the intention to set up a new South East Asia Command was announced. This Command was to relieve the India Command of responsibility for the conduct of operations against the Japanese in this theatre. Later, in August, Admiral the Lord Louis Mountbatten was appointed Supreme Allied Commander.

Although this would relieve me in due course of the planning and execution of future operations against the Japanese, there was much to be done during the intervening months, if continuity of effort was to be preserved until the new Command started to function and thereafter. During this time, therefore, at my Headquarters much work was done in the framing and examination of plans. These plans conformed with the decisions of the Washington and Quebec Conferences, and while at work on them I was in close touch with the Allied Chiefs of Staff.

Meanwhile, intensive training and preparation for the future continued in India. On the eastern frontier and along the lines of communication leading to it development proceeded so far as monsoon conditions would allow. The progress of these preparations and of work on the lines of communication is recorded in Part III of this Despatch. Before describing the progress of planning it is necessary, however, to explain the overriding effect of the meagre resources of India and of the severely limited capacity of the lines of communication on any military operations undertaken on the eastern frontier.

Although these conditions may apply to any theatre of war they exerted a particularly serious influence in this theatre for the following reasons:-

Firstly, the original conception of the load to be placed on the lines of communications, though based on sound reasoning at the time, had proved to be too small.

Secondly, in addition to securing the purely military needs of the land and air forces engaged with the enemy, including the large demands of the air transport route to China, the lines of communication had to cope with heavy civilian requirements, such as those of the tea and jute industries, indispensable to the war effort of the Allied Nations.

Thirdly, the normal economic life of Assam and Eastern Bengal had also to be sustained and this entailed the transportation of large quantities of commodities over the railways, rivers and roads which constituted the lines of communication serving the China-Burma-India theatre of war.

This was the maintenance situation, and on the 7th August I issued an instruction to my Long Term Administrative Planning Committee to examine the problem. Any feasible short term measures for expansion were also to be examined, and an account of these as well as the results of the examination by the Long Term Planning Committee will be found in Part III. On the 17th August, my Quarter Master General's Staff (Transportation Directorate) produced two documents on the provision of Transportation Stores in India for 1944–45. The first of these documents described the foundations on which our administrative preparations for the operations of the South East Asia Command were built, whilst the second afforded some idea of the magnitude of the transportation problem involved.

In reading, therefore, the account of operational planning which follows and the record of administrative progress and development set out in Part III of this Despatch, the above facts require to be remembered as their influence affects all plans for operations based on India against the Japanese whether on the land, the sea or in the air.

2. Plans considered as the Result of the Washington Conference.
When I took over command, planning was proceeding on the lines laid down by the Washington Conference of May, 1943.

It had been decided at this Conference that priority should be given to increasing the air transportation route to China to a monthly capacity of 10,000 tons by the early autumn of 1943. Bracketed with this as a first priority was the development of air facilities in Assam with a view:-

(*a*) To intensifying air operations against the Japanese in Burma.
(*b*) To maintaining increased American air forces in China.
(*c*) To keeping up the flow of airborne supplies in China.

Examination of this problem had been proceeding at India Command Headquarters, and on the 2nd July I came to the conclusion that, since priority was to be given to the air lift for China, the limitations of the Assam line of communications would not permit intensive land operations to be carried out. I considered the implications of this conclusion also in relation to the prospect of amphibious operations against Akyab, because I felt that the successful accomplishment of the latter was important for many reasons, including the need to raise the morale of the Army in India to the highest pitch. A summary of my recommendations was sent to the Chiefs of Staff on the 2nd July, 1943.

At this time it became clear that the capacity of the air transport route to China was already falling short of the target, and during July only 3,451 tons (as against a target figure of 7,000 tons) were actually delivered to China. The reason was the lack, as yet, of a comprehensive maintenance organisation and servicing facilities.

The effect on our airfields of monsoon conditions was not a factor in the failure to reach the required tonnage.

On the 18th July, ill fortune beset the line of communications to the Eastern Army in the form of a serious breach on the main line of the East Indian Railway and on the Grand Trunk Road, north-west of Calcutta. This breach was caused by widespread floods resulting from the river Damodar bursting its banks and changing its course, and it came at a time when transportation on the line of communication was already in arrears owing to various unforeseen causes and also when demands on its capacity were already increasing. It now began to be seen (as already recorded) that the long term development of the line of communications so far planned (which in any case could not be fully effective till the autumn of 1944) was going to be inadequate; and various measures for short term improvement were urgently considered. The situation in regard to communications in North East India at this time and its relation to the various projected operations, was communicated to the Chiefs of Staff on the 13th August 1943.

3. *Plans reconsidered as the Result of the Quebec Conference.*
On the 25th August I received the decisions of the Quebec Conference in so far as they affected the India Command. In these the previous decision of the Washington Conference was modified in so far as it was now resolved to give first priority in our war effort in this theatre to the land and air operations which would be necessary to establish land communication with China. It was also decided to continue to build up and increase the air routes and air supplies to China, and to develop the resources of that country in order:-

(*a*) To enable her to continue her struggle against Japan.
(*b*) To intensify operations against the Japanese.
(*c*) To maintain increased U.S. armed forces in China.

Furthermore, while the possibilities of developing the air route to China to enable us to deploy all the heavy bomber and transport aircraft likely to be available for the South East Asia theatre and China in 1944-45, were to be studied, a directive to the Supreme Allied Commander, South East Asia Command mentioned an eventual monthly lift of 20,000 tons as a target for the air ferry to China. No specific date, however, was fixed for this.

I now examined the operational programme for the future, so far as this had been planned, in the light of the Quebec decisions. The paragraphs which follow deal consecutively, and under their appropriate headings, with the various projects examined. In each case the narrative embraces broadly the conclusions reached up to the time I handed over to the Supreme Allied Commander, South East Asia Command.

4. *Plans for Land and Air Operations in Upper Burma.*
Plans for operations in Upper Burma had been under examination for some time, and, as soon as the decisions of the Quebec Conference were known, these plans received priority of attention over other projects.

The resolve was to conduct vigorous and aggressive land and air operations at the end of the 1943 monsoon, from Assam into Burma *via* Ledo and Imphal, and this was to be in step with an advance by Chinese Forces from Yunnan. The object was to contain as many Japanese Forces as possible and to cover the air ferry route. It was to be an essential step towards the reopening of land communications with China by means of a road from Ledo *via* Myitkyina. The new road would connect with the existing road north of Lashio.

Here again it is necessary not to lose sight of the over riding factor of the extremely limited capacity of the Assam L. of C. It was only possible to plan operations for a force within the maintenance capacity of that artery. If the forces or scope of operations were to be increased, it could only be done at the expense of other demands on the L. of C., and in particular that of the air lift to China.

By the 7th September, I was able to give the Chiefs of Staff a summary of suggested plans for land and air operations in Upper Burma in 1943-44. Chinese operations should take place as already planned from Yunnan and Ledo. It was only in respect of the plan for the British Forces that alternatives existed, and in this, physical considerations limited the plans for an advance into Burma from the Imphal – Tiddim area to two possibilities:-

An advance to the area Kalewa – Kalemyo, and thence to Ye-U.

An operation for the capture of the Indaw area (with its airfields) by airborne assault, followed by an advance overland to consolidate the capture. This force would depend on air supply until the Chinese advance from the north opened a route for maintenance by land.

In both plans the use of long range penetration forces was included; but more particularly did they figure in the second as a means to distract the enemy and disrupt his communications – thus reducing the hazards of the temporarily isolated force at Indaw.

Initially I favoured the first alternative, but the Chiefs of Staff inclined to the latter plan, stressing the following considerations:-

(*a*) The importance of the early seizure of a locality directly enabling us to join hands with the Chinese advances from Ledo and Yunnan.

(*b*) The element of surprise and the greater scope for employment of long range penetration groups.

(*c*) Greater economy in lift on the Assam L. of C.

Further and more detailed examination was therefore made, and as a result, and in view of the weight attached to (*a*) above, I agreed that the second plan was preferable.

On the 27th September, I cabled to the Chiefs of Staff a report on the progress made to date, and the conclusions reached.

The chief features of the plan at this stage were as follows. The Indaw airfields were to be seized by parachute troops, and thereafter a division (less one brigade) was to be flown in in seven days. A third brigade group with mules and jeeps was to advance overland from Imphal to Indaw. This was to be coupled with a limited offensive/defensive operation southwards from Tamu, as well as with the Chinese advances from Ledo and Yunnan on Myitkyina, Bhamo, and Lashio. Offensive operations in Arakan were also to be timed to take place so as to have the maximum distracting effect on the enemy. Finally (and of great importance) the advance of the main forces towards their objectives was to be preceded and assisted by long range penetration forces.

The plan involved the use of transport aircraft on a very large scale. It was thought that this would amount to between 18 and 23 squadrons, depending on the treatment found necessary for the surface of the Indaw airfields. The Chiefs of Staff, however, cabled on the 7th October that provision of aircraft on this scale was quite out of the question, and that a total of 151 transport aircraft (six squadrons) was all that were likely to be available. Accordingly, the matter was further examined, and on the 13th October I sent the Chiefs of Staff a modified plan, which, while not so satisfactory as the original, nevertheless appeared to be feasible.

The main modifications were:-

(*a*) Fighter squadrons would be located at Indaw during the dry weather only.

(*b*) The original air landing force of one division, less one brigade, would be flown in over a fortnight instead of a week.

(*c*) The parachute force would be retained, in order to strengthen the garrison, until the operational situation permitted it to be flown out.

(*d*) The delivery of engineer stores would be spread over a longer period by commencing delivery earlier.

Even with these modifications, however, the requirements of transport aircraft, while much less than they were in the original plan, were still greatly in excess of 151. In fact, 290 would be required in the worst case, and 263 in the best case – *i.e.*, 12 and 11 squadrons respectively, as against 23 (maximum) in the old plan.

I continued to look for means to make further reductions in the requirement of troop aircraft, but any such reductions could only be small unless the plan was still further radically altered. It became clear that, unless the additional aircraft could be provided, the capture of Indaw should not be attempted, and I suggested as a means to augment the supply that some aircraft might be made available from the ferry route.

As regards the enemy forces that might be disposed to meet our offensive operations in the Burma Theatre, a summary in regard to the situation in November, 1943, is given in Part II "Operations and Intelligence".

Briefly, there were five Japanese Divisions. The bulk of one (55th) was in Arakan; one (33rd) was in the Chin Hills; one held the Mawlaik Homalin area; and two (18th and 56th) covered the area of North Burma to the Salween.

5. *Plans for Operations on the Arakan Coast.*

At the Washington Conference of 12th to 25th May, 1943, it was resolved to capture Akyab and Ramree Island by an amphibious operation; also, possibly, to exploit any success gained. This was part of the general pattern of offensive operations in the South-East Asia Theatre, and plans were being formulated accordingly. It will be remembered, however, that at this time first priority on our resources was still allocated to the air ferry to China.

In my view the success of the attack on Akyab was of great importance both from the point of view of the Army and public in India, and of public opinion in Europe, America and China. The island was already strongly fortified and formidable. I considered two assault brigades would be necessary in the first flight, and a third, loaded with its own assault shipping and craft, as a follow-up. Three to four (land based) fighter squadrons would be required over Akyab during daylight, and convóys would be protected by carrier-borne aircraft.

Additional to the above plan, I considered that to ensure success we should operate offensively by land down the Arakan coast with up to two divisions. One long range penetration group would operate in the Kaladan River area.

A further important reason for this land advance was the capture of the Maungdaw airfield. With this in our hands shore-based fighter support could be given to the amphibious attack on Akyab.

As regards Ramree Island, unless separate shipping for an assault on this locality was to be allotted, this would either have to be taken by a surprise attack immediately after the capture of Akyab, or the attack would have to be postponed to a date three to four months later and then carried out by two assault brigade groups and one built-up division.

Fuller details of these plans including estimates of possible Japanese strength in Akyab and Arakan were cabled to the Chiefs of Staff on the 2nd July, 1943.

In the meantime, however, further and more detailed examination of the project for operations on this coast was taking place, and I found it necessary to amend my views. On the 22nd July, therefore, I cabled to the Chiefs of Staff a revised plan. The salient points of this were as follows:-

(*a*) In view of the special difficulties of an assault on Akyab, the following would be required:-

Three assault brigades.
One follow-up brigade.
One floating reserve brigade.

The following shipping and craft would be required in addition to that allotted or already asked for:-

Three Landing Ships Infantry, each with twelve Landing Craft Assault and crews.
Six Landing Craft Infantry (Large), complete with crews.
Twenty-one Landing Craft Tank (Support), complete with crews.

(*b*) It was clear from the above that we should not have sufficient resources to assault both Aykab and Ramree simultaneously.

Moreover, if Ramree was strongly held, this would require two assault brigades, and the interval between the assaults could not be less than 3 months;

e.g., if Akyab was assaulted on the 1st January, the assault on Ramree could not be before the 1st April, and probably later. This would be very near the monsoon, and the practicability of the operation was doubtful.

(*c*) A surprise attack consisting of a quick follow through by one brigade group from Akyab could not be done. The only possibility, therefore, of opposition at Ramree was expected to be slight, would be to use the shipping again of the Akyab assault troops to embark one fresh brigade group from east coast ports of India for an assault about a month after the Akyab assault. With the resources available, this brigade group could not be fully trained, but it would be possible to have it ready trained and waiting, if the additional craft and shipping demanded could be made available.

(*d*) The garrison of Ramree would have to be one division during the monsoon, plus a large force of naval craft to watch the approaches to the island. It was unlikely that we would be able to construct an all weather airfield before the monsoon broke.

The possession of Ramree island would:-

(i) Give depth to air defence,

(ii) Help air operations against Burma, Malaya and Sumatra.

(iii) Constitute a threat to Taungup which might contain enemy forces.

At this stage of planning the flood breach on the main East Indian Railway line upset our calculations. It was seen that, as a result of this calamity, land operations in Arakan were likely to be delayed, and the assault on Akyab might therefore have to be postponed to mid- February. On the 13th August I considered a suggestion that had been submitted to me by my Force Commanders that the plan for the attack on Akyab should be by means of "staggered assaults". I directed that an alternative plan should be framed embodying this principle.

The decisions of the Quebec Conference were now received on the 26th August. In so far as operations on the Arakan coast were concerned, preparations were to continue for an amphibious operation in the spring of 1944. Pending a decision on the particular operation to be carried out, the scale of these preparations was to be of the order of those contemplated at Washington for the capture of Akyab and Ramree. This and other operations in the South East Asia Theatre were to be considered in their relation to one another. In the meantime I had come to the conclusion that the capture of Ramree Island was not essential in connection with the other operations contemplated for the coming dry season of 1943–44. The reasons for this (which did not apply to Akyab) were cabled to the Chiefs of Staff on the 29th August, 1943.

They were as follows:-

(a) Ramree Island was not considered essential for other operations in 1943-44. It was only valuable in conjunction with other movements further down the coast.

(*b*) There was no time to complete an airstrip to all weather standard.

(*c*) The above was not applicable to Akyab which would be of greater assistance to obtain air superiority.

(*d*) In view of the decision to break up the 70th Division to form long range penetration forces, there would only be five assault brigades in India (*i.e.*, the 2nd and 36th Divisions). All these were required for Akyab.

On the other hand the military advantages of the capture of Akyab alone (and contrasted with Ramree) were definite. I cabled them to the Chiefs of Staff on the 4th September.

They were:-

(*a*) The removal of the Japanese threat to Chittagong.

(*b*) The number of troops required for the North of Akyab would be reduced, as also the maintenance tonnages.

(*c*) We would gain advanced airfields for attacks on enemy communications in Burma.

(*d*) The air warning system would be improved.

(*e*) An attack on Akyab would force the Japanese Air Force to fight.

Further examination of the Akyab and Arakan operations by my staff and force commanders continued. It was established that the personnel lift would not be less than 50,000, and the Chiefs of Staff were advised accordingly. They agreed to make personnel ships available for 50,000; but asked that efforts be made to confine the lift to this figure, as shipping for more could only be provided at the expense of other operations.

6. *Plans for the Recapture of the Andaman Islands.*
The principal value of these islands to us would be in connection with operations further south towards Sumatra and Malaya. In particular, the facilities their possession would afford for photographic reconnaissance and intelligence was a factor that might even make their capture an essential preliminary to other operations, either in this direction or towards the Burma coast. A summary of the situation regarding intelligence and photographic reconnaissance, and the influence thereon of being able to use the Andamans, was cabled to the Chiefs of Staff on the 11th October, 1943.

A further important consideration was the denial of the Andamans to the enemy as a useful forward base for refuelling submarines. At the same time, the fact that operations against the Andamans involved certain risks was not lost sight of, and it was fully realised that their possession might prove a liability as well as an asset. Lying within a semi-circle of enemy air centres, the airfield in the Andamans might be difficult to operate in the face of enemy bombing, and there was thus a risk of our troops being left without air support. Moreover, though the islands might not be difficult to capture, the reinforcement of isolated forces there might be a constant drain on our resources.

On the 13th August, I suggested to the Chiefs of Staff that if an assault on Malaya was definitely decided on for 1944-45, it would be desirable to divert resources from the capture of Akyab to the capture of the Andamans in the spring of 1944. By the 4th September an outline plan had been prepared which showed that the operation could be undertaken, subject to certain modifications, with the forces needed for the assault on Akyab.

This proposal, however, being inter-related with plans for other amphibious operations was still undecided when responsibility passed to the South East Asia Command.

7. *Plans for Operations against Sumatra and Malaya.*
After the Washington Conference in May, 1943, an outline plan was prepared for the capture of North Sumatra. This was to be immediately followed by a landing near Penang, with the object of reconquering the Malay Peninsula. The Chiefs of Staff accepted this as a basis for more detailed staff study, which commenced at my Headquarters accordingly. In the meantime the Quebec Conference called for a study of:-

(*a*) Operations against Northern Sumatra for the spring of 1944.
(*b*) Operations through the Malacca Straits and Malaya for the direct capture of Singapore.

With regard to the first, the conclusions reached were that the forces would be far in excess of those required for the capture of Akyab; and that isolated long range penetration operations, without the support of main forces could not achieve the capture of Sumatra. Regarding the second, this was at first scheduled for as early a date as might be practicable, but was subsequently deferred to the end of 1944 or early in 1945. Both these projects now took priority in consideration over the dual operation that was earlier being examined and was still under examination in November.

8. *Moulmein and the Isthmus of Kra.*
A study of possible operations through the Moulmein area or Kra Isthmus in the direction of Bangkok, was commenced as a result of the decisions of the Quebec Conference. A target date for the late spring of 1944 was given. Preliminary examination however was not very favourable.

9. *A Bomber Offensive on Japan from China (American Plan).*
Early in September, I received information from Washington of an air plan for a bomber offensive to accelerate the defeat of Japan, which had been prepared at Quebec by the American Air Planning Staff.

The general idea was to bomb Japan itself with a bomber force built up at Changsha. This force was to be maintained by a fleet of transport aircraft based on Calcutta, with a staging area at Kunming.

I cabled to Washington on the 8th September my comments on this plan, making clear the obstacles to it. The scheme postulated an increase in capacity of the port of Calcutta that was more extensive than anything previously envisaged. There were no administrative or constructional plans in existence for any such major port development. The idea also demanded the development of 45 airfields in the Calcutta area, for which suitable sites (near existing communications) could not be found in the time, and the petrol lift was beyond the capacity of existing transportation facilities.

Later in September, I received from American H.Q. in New Delhi their reactions to the above Quebec Air Plan. They agreed with me that the original plan was administratively unsound, and put forward an alternative scheme for bombing Japan with aircraft based partly on Calcutta and partly in China. The effect of this would be that India would have to prepare seven airfields by August, 1944.

On examining this alternative plan, the conclusion was reached that it also could not be achieved by the date given. Moreover, a special P.O.L. port on the Hooghly would be required, and the port capacity of Calcutta itself would have to be increased. I ordered a reconnaissance of the various possibilities of this plan to see how much could be done.

10. *Future Operations Southwards from North Burma for the Reconquest of the Country.*
The Quebec Conference decisions received on the 26th August included instructions to study future plans for these operations. The possible date was to be November, 1944, and examination was put in hand on the following assumptions:-

(*a*) That land and air operations for the capture of Upper Burma would be launched in mid-February, 1944.
(*b*) That offensive operations would be carried out on the Arakan coast in the spring of 1944.
(*c*) That we capture either Akyab or North Sumatra in the spring of 1944.
(*d*) That an airborne and other forms of attack on Rangoon would be included.

Plans for this major enterprise were still in process of being examined when operational planning was taken over by the South East Asia Command.

11. *Summary in regard to Operational Planning.*
In the period covered by this Despatch, much of the planning commenced under my direction could not be completed and was passed on in a fluid state to the Supreme Allied Commander, South East Asia Command. This was indeed only to be expected, and the changes of policy that resulted from the Quebec Conference also had a retarding effect on the progress made.

Although many of the conclusions reached during the period were in fact negative in character, much valuable work was nevertheless done. Schemes were explored which may well prove to be of use in the future. Clearly the main conclusion that emerged was the inadequacy of previous long term planning of base, transportation, and administrative resources. This is no reflection on work and preparation that had gone before. Developments in a theatre of war, and requirements in resources that follow as a result, are impossible to foresee.

We now look to the future in the hope that our long term planning in these directions undertaken during the period, is based on a sufficiently comprehensive scale to meet all needs. These things remain the responsibility of the India Command.

With the establishment of the South East Asia Command, my planning staff were transferred in a body to that H.Q. and continuity of work and effort was thus ensured in the operational planning room.

PART II – OPERATIONS AND INTELLIGENCE.

1. *Land Operations.*

In June, 1943, we were in contact with the Japanese on four fronts:- in Arakan; on the Chindwin; in the Chin Hills; and in North Burma.

2. *The Arakan Front.*

In Arakan, after the evacuation of Buthidaung and Maungdaw (in the final stages of our retirement from the Mayu Peninsula in the early part of the year) the 26th Indian Division took up positions covering Cox's Bazar. Our forward areas extended in the coastal region from the Teknaf Nhila to Bawli Bazar (held by one infantry brigade group),while inland across the Mayu ridge another brigade group held the area Taung Bazar – Goppe Bazar.

After following up our retirement in the first instance, the enemy had himself withdrawn to positions covering the Maungdaw – Buthidaung road, and both sides had settled into the above positions for the monsoon period.

Generally speaking, other than patrol activity, nothing of any significance occurred on this front during the period of this Despatch. Patrols, however, were used by us not only to get information and keep touch with the enemy, but also to build up the confidence of our troops in the forward areas. This, it must be admitted, had been somewhat shaken by the experiences of the previous Arakan campaign, and it was hoped by constant and energetic patrolling to accustom the troops in the forward areas to work in the jungle, and gradually to acquire a moral ascendency over the enemy.

To this end the troops worked splendidly under difficult conditions, and much success was achieved. In numerous brushes and encounters during this period of static warfare our patrols inflicted many more casualties on the enemy than they suffered themselves, and in spite of depressing monsoon conditions there was a general rise in morale.

Noteworthy among such minor affairs on the Arakan was a raid on Maungdaw (to obtain identifications) carried out between the 5th and 7th July. Two companies of a British battalion (1st Battalion The Lincolnshire Regiment) with a M.G. section and a 3" mortar detachment penetrated to Maungdaw and completely occupied it.

The main raiding party of one company landed by sampans from a river steamer in the Pyinbu Ghaung (four miles N.N.W. of Maungdaw). Stiff enemy opposition was encountered and overcome, an enemy M.G. post being stormed and six Japanese killed. Our troops withdrew according to plan after the raid, having killed twenty-one Japanese and wounded at least seven. Our casualties were seven killed (including one Viceroy's commissioned officer) and eight wounded. The capture of a mail bag in Maungdaw secured the required identifications. The total enemy strength engaged was estimated to be two companies. A further raid by another British battalion (1st Battalion The North Staffordshire Regiment) ten days later to establish road blocks on the Maungdaw – Buthidaung road resulted in one Japanese officer and twenty other ranks being killed and forty others (estimated) killed or wounded, at a cost to ourselves of one British officer wounded and missing, and two British other ranks killed.

The 26th Indian Division held the forward area in Arakan throughout the monsoon, until at the beginning of October, the 7th Indian Division relieved it, the 5th Indian Division also moving into the area. H.Q. 15 Corps (Lt.-Gen. W.J. Slim), moved to Chittagong and became responsible for operations south of (exclusive) Chittagong from the 1st November, 1943.

The enemy forces in Arakan opposing us during the period were the 55th Japanese Division with H.Q. at Akyab. This Division had only two regiments in this area, the third having gone to New Guinea. Possibly a battalion of the 33rd Regiment was also in Arakan at the end of October, 1943.

Such then was the position in Arakan when operational responsibility was assumed by the South East Asia Command.

3. 4th Corps Front.

The 4th Corps (Lt.-Gen. G.A.P. Scoones) has been responsible for the front east and south of Manipur since 1942. Its Headquarters were at Imphal and its front which extended from the Chindwin east of the Kabaw Valley to the Chin Hills south of Tiddim, was held by the 17th Indian Light Division and the 23rd Indian Division. The 4th Corps was in fact responsible for the whole front up to the Chinese Yunnan frontier, excluding the portion held by the Chinese American Task Force.

When the Army in Burma withdrew in June, 1942, it passed through rearguard positions on the high ground about Shenam between Palel and Tamu. The enemy did not pursue across the Chindwin, and we moved forward again later to our present positions. During the monsoon, in order to avoid malaria, our forces were held back on the high ground about Shenam.

In the dry season 1942-43, the 23rd Indian Division with Headquarters at Tamu patrolled across the Chindwin to the east, and the 17th Indian Light Division was fifty miles down the Tiddim road. The latter was watching the enemy in the Kalemyo area, and maintaining contact with our levies in the Chin Hills. This Division, during the summer, had one brigade forward in the Tiddim area. The rest of the Division was kept at Shillong carrying out training.

The course of events on this front was similar up to early November to that in Arakan, *i.e.*, nothing of importance was attempted by either side beyond patrol activity. In early November, however, the enemy showed signs of moving, and there was evidence of Japanese reinforcements reaching this area.

On the 5th November the enemy advanced into the Chin Hills with between five and nine companies of infantry. Our Irregulars after a gallant resistance were driven out of Falam, and the Japanese occupied that place and Haka, twelve miles south of it. A week later the enemy advanced from the Dolluang area, and on the 13th November drove back our weak detachments on the road to the north of Fort White, thereby isolating the latter post. The enemy strength in this area was two to three battalions with some field artillery. Our forces consisted of one Indian battalion, much below strength, with one company of a Gurkha battalion under its command; also one section of a mountain battery (3.7″ howitzers).

They were holding very extended positions, and the enemy attack came from the northwest after an encircling movement successfully hidden from us. It was clear that the Japanese had detailed knowledge of our positions, and so were able to advance from a direction least exposed to the fire of our troops.

During the fighting which ensued the enemy suffered heavily while our losses were light. We evacuated the Fort, which lying in the valley bottom was of little tactical or strategic value, and retired to positions on Kennedy Peak.

4. *The Chin Hills.*
Between the 4th Corps front and Arakan, lie the Chin Hills. This area was very thinly held by the Chin Hills Battalion and the Chin Levies. The Chin Hills Battalion was a part of the Burma Army and stayed in the Chin Hills after we evacuated Burma. Its officers were British, and it had one company of Chins; and three companies of Gurkhas or Kumaonis.

The Chin Levies were irregular troops with a small number of British officers, and one of the reasons for keeping regular troops as far south as Tiddim was the desirability of providing support and backing for these irregulars.

The strategic value of the Chin Hills area was that it covered tracks leading through Lungleh to Chittagong and to Aijal. It also lay on the flank of the enemy line of communications through Gangaw to Kalemyo. Communications, however, in the area were bad. Except for the road south from Imphal, which was being built and was often blocked during the monsoon, there was only a porter track leading into the area from the west. Supply of troops in the area had therefore to be carried out to a great extent by air.[1]

Except patrol activities and the Japanese advance to Falam and Haka in early November there were no operations of importance in this area.

5. *Chinese Forces and the U.S.A. Task Force in India.*
Earlier Despatches from the India Command have described how Chinese Forces first came to India in 1942. Their training was carried out here by the United States Army. A road from Ledo in Assam to connect eventually with the Burma – China Road, was also commenced by us and carried on by the U.S. Forces.

The two enterprises have since become closely allied, since two of the Chinese Divisions (22nd and 38th) moved to Ledo, and the construction of the road has been protected by the 38th Chinese Division. Part of one regiment of this

Division was located in advance of roadhead and was maintained by air. The 22nd Chinese Division completed its move from Ramgarh to Ledo in October, and was available to support the 38th Chinese Division if required. A third division (30th) was in process of arriving from China by air in November. During the monsoon progress on the Ledo Road was slow. Nearly all the engineering effort was absorbed in repairing washouts and adding extra shingling to the surface of the road already built. By the 15th November the road had been surveyed up to 99 miles from Ledo, bull-dozers were working at the 79th mile, and 48 miles of metalling had been completed.

As soon as more rapid progress at roadhead became possible, the Chinese 38th Division advanced southwards towards the upper reaches of the Chindwin. Some minor clashes occurred with weak Japanese detachments in the Hukawng Valley, but up to the 15th November no serious opposition had been offered to the advance. By then the advanced elements of the 38th Chinese Division had reached the Tarung Hka about Ningbyen and the Tanai Hka south and south-east of Shinbwiyang. There were signs that the enemy was strengthening his forces in this area.

6. *North Burma.*

On the left flank of the Chinese American Task Force, based on Ledo, we held the country up to the Salween River with a very small number of troops based on Fort Hertz. This area was not controlled by the U.S. Forces.

Two companies of the Burma Army were based on Fort Hertz, and were supplied by air. In addition, there were some seven hundred and fifty Kachin Levies – irregulars with a few British officers. The Kachins were loyal and hated the Japanese intensely. They had much success in patrols and in laying traps for Japanese troops.

As a reserve in case of emergency one Indian battalion was kept in North East Assam at call. The need for it did not arise, which perhaps was fortunate because it could only have been taken to Fort Hertz by air, and then only if the necessary aircraft could have been spared from other operations.

Dispositions of the levies have varied somewhat from time to time, but generally speaking they held as far south as Sumprabum, and a few detachments were east of the Mali Hka.

A complication in North East Burma was the presence there of certain Chinese whose arrival was first reported early in July. They appeared to be weak irregular armed forces, who were apparently expected to live on the country. The Kachin country however is extremely poor, and can barely produce enough for the Kachins themselves to live on. The presence of the Chinese was embarrassing. Indeed, the Kachins were nearly as hostile to them as they were to the Japanese. Urgent steps were therefore taken to secure their withdrawal by representation to Generalissimo Chiang Kai Shek through H.B.M.'s Ambassador in Chungking. Eventually, except for a few small detachments, they left the area and went back across the Salween to China early in September.

Subsequently, at the request of General Cheng Po, the Commander of Chinese Guerilla Forces, an operational boundary was fixed between the British and Chinese Forces in North East Burma. This was done in order to define the area in which the British and Chinese were respectively responsible for preventing Japanese infiltration. The boundary runs roughly in a north and south direction near the Burma – Yunnan border, and the arrangement made was that our Forces would be responsible to the west, and the Chinese to the east of this line.

7. *Ceylon Army Command.*
There were no active land operations in the Ceylon Army Command during the period under review. The Japanese, however, carried out several air reconnaissances, and two of their aircraft were destroyed.

The arrival of the 11th East African Division was completed, and intensive training was carried out by this formation.

In August a new defence scheme for Ceylon was approved as a result of a re-appreciation of the role of the Army in that Command. It included the reorganisation of the garrison on the arrival of the East African Troops.

On the 10th September the Italian warship Eritrea, acting on the orders of Admiral Sir Andrew Cunningham, put into Colombo.

On the 1st September the shore organisation of the Eastern Fleet arrived in Colombo, and on the same date also, the Rear Admiral, Naval Air Stations, Indian Ocean, set up his Headquarters there.

In the Maldive Islands, a new flying boat base was established during the period at Kalai. Intensive constructional work at Addu Atoll continued.

The Japanese about once a month made air reconnaissances of Cocos Island.

8. *Operations of the Royal Indian Navy.*
H.M.I. Ships "Jumna" and "Sutlej" operated in the Mediterranean with the Royal Navy during the period. Otherwise, normal escorts were provided for convoys to and from Aden, the Persian Gulf, Colombo and along the coasts of India. In the course of these escort duties a number of depth charge attacks were made on enemy submarines with unknown results.

THE AIR.

9. *General.*
The monsoon inevitably curtailed operations in the air, but not to the same extent as on land. From time to time all-weather runways were flooded, and throughout the period fair-weather strips were unusable. Administration was also hampered by breaking of rail and road communications and the rupture of signal channels.

Nevertheless, unlike the Japanese who practically discontinued air operations during the rainy season, we continued to be active in the air as far as conditions allowed, and we prepared for the dry weather by training and equipping squadrons, and building up reserves of supplies.

An important development was the improvement in meteorological services. It was found possible to establish what can and cannot be done from the air over North East India and Burma during the monsoon. In particular, monsoon conditions were found not so very bad over central Burma, and it was generally possible to locate targets on enemy lines of communications. Moreover, given reliable route forecasts of weather over enemy territory, night bombing was practicable over a wide area. In fact, unless all-weather airfields are actually flooded, large scale air operations can be undertaken safely even at the height of the monsoon.

The extent of our air effort during the period under review is given under the appropriate headings in the paragraphs which follow, and the training and administrative side of it is dealt with in Part III of this Despatch.

10. *Aircraft Flow and its Effect on Operations.*
There was a great increase of aircraft held in the Command, and obsolescent types were largely replaced by modern aircraft. In all there were in India the following aircraft of all types, 2,453 on 25th June, and 3,699 on 17th November, 1943.

The most important development, however, was the extensive modernisation of our fighter defence. Hurricanes rose from 677 to 1,088. Spitfires increased from 13 to 153. They had a most decisive effect on operations, though this did not fully develop till later. Spitfires went into action in November for the first time, and not being supplied with long range tanks could only operate over our own territory thus having no chance to meet large enemy air forces. Prior to this the enemy had been able to carry out reconnaissance flights with impunity by flying at great heights and out-distancing the Hurricanes. The first three reconnaissance aircraft the enemy sent over after the Spitfires arrived were all destroyed, and the enemy did not again attempt a reconnaissance or a raid in the area where the Spitfires were located.

So important was the success of the Spitfires that my Air Officer Commanding-in-Chief asked the Chief of Air Staff urgently for the flow to be increased as far as possible, and the great successes later against large enemy formations fully justified the request.

11. *Expansion of Squadrons and their Distribution on the 15th November*, 1943.
Although a considerable inflow of aircraft had occurred, our actual front line air strength had not increased very greatly by November.

The target for the end of 1943 was 76 squadrons. In detailed planning, however, targets agreed on from time to time with the Air Ministry have been substituted. Forward administrative planning and organisation was finally based on the 146 squadron target, which is what has been promised on conclusion of the war with Germany.

12. *The 10th U.S.A.A.F.*
While dealing with the developing strength of air power in this theatre, it is appropriate to mention the American Air Forces. My R.A.F. Headquarters have

been in constant touch with the U.S. Air Force, and there has been perfect co-ordination of air operations between the two. In general, the 10th U.S.A.A.F. attacked distant objectives over Burma by day; R.A.F. medium and heavy bombers operated by night; and R.A.F. fighters and light bombers attacked by day objectives within 250 miles of the forward airfields. The introduction of Mustangs (A.36's and 51's) to augment our attacks on enemy communications in forward areas was notable, and the American fighter strength was employed to protect their airfields in Assam and sometimes to escort day bombers and supply dropping aircraft.

The air ferry to Kunming carried an increasing tonnage to China. In June the total was 3,100 tons, and in October 8,632 tons.

13. *Enemy Air Effort.*
I have already remarked that the enemy practically ceased operations in the air during the monsoon period. A few intercept sorties in Burma and some recon-naissance flights were all that were undertaken. Presumably the bulk of enemy squadrons were withdrawn for rest or training.

There was, however, an increase in October and November and raids were carried out on Chittagong, Agartala, Fenny, Palel, Imphal, Khumbhirgram, and Tiddim.

Reconnaissance aircraft appeared a few times also over the Madras coast and Ceylon. Two of these were shot down in October and November by our Beau-fighters. The enemy fighter defences and warning system in the Andamans, Nicobars and over Northern Sumatra were fairly efficient, and in each of these areas we lost Liberators shot down while engaged in photographic reconnais-sances.

AIR OPERATIONS.

14. *The Bengal Command.*
In June, 1943, dispositions of squadrons were as follows:-

In forward airfields	5 Hurricane Squadrons.
	1 Beaufighter Squadron.
	1 Blenheim Squadron.
	1 Bisley Squadron.
At Cox's Bazar	1 Hurricane Squadron (detachment).
In Assam	1 Bisley Squadron.
	1 Mohawk Squadron.
In second line airfields (in Jessore round Calcutta)	3 Bomber Squadrons.
	5 Fighter Squadrons.
	1 Photo Reconnaissance Squadron.
	1 Transport Aircraft Squadron.
Training at Digri and Salbani	3 Vengeance squadrons.

Until the weather improved at the end of September this distribution remained substantially unchanged.

The policy regarding the employment of these forces during the monsoon had been laid down as follows:-

To maintain a forward fighter offensive policy.

To ensure the continuance of local air superiority,

To protect our costal shipping southwards from Chittagong.

To attack enemy occupied airfields wherever possible.

To attack enemy lines of communications and shipping in the enemy forward areas.

Actually, while the maintenance of air superiority remained a primary task, medium and heavy bomber effort was concentrated on attacking L. of C. targets.

15. *Strategic Bombing.*

In June/July heavy and medium bomber operations were much handicapped by bad weather and shortage of spares. Nevertheless, the high percentage of successful sorties under difficult weather conditions during this period reflects great credit on the crews concerned.

Between June and August the 10th U.S.A.A.F., operating by day inflicted considerable damage on the Thilawa and Syriam oil installations and took toll of railway rolling stock. The Myitnge Bridge was cut and the Gotteik Viaduct damaged. Enemy vessels off the coast of Burma or near the Andaman and Nicobar Islands were also attacked with success.

As a result of continued reconnaissance and attacks on shipping, enemy use of the port of Rangoon practically ceased during the period.

During the whole period U.S.A.A.F. bombers shot down twenty-four enemy aircraft, probably destroyed eighteen and damaged thirty-one.

16. *Tactical Bombing.*

The 4th Corps was effectively supported by attacks on the Japanese bases at Kalewa, Kalemyo and on other similar targets. In August light bombers co-operated with land forces in raiding operations, thereby obtaining useful experience of co-operation in jungle country. In this it was found that our existing ground to air radio telephony control arrangements were inadequate, and methods such as the use of smoke mortar bombs to indicate enemy targets close to our own troops and positions were developed.

By the middle of September, Vengeances almost entirely replaced Blenheims for day tactical bombing, and the pilots of these machines rapidly became skilled in the identification and bombing of small camouflaged targets.

17. *Fighters and Fighter Bombers employed offensively.*

Aircraft were deployed to support both the 4th Corps front from Assam to the Southern Chin Hills, and the 15th Corps front in the Arakan. Weather conditions, however, restricted land activity; and fighters were confined to answering calls for support from our land patrols, and to attacking enemy forward positions and their lines of communication immediately in rear.

On the 15th Corps front our offensive air operations made the enemy progressively more cautious in the siting of his monsoon quarters. Our attacks also considerably reduced his freedom of movement, and often he was only able to move by night or in bad weather.

The enemy reacted strongly to our attacks by placing light anti-aircraft defences at or near all likely targets, and thereafter this type of attack proved more expensive for our own aircraft. The damage inflicted upon the enemy, however, fully justified such losses as we incurred.

18. *Maintenance of Air Superiority.*
We were ready for the enemy when towards the end of the period he resumed operations in the air. The results, however, of our efforts, to intercept his raids were disappointing because of advantages the enemy aircraft had over the Hurricanes which formed the bulk of our defensive force. Whenever contact was made, however, attacks were carried out with vigour, and losses as high as could be expected were inflicted by the Hurricanes. However, as already mentioned, the first appearance of our Spitfires altered this.

During the whole period our air superiority was definitely unchallenged, and with the expansion and re-equipment that has been carried out it should remain so.

19. *Fighter Reconnaissance.*
Hurricanes accomplished a particularly satisfactory task in their reconnaissances in support of the 4th and 15th Corps. Their assignments included photographic reconnaissance of the enemy's forward positions, tactical reconnaissance in tracing enemy movements in the immediate rear of their forward positions, and continual survey of the rearward lines of communication. Bengal Command was also responsible for seaward reconnaissance to a depth of twenty-five miles from the coast along the whole Sunderbans and Arakan coastline, from Calcutta to Pagoda Point. This work, done as it was in the worst part of the monsoon weather, was of great merit.

20. *Air Supply.*
Isolated radar and Observer Corps posts cut off by the monsoon rains were supplied by air. Also the almost daily service to and from the forward areas transported essential spare parts, the lack of which was keeping operational aircraft on the ground.

The main tasks however, of the squadron engaged on this work were for the Army. It followed up its successful work in supplying the Long Range Penetration Brigade in its raid during the spring of 1943 by supply dropping in inaccessible country where, without its aid, land detachments could not have been maintained. It carried out 1,100 sorties, and almost 1,200 tons of supplies were dropped.

21. *Air Operations for the Defence of India's Coastline and Ceylon.*
Two groups comprising twelve squadrons were allocated to this duty. Operational control of all general reconnaissance in this sphere was vested in the

headquarters of one of these groups under the strategical direction of the Air Officer Commanding-in-Chief, modified from time to time by mutual agreement with the Commander-in-Chief, Eastern Fleet.

Control of operations in the Arabian Sea was also strengthened, and a Naval Air Operations Room established at Bombay.

The threat of seaborne attack against India and Ceylon receded, and we should get at least two or three months warning of any such enterprise. We relied therefore on our existing strength in coastal areas for immediate air defence, while taking all necessary measures for expansion and reinforcement that did not actually involve the holding of aircraft, *e.g.*, organisation of fighter control, installation of communications, etc.

22. General and Photographic Reconnaissances.
The strengthening of our island bases at Addu Atoll and Diego Garcia and the retention of Cocos Island, extended the range of our general reconnaissances.

Considerable development of photographic reconnaissances also took place. Strategical photographic reconnaissances of enemy occupied territory in Burma, China, Assam and the Andamans were carried out.

The main task, however, was greatly increased intelligence cover of Sumatra, Malaya, the Andamans and Nicobar Islands.[2] Mosquitos were only able to cover the Northern Andamans, and it was therefore necessary to use Liberators also, based in Ceylon and on the East coast of India.

23. Air Operations on the North West Frontier.
Modern high speed aircraft were used on the North West Frontier of India for the first time. There were however, no tasks of any importance to carry out.

North West Frontier operations are now purely an Indian Air Force commitment, and the Frontier area has served as a useful training ground for its squadrons. Intelligence and photographic facilities have been developed, the Kohat runway extended, and organisation undertaken to modernise what has hitherto been a most backward area from the point of view of the air forces.

24. Balloon Barrages.
Subject to weather conditions, balloons were flown continuously at Calcutta for the protection of the Docks area and Howrah Bridge, also at Jamshedpur to defend the Tata Iron and Steel Works, and at Colombo to protect the harbour and dock installations and certain parts of the city. The barrage at Trincomalee, originally intended for the protection of the oil tanks and consisting of some seventeen balloons only, was extended to include in its scope the whole Naval anchorage at Trincomalee – China Bay. Additional commitments undertaken in November included the defence of the harbour and docks at Chittagong, and balloon protection for merchant shipping and Fleet auxiliaries.

Subsidiary operations have included the flying of balloons at 1,000 feet on patrol ships which go out daily at dawn to guide friendly submarines into harbour.

Captains of these submarines speak highly of the assistance in locating the patrol ship provided by the flying of these balloons. Submarines are frequently well off course, and time is saved and danger averted by this method of homing. Moreover, balloons have been flown for anti-aircraft calibration, radar calibration and meteorological purposes.

In no cases have the areas provided with balloon protection been subjected to low level air attacks. During the monsoon period one new squadron and nine ancillary units were formed.

25. *Air Sea Rescue.*
Owing to the shortage of Air Sea Rescue aircraft and marine craft, few units had been brought into operation as yet, and the important work of rescuing the survivors of shipwrecked vessels or "ditched" aircraft had devolved on operational squadrons. Twenty-one incidents were recorded, ten of which occurred in the Bay of Bengal, two in the Arabian Sea and eight off Ceylon, involving in all one hundred and eleven persons, of whom sixty-nine were rescued. The credit for most of this work is due to General Reconnaissance Squadrons, but one of the Chittagong Air Sea Rescue units, in its first operational sortie, succeeded in rescuing three out of five members of a Wellington. On a further occasion Lindholme dinghy gear, which has now been distributed, was successfully dropped to a distressed U.S.A.A.F. aircrew.

26. *Estimates of Results.*
The decision to operate during the monsoon season has been more than justified by the results achieved.

Attacks on shipping by the U.S.A.A.F. and on the port of Rangoon by both U.S.A.A.F. and R.A.F. aircraft more or less prohibited the use of this port to the enemy. Similarly, Akyab was consistently bombed.

The new Burma Siam railway was under construction during the period by the enemy (who used prisoners of war labour for it under conditions of bestial cruelty) and has since been completed. This probably eliminated the port of Rangoon as a link in the enemy line of communication, and reduced its importance as a target for our bombers. At the same time it remained to be seen how far this new railway was itself vulnerable to air attack, in spite of the enemy's duplication of bridges and other measures to preserve it from interruption.

An estimate of the damage to transportation facilities can be gathered from the following table of claims for the period made by the Bengal Air Command:-

Sampans destroyed	160
Sampans damaged	2,624
Power driven water craft and barges destroyed	12
Power driven water craft and barges damaged	193
Locomotives destroyed	9
Locomotives damaged	143

Rolling stock destroyed	27
Rolling stock damaged	464
M.T. destroyed	42
M.T. damaged	142

Much of the material enumerated above cannot easily be renewed.

As regards casualties inflicted on the enemy, intelligence reports showed that attacks from the air had great effect. In Arakan where most of such attacks were made, enemy losses were conservatively put at 500 killed and many more wounded from June to September. Our losses during the period under review were thirty-one aircraft, including four destroyed on the ground at the beginning of November.

27. *Morale of Air Personnel.*

The strain of maintaining a continuous effort and carrying out operations, in very trying heat and humidity undoubtedly had its effect at times on the morale of the men. This was remedied by maintaining a high standard of training, with the result that the fighting spirit of all was high when the period ended.

I cannot commend too highly the manner in which the men of ground organisations carried out their duties during very bad monsoon conditions. If any are to be singled out, I would mention the maintenance personnel who never failed to keep the serviceability of operational aircraft at a high standard, and I would also pay particular tribute to the ranks employed at radar units and wireless observer posts. Many of these detachments were completely isolated for long periods, and had to be maintained by air alone.

INFORMATION OF THE ENEMY.

28. *Enemy Situation in Burma on the 15th November, 1943.*

Throughout the monsoon Burma was held by the Japanese with four divisions. By the 15th November a fifth Japanese division had arrived in Burma, and the dispositions of Japanese forces in the country were believed to be:

Arakan	55th Division less one regiment in the South West Pacific.
	213th Regiment of 33rd Division.
	2nd Battalion 214th Regiment (less one company) of 33rd Division.
Chin Hills and Atwin Yomas	33rd Division less detachments in Arakan.
Mawlaik exclusive to Homalin inclusive.	New Division less one regiment.
Hukawng	}
Myitkyma	} 18th Division
Laukhaung	}
Htawgaw	}
Salween	56th Division.

29. Up to the 15th November the general picture on the enemy side appeared to be as follows:-

Arakan. – The Japanese were generally on the defensive, but had reacted somewhat to our advance down the main Mayu range and were attempting with no success to oust us from our forward positions there.

Chin Hills. – The Japanese had advanced. As already described, they occupied Falam on the 7th November, Haka on the 11th November, and Fort White on the 15th November, but their offensives in Manipur and Arakan were not to develop till later.

Chindwin. – The Japanese were moving forward to their pre-monsoon locations, and there were indications that the new Division was taking over more front than had originally been held by the 18th Division. There were then no indications that the Japanese intended to cross the Chindwin in force.

Hukawng Valley. – After a slow start (probably owing to being upset by the Chinese advance) Japanese reinforcements began to arrive in the Hukawng Valley about the 7th November.

Sumprabum Area. – Sumprabum was reinforced by the enemy to a strength of two companies about the 10th November, and at the same time the Japanese strength at Ninchangyang in the South Triangle was increased to five hundred.

Salween. – The likelihood of any large scale Japanese operation across the Salween seemed to have receded by the 1st November. It appeared, however, that contrary to their former practice, the Japanese now intended to hold the area which they had occupied North-East of Tengchung.

30. *The Civil Affairs Organisation in re-occupied Territories of Burma.*
This service has functioned satisfactorily throughout the period, in those parts of Burma under our control.

The only area where any notable advance and re-occupation by our forces of Burmese territory took place, was in that of the Chinese-American Task Force (C.A.T.F.) described above – i.e., towards the Hukawng Valley. As this became in fact an American zone, the question arose as to how the administration of civil affairs in these re-occupied territories should be organised. A small civil affairs organisation had been functioning in the American zone for some time, but it became necessary to expand this and put it on a proper basis. A conference therefore was held (before the advance began) between the General Officer Commanding-in-Chief, Eastern Army, the (American) Commanding General of the C.A.T.F. and the (British) Chief Civil Affairs Officer, as a result of which a satisfactory solution was reached.

It was decided that a senior Civil Affairs Officer should be attached to the Headquarters of the C.A.T.F. as a political adviser, co-ordinator, and liaison officer with junior Civil Affairs officers and the local population. The Civil Affairs Section, which also had been started with the Rear Echelon at Delhi of the headquarters of the American Forces, was also to maintain close touch with my

General Headquarters. These arrangements, and the fact that there is little difference between American and British ideas on the functions of Civil Affairs services, rendered the position of our Civil Affairs officers working under the C.A.T.F. perfectly satisfactory, and the work proceeded smoothly as the advance progressed.

31. *Internal Conditions in India.*
Peaceful conditions have continued throughout India, and there was no renewal during the period of any outbreaks like those of August, 1942. The possibility of disturbances occurring on the anniversary of these outbreaks was however guarded against in those areas where they were thought likely. On the approach of the 9th August, the anniversary of Mr. Gandhi's arrest last year, additional troops were placed at the disposal of the commanders concerned. In addition, protective measures were taken on all the more important railways in the Central Command from the 7th to the 17th August.

32. *The Economic Emergency and Famine in Bengal.*
A far more serious internal problem, and one which may become dangerously acute if India's resources are still further taxed, was the economic one.

The causes of this, and the manner in which the problem is linked with military expansion and the support of the forces based on India, has been indicated elsewhere in the paragraphs dealing with long term administrative planning. Other factors in the civil sphere, such as the results of harvests, the loss of the rice imports from Burma, the hoarding of food grains and other commodities, difficulties of civil transportation, etc., have undoubtedly affected the situation in one way or another.

The outcome has been famine in certain parts of the country, notably those where the staple food is rice. In particular, Bengal suffered acutely, and here, at the request of His Excellency the Viceroy for military aid in relief of famine distress in Bengal, I approved, on the 1st November, the following plan for the employment of military resources:-

(*a*) An organisation under command Maj.- General A.V.T. Wakely, in the appointment of Director of Movements Civil Supplies, working under the Bengal Government.

(*b*) A second organisation under command Maj.-General D. Stuart, Commander 303 L. of C. Area, reinforced by additional troops to be drafted into the area.

Lt.-General A.G.O.M. Mayne, General Officer Commanding-in-Chief, Eastern Command, was appointed Supreme Military Liaison Officer between the Bengal Government and the military authorities.

The duty of Maj.-General Wakely's organisation was to transport food-grains and other supplies from Calcutta and other outside sources to main distribution centres in the distressed areas by the maximum use of all available transportation methods.

Maj.-General Stuart's command reinforced by-

One Indian motorised brigade.
Five Indian Infantry battalions.
One Indian General Hospital.
Two field ambulances.
One Casualty Clearing Station.

and certain engineer and supply units assisted the civil organisation in the transportation and distribution of foodstuffs forward of main distribution centres and in medical relief.

By the night of the 15/16th November reinforcements were already operating in the Dacca area, and more were due to arrive on the 19th November and subsequent days. Advanced parties were already on the ground carrying out detailed reconnaissances.

Prior to the arrival of these additional troops, the transportation of food-grains commenced under Maj.-General Stuart's organisation using transport and internal security troops already available in Bengal.

In addition to the provision of units, medical assistance was provided in the form of 101 medical officers, of whom 11 were specialists in hygiene. These officers commenced to arrive on the 15th November and they were sent immediately to distressed areas.

On the 15th November, within a fortnight of the inception of the project, military aid had already achieved very satisfactory and promising results. The output of relief supplies from Calcutta to the districts had been doubled, public confidence in the efficacy of relief measures had been partially restored and, in consequence, the price of food-grains in the districts had been substantially lowered.

This relief work, both economic and medical, was still in progress at the end of the period, for the emergency in Bengal had by no means ended by then.

33. *The North West Frontier of India.*

The tribal areas of the North West Frontier continued quiet, and except for occasional acts of kidnapping, sniping, etc., by gangs of bad characters, there was no hostile activity on our side of the international frontier.

As regards the general outlook across the frontier, with the removal of the threat (from the Caucasus) to Persia and the North West Frontier, and the turn in the Allied fortunes in Europe, our policy underwent a change. The role of the land and air forces in North West India was restricted to exercising tribal control. The forces available for this were those normally allocated to Frontier Defence and Frontier Defence Reserve; but at the same time I warned the Commander of the North Western Army that it might be necessary to draw on them for commitments in the East of India.

With this reservation therefore, I directed that the general policy was to maintain our existing position in the tribal areas, and that action taken in pursuance of it should as far as possible be designed to avoid the creation of situations demanding the employment of forces additional to those at the disposal of the Commander of the North Western Army.

PART III – ORGANISATION, TRAINING AND ADMINISTRATION ORGANISATION.

1. *General.*

During the period covered by this Despatch much attention was given to the organisation of the Army in India. Many of the changes and innovations were the result of experience gained during the fighting of the previous dry season, and some were far-reaching in character.

In the re-organisation of the composition of divisions the following principles were observed-

The existing composition was to be disturbed as little as possible.

Vehicles with less mobility than the 15 cwt. four-wheel-drive truck were generally to be eliminated.

The number of vehicles was to be reduced to the absolute minimum, and those kept were to be for the carriage of essential fighting equipment only.

A Divisional Headquarters battalion was introduced. This had the same War Establishment as other infantry battalions, and replaced divisional defence and employment platoons and brigade defence platoons.

The need for the closest possible support of infantry by artillery in country where the normal 25 pounder artillery regiment could not operate was met by providing 3.7″ howitzers and 3″ mortars.

In light divisions the brigade light reconnaissance battalions were to be replaced by one divisional light reconnaissance battalion.

The most far-reaching and revolutionary of the innovations however, was that initiated by my predecessor in the form of long range penetration (L.R.P.) groups. These are dealt with separately in the paragraphs which follow, and their expansion formed a major feature of the re-organisation that took place.

In the lower formations and units various changes affecting the artillery, motor battalions, infantry (both British and Indian), Indian machine gun battalions and Royal Indian Army Service Corps were introduced. These affected types and weight of equipment as well as the number and grouping of personnel and the ranks of junior commanders.

2. *Changes in Order of Battle of the Forces in India.*

The Supreme Allied Commander South East Asia Command began to function from midnight of the 15/16th November. From this date the Fourteenth Army and the Ceylon Command (including the anchorages of Addu Atoll, Diego Garcia and Cocos) came under his command, except for certain administrative and training matters which my headquarters continued to handle until the newly formed 11th Army Group headquarters staff was in a position to take them over.

Earlier, various important changes took, place of which the most important were:-

(*a*) The splitting of the Eastern Army on the 15th October into the Eastern Command (under Lt.-General A.G.O.M. Mayne) and the Fourteenth Army under General Sir George Giffard).

(*b*) The disappearance of the Indian Expeditionary Force and its redesignation as the 33rd Indian Corps.

With regard to (*a*) the boundary between the two was the River Meghna from its mouth to the north as far as its junction with the Assam – Bengal boundary at Lakhai, and thence the Assam – Bengal boundary. The Fourteenth Army was an operational headquarters under the new organisation of the South East Asia Command, while the Eastern Command was a static formation under the India Command.

As regards (*b*) the Indian Expeditionary Force Headquarters (I.E.F.) had been formed in February 1943 under the orders of the Governor General in Council, and was designed to take charge of all overseas operations launched against the Japanese from India. Its original Commander was A/Maj.-Gen. T.J.W. Winterton, but General Sir George Giffard, was appointed to succeed him on the 31st March, 1943.

Early in September the I.E.F. was redesignated the 33rd Indian Corps.

3. *Long Range Penetration Groups (L. R. P. Groups) – Their Expansion and Organisation into a "Special Force."*

Lord Wavell's last Despatch gave an account of the experiment in long range penetration carried out in the spring of 1943 by the 77th Indian Infantry Brigade under Brigadier (later Maj.-Gen.) O.C. Wingate.

The success of this Brigade in traversing North Burma (being maintained entirely by air supply and what they could purchase locally), and the inability of the Japanese to obliterate it, opened up new possibilities.

One of the features of this operation had been that the Brigade had adopted an entirely new organisation for its raid, and had undergone much special training with particular equipment prior to embarking on it.

Briefly, under this new organisation, the battalions of the Brigade had been broken up and re-organised into a number of columns. The Brigade itself had been termed a "Long Range Penetration Brigade" and there were seven columns, each about half a battalion strong, in it. Each of these columns was a self-contained unit under its own commander, with its own facilities for receiving supplies by air, and for intercommunication. Each was moreover organised and trained to fight as a highly mobile tactical unit in the jungle. The Brigade had no artillery or motor transport, but units had medium machine guns and mortars. It moved on foot through the jungle with the minimum of pack transport, and aimed at disrupting the rearward organisation of the enemy. To effect this it relied on its great mobility and its complete independence of any fixed line of supply.

When the detachments of 77th Brigade came out of Burma it was collected at Imphal and officers and men were sent on leave. Major-General Wingate came to New Delhi and, after discussing with me and my staff the lessons to be drawn from his recent operations in Burma, went to England where he was again able to explain his ideas. These were examined prior to, and at the Quebec Conference, and it was finally decided to make a greatly extended use of long range penetration forces. My views on the employment of these forces were sent to the Chiefs of Staffs on the 9th August.

I considered that the timings and areas of employment of L.R.P. Groups, are governed by the activities of the main forces. Without exploitation by the main forces concerned, operations by L.R.P. Groups are unjustifiably costly against a first class enemy and achieve no strategic object. These Groups are not capable of achieving decisive results against organised forces of all arms. Their role is not to fight, but to evade the enemy and by guerrilla tactics to harass him. I emphasised that unless the main forces can take advantage of the situations created by these Groups, the latter's efforts are wasted. In addition subsequent Japanese retaliation against Burmese who have helped these Groups, only made them less willing to help in the future.

4. It was now decided to form a L.R.P. force of six brigades in the first instance for Burma operations and to increase these to eight later on. Each brigade was to be organised in two "wings" and to consist of eight columns, each three hundred and forty strong – a total in all of some 1,000 officers and 25,000 men. There was to be a Force Headquarters whose functions were in the first instance to deal with policy and to organise and train the "L.R.P." or "Special Force" as it was now called.

By the time these decisions were taken the leave of the original 77th (L.R.P.) Brigade was over, and it was reformed near Jhansi in August.

Meanwhile, a second long range penetration brigade (111th Indian Infantry Brigade) had been forming in the same area.

5. It was now decided to transform the 70th British Division, which was in Bangalore at the time, into the Special Force, and it was moved to Nowgong early in October for this purpose.

The 77th and 111th Indian Infantry Brigades were increased from six to eight columns each, by the addition to each of an extra British infantry battalion. The 3rd West African Infantry Brigade, which arrived at Bombay on the 4th November, joined the Special Force in mid-November.

An American L.R.P. Brigade (5307 Provisional Regiment) arrived in India and moved to Deogarh near Lalitpur early in November for training, but was not incorporated in the Special Force.

The 70th British Division completed its special training as L.R.P. brigades in the Nowgong area by the end of October. Two extra British Infantry battalions were added to the Division to enable the requisite number of columns to be formed.

Troops other than infantry which were absorbed in the Special Force, included two field artillery regiments, an anti-tank regiment, a reconnaissance regiment, and two regiments of the Royal Armoured Corps. On joining the Special Force, the men of these units severed for the time being their connection with their original arm of the service.

6. The Special Force Headquarters opened at Gwalior on the 25th October, for the training, organisation and administration under H.Q. Central Command of all L.R.P. forces and later as required by South East Asia Command for their operational control. This headquarters was formed from resources made available from the 70th Division and from personnel from the United Kingdom. Its more important appointments were duplicated to allow of training and planning to proceed concurrently, and it provided staffs where necessary for wings of the L.R.P. brigades.

This was the general position of the Special Force in November, and while the training of it continued under me, it operated later in strength against the enemy communications in North Central Burma under the direction of the Supreme Allied Commander South East Asia Command. The untimely death of Maj.-Gen. Wingate at the outset of these operations was a tragic loss to the Force which had been his conception from the start.

7. *Airfield Defences.*
Another extensive development was in the land defence of airfields and air force installations. The existing policy held good whereby general and local land defence was the task of the Army; but the R.A.F. were now to assist to the limit of their own available resources. Extensive camouflage measures were undertaken to conceal airfields in the vulnerable area of the Provinces of Assam, Bengal, Bihar, the southern districts of Orissa, and in a coastal belt of twenty-five miles from Orissa to Cape Comorin.

To obliterate the traces of recent construction constituted a major difficulty, and a vast campaign of grass and creeper growing had been undertaken. The camouflage of the strips themselves remained, however, the main problem owing to lack of materials, transport and labour. Nevertheless progress was made. Dummy aircraft of various designs were manufactured and put in use, and thirty decoy sites in Bengal had been projected as a defensive measure against night attack.

8. *Chemical Warfare and Special Weapons.*
The use of gas by the Japanese seemed unlikely, particularly so in view of the strategical conditions on the Burma front.

In order to lighten the load on the individual fighting soldier, I decided, with certain exceptions, to withdraw respirators and anti-gas equipment from formations and units joining the field army. Exceptions were the crews of tanks and carriers. The equipment withdrawn was, however, stored in forward ordnance depots under special arrangements to admit of its being rapidly issued in emergency. Anti-gas training also continued, and a high standard was maintained, and for security reasons Commanders were directed to exercise discretion in promulgating this policy.

9. *Flame Weapons and Coloured Smokes.*
A number of flame weapons, both man-pack and carrier-borne, were ordered from England for 1943 and 1944, but their tactical use, the arm of the service that will use them, and the scales and method of maintenance in the field remain to be decided after trials and demonstrations have been carried out.

While it was decided to use coloured smokes with mortars and certain smaller calibre guns, none were yet available for these weapons. Two thousand coloured smoke generators only were provided from England, and small quantities of grenades, filled with red and yellow smoke only, were available from indigenous production in India.

TRAINING

10. The experience gained in recent operations and in Arakan exposed various shortcomings in our training, and this gave rise to many of the measures carried out during the period under review. Indeed, some of the measures introduced constituted fundamental changes in our policy and practice in regard to military training as a whole. In addition to the expansion of our training framework in various directions, much reorganisation and improvement of existing training formations, and installations was effected. The most important of these developments are summarised below.

11. *The selection of candidates for commissions.*
Since the war expansion of the Indian Army began, selection has been by means of interview boards. These boards consisted originally of certain senior civil and military officers, and were district and provincial in character. Though this system had met with considerable success, there was a high subsequent wastage at Officers' training schools. During the period, these boards were centralised in General Headquarters, and scientifically organised on the system already evolved in the United Kingdom. By these means it was hoped to save time and effort, as well as to select the embryo officer at the outset for the work to which he was most suited.

Similarly selection of officers for the Women's Auxiliary Corps (India) was commenced by means of interview boards on the same lines.

12. *The Training of Officers.*
In order to provide the large number of staff officers that were required for static formation headquarters, it was decided in August to start at the Staff College a series of short courses, each of 60 students. The students for these short courses were primarily selected from those who were over age for the ordinary Staff College course, and physically incapable of carrying out staff duties in active formations.

The syllabus for instruction at the Tactical School was completely revised to cover jungle warfare and warfare in Eastern countries rather than desert warfare on which its efforts had primarily been concentrated.

It was found necessary to start at Ahmednagar a new special Officer Cadre Training Unit (O.C.T.U) for the Indian Armoured Corps.

A further officer cadet training unit was also started at Dagshai for the training of cadet officers for the Women's Auxiliary Corps (India).

An effort was made to improve the training in University Officers Training Corps (U.O.T.C.) and thereby attract more candidates through that channel for commissions in the army. Cadets of U.O.T.C.s can now obtain Certificates "A" and "B" for which syllabi have been laid down by General Headquarters. Those who qualified for these certificates gained certain advantages, if and when they were selected, and went to Officers Training Schools.

In order to give as many officers as possible practical experience in the more modern methods of fighting the Japanese in jungle country, fifty officers from the India Command were sent to Australia and New Guinea, where they were to be attached to fighting units of the Australian Army for about three months.

In order to train and bring up to date senior officers of the Army and the Royal Air Force in problems of air support in eastern theatres, two courses were held in Simla in July which the majority of Brigadiers General Staff and General Staff Officers 1st Grade of divisions and a large number of Group Captains and Wing Commanders R.A.F. attended. Considerable value was gained from these inter-service discussions.

13. *Initial training of the soldier.*
It was apparent that the basic training period for infantry recruits was too short and it was decided to increase the total period of training to eleven months, nine of which to be spent in basic training at regimental centres, and two in special jungle training divisions.

Similarly it became necessary to increase the period of mechanical transport training for recruits from fourteen to twenty weeks. This again was likely to be increased to twenty-four weeks, and would ensure that the recruits obtained at least 120 hours' driving training before being posted to an active unit.

The training carried out in reinforcement camps on the lines of communication was also much improved with the help of the active divisions which depended on these camps for reinforcements. These divisions have been able to provide instructors, and a considerable increase in equipment has also been made available.

14. *Training in Jungle Fighting.*
A second jungle warfare school was opened at Shimoga in Mysore State, to train instructors both British and Indian in the technique of living and fighting in the jungle.

The Jungle Warfare Training Centre at Raiwala, which was originally designed to give recruits training in jungle fighting, was not now needed for this purpose, since the jungle training divisions had come into being. It was used, therefore, for training complete units, and all three battalions of the 50th Indian Parachute Brigade were trained at this centre.

In order to inculcate the higher degree of accuracy and better ammunition control that has been found necessary in jungle fighting, greater stress was laid on quick and accurate snap shooting and less on rapid fire. Psychologically this was having encouraging results.

15. *Collective Training.*

In order to carry training for fighting in the jungle a step further, the 14th Indian Division at Chhindwara and the 39th Indian Division at Saharanpur were converted into jungle training divisions.

Each Indian infantry regiment had its training battalion in one or other of these divisions. Similarly in the case of British reinforcements, it was necessary not only to give basic training to many of the infantry reinforcements who lacked it on arrival from the United Kingdom, but also to give them training in jungle fighting methods. For the first task the 13th Bn. The Sherwood Foresters was temporarily converted into a basic training unit and stationed at Jubbulpore.

For jungle training of British Troops the 52nd Infantry Brigade was formed at Budni in Bhopal State. It consisted of the 20th Bn. The Royal Fusiliers, 7th Bn. The South Lancashire Regt. and 12th Bn. The Sherwood Foresters. Here British infantry reinforcements did two months' training in the forest before going to active battalions.

Collective training in jungle fighting was also necessary for those formations being trained for combined operations.[3] In order to meet this need, both for those units already under training in India in an amphibious role, and for others that would arrive in India in the future, a training headquarters was created. Each of the two wings of this headquarters was designed to organise the collective training of one division at a time in combined operation and jungle warfare.

16. *Engineer Training.*

The need in this Command for a school of military engineering had been felt for some time, to relieve existing engineer training centres of special training commitments for which they were not designed. A school was accordingly planned during the period, which when in being, would give technical post-graduate training to selected young officers, deal with the training of M.E.S. personnel, and generally standardise engineer instruction to a greater degree than hitherto.

Additionally the school of military engineering would centralise all engineer officer cadet training in India.

Another engineering training establishment started was the Obstacle Assault Centre. This contained both engineer and armoured corps elements, and dealt with problems of the assault against Japanese defences and other obstacles.

17. *Combined Operations – Organisation and Training.*

On the 20th June, 1943, the Combined Operations Directorate at G.H.Q. consisted of a Group Captain R.A.F. (Director), a Military Member (Lt.-Col.), and a

Naval Member (Lt.-Commander). These were assisted by a small inter-service staff.

The Director also acted as a member of the Air Staff dealing with combined operations questions, while the Military Member was an integral part of the Staff Duties Directorate at G.H.Q.

The responsibility for all training for combined operations passed to the Headquarters Indian Expeditionary Force (I.E.F.) on its formation in April 1943, but it soon became apparent that this was not satisfactory. Force commanders were only charged with training of forces allotted to them for a specific operation, whilst at G.H.Q. it was necessary that the future policy governing combined operations should be formulated and preparations made to carry it out. Moreover advice was constantly being sought by my planning Staff on combined operations questions in connection with the many plans under consideration.

An immediate re-organisation of the Combined Operations Directorate was therefore essential so that it could resume its proper functions. I took the first opportunity of discussing this with the Commander-in-Chief, Eastern Fleet, and early in August the Chiefs of Staff approved of a Rear Admiral as Director, and a Captain R.N., a Brigadier, and an Air Commodore as Deputy Directors of a reconstituted Directorate of Combined Operations at G.H.Q. of the India Command.

The responsibilities of the Directorate were laid down as follows:-

(*a*) In all matters of combined operations to advise the Supreme Commander, South-East Asia Command and Commander-in-Chief, India, and to give direct counsel to such other authorities as might be authorised from time to time.

(*b*) To maintain close liaison with the Chief of Combined Operations and other D.C.O.'s and to disseminate doctrine regarding combined operations.

(*c*) To guide all preliminary training in combined operations. To control basic training for the assault, for all three services at combined training centres and landing craft wings of the R.I.N., including the training headquarters and staffs in planning and preparation of operations.

(*d*) To advise on the organisation and equipment of all forces detailed for the assault in a combined operation. This included direct contact with the Senior Officer Assault Ships and Craft.

(*e*) To advise on any special training required by troops to be landed over beaches.

(*f*) To arrange for the trial and development of landing crafts and specialised equipment for combined operations; to make recommendations for their provision; and to develop special technique in combined assault. These matters were to be treated with particular reference to the waters and terrain likely to be encountered in operations in South-East Asia.

(*g*) To advise the Joint Intelligence Committee of any special type of information required, or action to be taken in connection with combined operations.

(*h*) On the appointment of Force Commanders for a combined operation, to render them assistance in every way possible.

18. *Training for Combined Operations.*
The provision of landing craft and stores for combined operations, and the maintenance of equipment were made the responsibility of the Supreme Allied Commander, South-East Asia Command.

The question as to whether the Director of Combined Operations (India) should remain under the Commander-in-Chief India or should transfer to the South-East Asia Command was also discussed at length, and it was agreed that it was better that he should remain under the Commander-in-Chief India, at any rate for the time being.

Rear Admiral E.H. Maund was appointed by the Admiralty as Director on the 25th August, and arrived in India on the 16th October.

In the meantime future training policy had not stood still.

The question of giving basic and refresher training to amphibious divisions with their naval and air components was investigated in detail. There were two main problems. The basic and refresher training for those divisions in India, and the refresher training for those divisions who must come to India from other places before operations could be mounted. Two overriding factors affected these problems, the monsoon and the difficulty of moving large bodies of troops over great distances on the already overstrained railways of India.

We already had one combined training centre on the West coast near Bombay. As training had to be complete by early December of 1944, a second centre was clearly necessary, and Cocanada on the East coast, though by no means ideal, was selected as the only practical site available.

The Cocanada Training Centre was developed to provide wet-shod training for an assault brigade group and a beach group, together with their quota of divisional, corps and army troops, and their R.N. and R.A.F. components.

These two centres represented the limit of India's capacity in the matter of combined operational training facilities. Even for the second centre it was not possible to find in India the requisite officers for the instructional staff.[4]

19. *Manpower and Craft for Combined Operations.*
As regards actual hands for the special formations required, large numbers of Royal Navy personnel entered the country during the period of this Despatch. In addition the Royal Indian Navy continued to train crews for landing-craft.

Originally the R.I.N. were to train sufficient personnel for three assault brigade groups, but it was found that landing craft crews for two brigade groups was the most that could efficiently be produced from India at the present time.

Two afloat exercises took place during October and November whilst large "wetshod" exercises were prepared for December.

In the past our training had suffered from lack of sufficient landing craft, but during the period of this Despatch they came into the country in good number.

There was still however a shortage of assault ships for training purposes, and this was particularly felt in the case of "Landing Ships Infantry."

ADMINISTRATION.
Transportation and Supply.
20. *The General Situation and Future Plans.*
It has been recorded in Part I that early in the period covered by this Despatch it was necessary to recast our long term administrative plans, and that a directive giving data for preparing fresh plans for the future was issued to my Long Term Administrative Planning Committee on the 7th August; also that certain short term improvements on the Assam L. of C. were urgently considered.

With regard to long term planning, the Committee were able to furnish an administrative review in September 1943 covering the ground indicated to them in my above mentioned directive for plans for 1944–45.

Their general conclusions were disquieting. They showed that limiting factors in India as a whole were likely to exist under all the main headings of movement and transportation, construction of accommodation for stores and personnel, and provision of Indian manpower.

They also found that the number and capacity of India's ports (and the railways and roads serving those ports) together with the need to maintain the level of imports and exports so as to meet the requirements of India's production of war material and to maintain India as a secure base for operations, restricted at the present time India's capacity to launch amphibious operations.

They remarked that it would be essential for three and probably four of the divisions, likely to be needed for future operations, to by-pass India. It would also be desirable for subsequent maintenance to be partly by direct shipments from bases outside India.

Action to improve the transportation capacity of ports and roads leading thereto was a matter of urgent and major importance, and the following steps were suggested:-

(*a*) The provision of additional broad gauge locomotives and wagons.

(*b*) Development of rail and road approaches to the ports, and action to improve capacity, remove congestion and speed up the turn-round at and in the vicinity of ports.

(*c*) Improvements designed to increase port capacity – such as provision of additional moorings, port craft and other facilities, these measures to be put on a war time basis so as to give early results, as opposed to long term improvements of permanent post-war value.

(*d*) The development of small ports likely to be suitable for smaller assault shipping, etc. Also the use of the smaller ports for coastal traffic in order to ease the load on the railways.

(*e*) An increased use of these smaller ports for civil imports and exports.

Though this last named expedient might not be very desirable from a civil point of view, it would enable the larger ports to deal with a greater flow of military stores and traffic. To achieve results, however, diversion of civil traffic would have to take place well beforehand, as a permanent war-time measure.

21. These conclusions were so far-reaching that an examination of India's capacity to act as a base for the operations contemplated was necessary. For this an operational background was required with estimates of the forces. I therefore asked for this in a telegram to the Chiefs of Staff on the 14th September and received the required information on the 27th September. It conformed generally to my own estimates.

In the meantime examination of India's potential as a base for the operations of the South East Asia Command was taken in hand on broad Lines by the War Projects Co-ordination and Administrative Committee of the Government of India. Here I should mention that although this Committee comprised representatives of all civil as well as military organisations having to do with transportation and supply, it has been my constant concern to keep civil officials of the Government of India, including the Railways, informed and alive as to how their various spheres might be affected by developments. Accordingly, I held meetings with high civil officials from time to time with this end in view.

The War Projects Co-ordination and Administrative Committee, as a result of their examination, advised the Government that, in their view, demands likely to be placed on India in the normal course in order to carry out these long-term plans were probably not only beyond her capacity in the time available, but that the continuance of the strain on India's economy even at the existing level, for another two years, was likely to lead to most serious consequences. They advised certain measures to meet this dangerous situation, and classified them under two headings.

22. Firstly, there were measures designed to counter the menace of inflation and restrict or absorb surplus purchasing power in the country. These were as follows:-

(*a*) Enough silver should be imported to meet the pay and allowances of the additional United Nations Forces involved.

(*b*) The amount of pay which personnel of the United States Forces could draw in India, should be restricted as it is for Dominion troops.

(*c*) Enough canteen stores should be imported to absorb at least 50 per cent. of the purchasing power of the additional Allied troops required.

(*d*) Importation of certain specifically detailed consumer goods for the civil population – these, as in North Africa, to be demanded as essential on military grounds.

(*e*) Foodstuffs should be imported for the civil population.

23. The second series of measures recommended were designed to restrict to safety limits further demands on India for services and supplies for war purposes. They were as follows:-

(*a*) The volume of war production to which India is already committed should not be exceeded.

(*b*) New products for manufacture, or the expansion of existing production for war purposes, should only be undertaken if production could be achieved by June, 1944.

(*c*) As regards 1945, His Majesty's Government should be pressed to accept a drastic curtailment of demands on India for war supplies.

(*d*) Where necessary, military demands on indigenous production of articles essential to the civil population, of which there was a shortage, should be diverted elsewhere

(*e*) The fullest possible use should be made of the Central Provision Office's stocks as well as of the productive capacity in Eastern Group countries in order to relieve India.

(*f*) Sufficient transportation facilities whether by rail, road, inland water, or coastal shipping, should be reserved in order to maintain India's internal economy and productive capacity at suitable levels.

The above recommendations were accepted and telegraphed with observations in greater detail, by the Governor-General to H.M. Government (India Office) on 21st October, 1943.

24. The following short-term improvements on the Assam L. of C. were immediately considered-

(*a*) Increasing the number of train paths in Assam by various improvements in operation. One of these was supervision by military personnel[5] and, another, the relaxation of certain running precaution involving abnormal risks.

(*b*) The immediate increase of locomotive and rolling stock on the Bengal and Assam Railway by transfers from other parts of India – the latter to be replaced by fresh stock from the U.S.A. on arrival.

(*c*) The speeding up of river transportation by installation of navigational lights and by night running.

(*d*) The despatch by air from Calcutta to Assam airfields of stores destined for China.

25. *Progress in Manpower and Recruiting.*
I now come to the actual progress that has been achieved in pursuance of existing plans or policy.

It has been remarked above that one of the main headings under which limitations existed in regard to the total war effort of this country is manpower.

The problem became more complicated as the drain on the United Kingdom and India increased.

The shortage of officers in the United Kingdom coincided with heavily increased commitments due to the setting up of the South East Asia Command, and the formation of the Headquarters of the 11th Army Group and the Fourteenth Army. At the same time there was a decline in the intake to our officers' training schools in this country. As a result, when the period ended there was an acute shortage of officers for both the British and Indian Armies. (The officer situation in the Air Forces is dealt with separately in that portion of this Despatch relating to Air Force Administration.)

With regard to British other ranks, the supply from the United Kingdom was up to expectations apart from technicians. We were thus able to build up strength in the majority of arms, and in some cases even to increase their reserve.

As regards Indian other ranks, there was a decline in recruiting particularly during October and November.

The following are the figures:-

	I.A.	R.I.N.	I.A.F.	Total
June	50,713	594	2,750	54,057
July	50,161	630	2,574	53,365
August	41,354	544	1,936	43,834
September	39,705	604	1,609	41,918
October	33,879	627	1,367	35,873
November	35,597	582	1,564	37,743
TOTAL	251,409	3,581	11,800	266,790

The causes of decline are thought to be several. Clearly, the manpower of the races and tribes which furnished the bulk of recruits before the war had been heavily tapped since 1940, and the increasing opportunities for well-paid employment in civil labour conflicted with the attractions of service in the fighting forces.

Another complication was the ever-increasing demand for educated recruits to be trained as technicians. All services have required them, but priority was accorded to the Indian Air Force for the dilution scheme designed to conserve British manpower. Though the scheme helped the Air Forces (and their need was paramount) it tended to restrict the flow to the Indian Army of much-wanted educated personnel especially clerks.

Similarly the Royal Indian Navy suffered in the recruitment for its more highly educated categories. It obtained, however, the men it needed for its lower grades, and was able to take a higher proportion of these from Southern India.

Recruitment for the Women's Auxiliary Corps (India) averaged 400 per month in the first half of the period but fell to about 300 per month later. Here accommodation difficulties entailed the cessation of the publicity campaign and the intake fell as a result.

26. Line of Communication Development.
The last two Despatches from the India Command give details of the efforts made since early 1942 to build up our lines of communication in the extremely difficult zone comprising Assam and North Eastern India generally. During the period under review, progress was severely handicapped by the monsoon. This was only to be expected, but nevertheless much was done under adverse conditions. The

post of Inspector of Transportation, Assam, was created to supervise the working of the Assam line of communications. Also a Joint Transportation Committee, representing all branches and departments of the Government of India concerned, was set up to initiate, supervise and progress transportation projects of all kinds arising from the needs of the South East Asia Command. The rail and road facilities of the parts of Calcutta and Bombay were the first matters to receive their attention.

27. *Transportation by Rail and Road.*

Arrangements were made to increase the capacity of the Assam line of communication railways to 7,300 tons of military stores daily by the 1st January, 1946. This included doubling the line between Parbatipur and Ledo, building a bridge over the Brahmaputra between Amingaon and Pandu, and constructing a chord line between Namrup and Margherita.

The development of rail service to steamer landings on the Brahmaputra continued, but was subject to special hindrance by the monsoon. In particular, the bridging of the Kakila River (three 60 foot and two 20 foot spans) on the access line to the new river port Neamati (North of Jorhat on the Brahmaputra) suffered from monsoon floods.

Severe flooding prevented the completion of the Dohazari railhead by the target date of the 1st September. It has, however, now been completed. The works to increase the capacity of the railway between Dohazari and Chittagong were finished.

The bursting of the banks of the Damodar River on the 18th July and the consequent cutting of the main rail and road communications North-West of Calcutta have already been mentioned. As a result of these breaches, diversions of traffic had to be made. Two-thirds of the total Assam stores lift, and all traffic for East Bengal and Chittagong (with the exception of fifteen metre gauge wagon loads daily) was sent via Bombay and the sea routes to Calcutta or Chittagong, as long as the interruption lasted.

Among other short term means to improve the rail capacity of the Assam line of communication were the improvement in efficiency of operation by United States military personnel running the railway. This comprised some 4,600 U.S. army transportation troops who assisted in operating the Bengal and Assam Railway, and the view was expressed that an increase of as much as fifty per cent. was obtained by improved operation. A request for these railway troops was sent to the U.S.A.

Another handicap has been the shortage of locomotives in India, deliveries of which from overseas were awaited. During the period under review thirteen broad gauge "Eagle" and ninety-two metre gauge "Mikado" locomotives arrived. A number of the latter were taken into use on the Bengal and Assam Railway.

To increase the capacity of mechanical road transport, experiments and trials were successfully carried out with trailers, and it was decided to introduce these at the rate of 25 per general purpose transport company equipped with 15 cwt. trucks.

28. *Docks.*

The development of Chittagong port to meet operational needs has gone ahead. Additional moorings for deep sea ships were got from Calcutta, and most of the cranes taken from Chittagong under the denial scheme in 1942 have been replaced.

Dock labour as a whole gave little cause for anxiety, although the position at Vizagapatam for a time was not good.

A special joint investigation was held into the congestion in the Port of Calcutta. Relief measures included the provision of mobile cranes for heavy lifts, the improvement of rail facilities in depots, and the provision of tank transporters and additional motor transport for port operation.

29. *Inland Water Transport (I.W.T.).*

This service also has been handicapped by floods. Rapid erosion at several of the landing places on the Brahmaputra caused anxiety, but preventive measures succeeded in averting serious trouble.

In regard to river craft, India had requested the return from Iraq of certain river steamers which had been sent there from India earlier in the war. In addition to the arrival of these, ten paddlers, three screw steamers, and ten dumb craft were released from Iraq for use on the Brahmaputra. These craft began to reach India at the rate of two a month, the first pair arriving in October. Higgins barges also were brought into use on an increasing scale with good results.

For the transportation of oil in bulk by river, seventeen flats were converted for use as carriers on the Brahmaputra, to supplement the one solitary flat previously, available. Successful trials were carried out with "Airbags" for lifting sunken craft. An I.W.T. salvage unit was organised during the period and was equipped with a number of these bags.

30. *Supplies.*

The food scarcity in India[6] affected the supply to the Army of indigenous food-stuffs, and it was not possible to maintain reserves up to the normal level.

Early in November the situation was serious, especially in the Fourteenth Army area. Rice in particular was short, and the ration scale of rice was reduced by four ounces. This reduction was, however, replaced by an equivalent amount of other grain products. Stocks also of milk, ghee, atta, tinned vegetables and fruits, and fodder were very low. The shortage of tinned supplies was due to the difficulties in obtaining fresh supplies in the forward areas, so that more tinned substitutes had to be consumed than those for which provision had been made. The shortages of atta and ghee were due to the Food Department of the Government of India being unable to meet the Army's requirements; and that of fodder to the coal shortage, since coal is needed for baling purposes.

The supply situation in the Fourteenth Army improved latterly, but the stock position cannot return to normal until the Food Department can meet the Army's needs of atta and ghee, and until demands made to the United Kingdom for tinned supplies have been met.

Attempts to obtain by indigenous production, foodstuffs that are usually imported – *e.g.*, cheese, dehydrated vegetables, jam, etc., have not proved as successful as had been hoped. Among the causes were insufficient experience in processing, climatic conditions, lack of suitable machinery and packing material, and the difficulty of getting really suitable hygienic conditions in Indian factories.

The absence of suitable packing material in India also handicapped production of the light scale and composite rations. I therefore asked the War Office if the U.S.A. Forces "K" and "Mountain" rations could be provided for the India Command. These are extremely well packed, and are suitable for British Troops in a tropical climate. They are also suitable for air supply dropping.

In the meantime the existing special pack rations produced in India were found for various reasons to be unsatisfactory, and were revised.

The following are now prepared in this country:-

A 24 hour ration designed for assault troops and issuable up to 48 hours. Each day's ration is self-contained, in a carton, wrapped and sealed in wax proof paper.

A light scale ration designed for L.R.P troops and long distance patrols. These also are put up in daily self-contained packs.

A complete non-cooking ration with separate scales for British and Indian Troops.

31. *Remounts and Veterinary.*
A great increase in animal reinforcements was required in the cold season 1942–43 for the Eastern Army, and a heavy toll was taken by disease, especially surra.

In the period now under review, the extensive conversion of the Army in India to a mixed animal and mechanical transport basis caused a further large demand for animals. In fact by the end of the period, the number of animals in the Army in India exceeded any previously recorded figure even before mechanisation began, and it was expected, during 1944–45 to amount to some 125,000 animals. My Director of Remounts visited South Africa to contact Union Defence Force officials and the Remount Purchasing Officer there, since that country is now our main source of supply.

Imports from South Africa during the period came to 2,415 mules and 850 donkeys, while over 4,000 animals were bought in India. Arrangements were also made to import 1,500 mountain artillery mules from the U.S.A. under Lease-Lend arrangements.

During a period of twelve months in Assam and nine months in Arakan a total of 9,418 animal casualties occurred. Of these 34 per cent. returned to remount depots after treatment. The above total casualties exceeded our total purchases of mules and donkeys, etc., in South Africa for a corresponding period by 996.

The Chinese Forces in India received 422 horses, ponies and mules during the period. This made the total of animals issued to these forces 6,526, against their combined demand for 8,690.

Surra has continued in forward areas and during the period of this Despatch, in the 4th Corps area, 828 horses and mules were cured while 375 died of the disease. About a thousand were usually under treatment at any one time. Surra was also detected in Arakan in the middle of August, but only sixteen deaths occurred, while some 200 cases were generally under treatment.

32. Ordnance Services.
Advanced ordnance and ammunition depots were established at Gauhati and Kanglatongbi (near Imphal) and an advanced ammunition depot at Palel. These were in addition to the base and advanced depots already at Manipur Road. In Arakan, the existing ordnance field depot at Chittagong was expanded into advanced depots for ordnance and ammunition. Two new ordnance field depots were formed for divisions operating forward of Chittagong, and a further one at Comilla for air supply.

Ammunition laboratories and mobile ammunition inspection units were provided for both the Fourteenth Army and the Eastern Command.

Manpower in the ordnance services still remained a difficulty, and recruitment of educated types as N.C.O. clerks for office and store duties continued to be unsatisfactory.[7] Reinforcements, however, were steadily despatched to the Fourteenth Army for ordnance field units, and the strain was then eased.

33. The Electrical and Mechanical Engineers (E. & M.E.).
Generally speaking, the 1st and 2nd Echelon units of the service proved satisfactory, except the recovery company in the Light Division. For this a heavier vehicle for jeep recovery was found necessary and was provided. As regards actual 1st and 2nd Echelon repair of vehicles, this was satisfactory in so far as the supply of spare parts allowed.

A lack of 2nd Echelon wireless repair facilities was felt. This was remedied by the addition of wireless sections to each mobile workshop company in an operational formation, but in the meantime wireless repair suffered. There were no 2nd Echelon wireless repair facilities available at all; and wireless sets which could have been repaired in the field, had to be evacuated to base or command workshops for the purpose. This resulted in overloading these shops, and heavy delays in repairs. The lack of up-to-date wireless workshop sections has been due to a continued shortage of special test equipment and artificers from England.

With a view to providing some of these units India, wireless mechanics were under training in this country and the raising of nine workshop sections was commenced.

The great expansion of lines of communication continued to make heavy demands on E. & M.E. resources, principally in lines of communication recovery companies. In order to economise in mobile workshops on the lines of communication, sixteen station workshops were installed, thus releasing mobile units for the forward areas.

Road transport on the lines of communication, and in particular between Manipur Road and Imphal, continued to absorb a large amount of E. & M.E. maintenance. The thousand vehicles employed there were plying on a terrain in exacting conditions; and to a continuous "round the clock" running routine. The water-proofing of vehicles and equipment also required constant attention.

The first semi-mobile 3rd Echelon workshop to be raised in India moved to Imphal early in July. It was seriously delayed by the floods, and was not completely installed till three months later.

When the two training Divisions (14th and 39th) moved to Central Command to assume their functions,[8] the full complement of E. & M.E. divisional units accompanied them. These E. & M.E. units now take reinforcements from training centres up to fifty per cent. of their own war establishment for two months operational training before sending them forward.

ENGINEERING WORKS AND PROGRESS.

34. *Roads.*
As I have already remarked, the monsoon caused road work in certain forward areas to be limited to the repair of washouts and landslides. Very little new construction was possible while it lasted, but progress increased with the return of dry weather. When the Damodar floods seriously damaged the Grand Trunk Road, North West of Calcutta, engineer field units had to be used for the repairs, and the road was not in full service again till October. As regards the actual flood breaches on the river bank, work on these continued throughout the period and was only approaching completion at the end of it. Further projects to prevent a recurrence of the breaches were still being planned.

Efforts were made to accelerate completion of the access road from broad gauge railhead at Siliguri to the Brahmaputra ferry at Goalpara. Work on the Manipur Road base continued satisfactorily, and by October the base could be considered reasonably well provided with roads.

Satisfactory progress, however, with the roads of Nos. 3 and 4 Reserve Bases (both expanding 100 per cent.) at Panagarh and Avadi (near Madras) could not be made till the monsoon was over.

35. *Engineering Projects connected with Airfields*[9]
As in the case of roads, airfield construction was much hampered by heavy rains, and by the Damodar flood breach on the E.I. Railway. In spite of this, however, it is hoped that the bulk of the original airfield construction programme (details of which are given later under Air Administration) will be complete by the end of the year.

The prior importance early in the period of the air lift to China called for special measures to expedite the construction of the North East Assam airfields.

Considerable engineer resources were accordingly sent to this area so as to accelerate work on runways, taxi tracks and accommodation. In addition, a number of airfields had to be raised to heavy bomber standard.

Bulk petrol storage requirements at airfields also increased rapidly, and over sixty airfields required bulk storage capacity varying from 40,000 gallons to 300,000 gallons per airfield.

36. *Oil Projects.*

Most of the projects recommended by the Elderton Committee to deal with the supply of petrol, oil and lubricants (P.O.L.) in North East India, were started in the period, and by the end of it many were approaching completion.

At first, progress was poor because most of the stores which came from abroad were late in arriving, and difficulties were also experienced due to the monsoon. In particular, work was held up by the late arrival from the U.S.A. of certain essentials – particularly valves, victaulic fittings and pumping stations. These were originally promised in May, but first shipments were not received till September and October. Indeed fifty per cent. of valves and pumping stations had still not arrived by the 15th November.

Delivery of tankage to high priority airfields was however generally completed by the end of the period.

The expansion scheme of the Assam Company's oilfields at Digboi unfortunately had a series of setbacks. Instead of the hoped for increase on the previous production figure of 200,000 gallons of crude oil a day, there has been a drop to 160,000 gallons a day, and no improvement on this figure can be expected for the remainder of 1943. The reason for this was partly that existing oilwells have unexpectedly run dry, and partly that new drillings that gave promise of prolific production have, after all, proved disappointing.

A new thirty million gallon storage depot was planned near Budge Budge, and indents were placed for the necessary stores for this. It was to be the terminal for a pipe line project from Budge Budge to Dibrugarh planned by the Americans, and to be executed by them.

The production in India of containers for petrol remained disappointing throughout the period, in spite of strenuous efforts to develop local resources of this and petrol handling equipment generally. It had been estimated that production of 4 gallon drums would reach 180,000 in October, but in fact actual production was just under 44,000. Two Jerrican manufacturing plants however commenced to arrive in India and they were installed at Madras.

37. *Administrative Development in the Ceylon Army Command.*

The strength of the Ceylon Force increased slightly by some one thousand all ranks during the period under review. This, increase was distributed evenly among all arms.

A new Ceylon Signal Corps was constituted in November. Its first personnel were found by transfers of signalmen of the Ceylon Engineers.

The Ceylon Engineers were increased by the addition of a mechanical excavating company, and a motor boat company.

An extensive programe of war construction for coast defence, camps (for East African Troops and Royal Marines), installations and communications, was put in hand. A vegetable garden on a large scale was started on the uplands of Nuwara Eliya which was expected to supply most of the needs of the island.

As regards communications, it was decided to relay some sixty miles of railway line with heavier rails. When completed this was expected to relieve the shortage of light-axle load locomotives.

AIR ORGANISTATION AND ADMINISTRATION.
38. *Airfields*[10].

Up to June, 1943, the progress of airfield construction was behind schedule, and many airfields were still incomplete.

Actually, at the beginning of 1943 the main airfield construction programme in India included the building of 215 standard all-weather airfields. Some were to be "operational," *i.e.*, built to full scale with two runways and accommodation for two squadrons. Of this programme, which had initially been drawn up in March, 1942, five operational airfields were complete in all respects, and 88 had one all-weather runway ready (over 1,600 yards in length) by the end of 1942. In addition, sixty fair-weather strips or landing areas had been completed.

The increasing scale of offensive operations throughout 1943 entailed far more construction in the east than under the original plan. A number of fair-weather airfields had to be prepared in forward areas, with limited shelter type accommodation and tentage, and the decision to operate throughout the monsoon made it necessary to develop some of these as all-weather airfields with increased accommodation and accessories. A number of airfields was also completed in North East Assam to handle supplies to China, or on the supply route from the West for the same purpose. Moreover, in the same area certain airfields were developed from which the U.S. Air Forces could operate heavy bombers or defensive fighters.

In addition, the maintenance and reinforcing of the U.S. Army Air Force squadrons in Assam involved further construction in the southern, western and central areas. By November, 1943, a total of 34 all-weather airfields, and 11 fair-weather strips had been handed over to the U.S.A.A.F. Facilities were also given to them in certain other R.A.F. airfields.

In March, 1942, there were only 16 airfields possessing all-weather runways, of which four only were operational by modern standards. There were also twenty fair-weather strips. By November, 1943, there were 285 airfields completed and 15 under construction. Of this total, no less than 140 were complete in all respects, while 64 airfields had one all-weather runway ready, and a further 71 had fair-weather strips or landing areas, and were equipped in varying degrees with dispersal facilities and domestic and technical accommodation.

There have been great difficulties in the execution of this programme which has cost about fifteen million pounds. There has been a shortage of suitable constructional equipment and supervisory staff. Much of the work carried out by civilian contractors has not been satisfactory, and in all areas there has been delay due to bad communications or inadequate control. In the Punjab and United Provinces the Provincial Governments have given great assistance. In Eastern India, where the need was greatest, there has been less enterprise and efficiency. The fact remains, however, that the Air Forces in India can now expand rapidly with the sure confidence that there are suitable bases from which to operate. A tribute is due to the many military and civil engineers whose devoted work has made this possible.

39. *Manpower in the Royal Air Force.*
Perhaps the greatest problem in the expansion of the Air Forces in this Command has been caused by the acute shortage of suitable manpower. Other theatres of war, whose more imperative needs have quite rightly been given priority, appear to have exhausted the available manpower in the United Kingdom, with the result that this Command has often seemed to be situated at the end of a badly leaking pipe-line. To combat this difficulty, the substitution scheme, whereby local manpower is recruited and trained to fill existing vacancies in R.A.F. non-operational units, was decided upon at the end of 1942, and put into practice during the first half of 1943.

The output of trained manpower under this scheme was not adequate, however, to meet the demand caused by the expansion of the Air Command. As a result we had to subsist mainly on whatever drafts became available from time to time from the United Kingdom or other Commands.

An important and complicating factor in this situation was the increased variety of aircraft operating from India, and the consequent multiplication of requirements of the different categories of aircrew trained for each type. As advanced aircrew training facilities were strictly limited in the Command, the main solution to this problem consisted in placing more accurate and detailed demands on the Air Ministry for the personnel required. At the same time training facilities were developed and utilised to the maximum extent for converting surplus aircrews from one type of aircraft to another.

Ultimately, as a result of the manpower shortage throughout the R.A.F., an establishment ceiling was imposed on the Air Command in India. This ceiling limited the personnel expansion of the Command to a total of approximately 90,000 R.A.F. and 10,000 I.A.F. personnel to meet a target of 73 squadrons. Any personnel recruited into the I.A.F. however, under the substitution scheme would not be counted against this ceiling. A target of 140 squadrons will become operative after Germany has been defeated and personnel become available again from the west.

Actually the figures of air manpower for July and November, 1943, were as follows, but these contained deficiencies among some classes of personnel and surpluses among others which could not be adjusted by interchange, without training afresh:-

	July 1943	November 1943
R.A.F. Officers aircrew	1,718	1,851
R.A.F. Officers ground	3,250	4,314
I.A.F. Officers aircrew	320	432
I.A.F. Officers ground	453	694
B.O.Rs. aircrew	2,290	3,621
B.O.Rs. ground	61,005	74,929
I.O.Rs. ground	4,894	8,072
Enrolled followers	9,142	10,338
Temporary followers	7,202	11,410
Non-Combatant Service personnel	1,266	1,345
W.A.C.(I)s	1,060	1,346
Civilians	1,142	1,600
Total	93,742	119,952

The position now is that the manpower ceiling has almost been reached as regards R.A.F. personnel, and the provision for future expansion in this Command, the necessity for which no one can doubt, is a problem still to be solved.

That the W.A.A.F. should be brought to the rescue was an idea that did not come to fruit on within the period of this Despatch.

40. *The Indian Air Force (I.A.F.).*
Previous Despatches from the India Command have not so far dealt specifically with developments in this Service, and a stage has now been reached when a review of it is opportune.

The Indian Air Force has now almost reached the peace time strength of the Royal Air Force ten or eleven years ago. Numerous facilities for technical and flying training have been thrown open to the youth of the country who, as regards technical training, have realised the value of what was being offered to them and responded accordingly.

The process of expansion, however, has been so rapid that many difficulties have arisen.

The Indian Air Force is at the moment completely Indian, with the exception of a limited number of R.A.F. N.C.Os. No European can hold a commission in the Indian Air Force, which differs in this respect from the Royal Indian Navy and the Indian Army. Up till the beginning of 1942, R.A.F. officers did in fact command I.A.F. units without, however, being specifically commissioned in the I.A.F. After the success of No. 1 Squadron in the Burma campaign, policy was changed and since that date only one Royal Air Force officer (for a brief period of two or three months) has commanded an I.A.F. Squadron. It will be seen then, that as far as possible, the Indian Air Force as a service has been kept Indian.

In regard to efficiency, however, the I.A.F. up to November, 1943, had hardly succeeded as well as its first Squadron did in Burma. Owing to the rapid expansion of the Service since the outbreak of the War there is a definite lack of officers suitable for important commands. At the moment it depends almost entirely for its leadership on the limited number of officers who in pre-war days were trained at Cranwell. The intake of officers since war broke out has been large, and their training necessarily has been far less thorough than that given at Cranwell.

It is early yet to form any idea as to whether and to what extent the I.A.F. should be assisted by a cadre of R.A.F. personnel. Several completely Indian Squadrons will shortly go into action. If these acquit themselves well, their success will obviously reduce the number of R.A.F. personnel necessary to give assistance. It may, however, be necessary later to increase the R.A.F. element in I.A.F. Squadrons.

With regard to the recruiting of Indian manpower for the I.A.F. the rate of intake of the previous six months was maintained.

The rate of intake, although it only amounted to 60 per cent. of the target, was still six times greater than the 1942 average, and recruiting in fact has been successful beyond what was expected.

The recruitment of airmen with the ultimate object of finding suitable material as officers, presented some difficulty. Those few I.A.T.C. cadets who were keen to become pilots were not willing to enter the ranks and take their chance of being subsequently selected for pilot training, when they could probably obtain direct commissions in the Army or the Royal Indian Navy. The policy of commissioning from the ranks was vigorously pursued, but few of the men selected were good officer material, and fewer succeeded in completing their training as pilots. After the success of the campaign for technicians, however, an aircrew publicity campaign was launched, stressing the adventurous aspects of flying. Experienced officers were detailed to tour India, with the result that a list of over 400 candidates was obtained for interviews by the Officers' Selection Board.

Moreover the Air Training Corps, which is already functioning in six universities and is due to begin shortly in two others, has now been converted to an organisation for the production of general duties officers. On the other hand the number of recruits required to keep up the ten I.A.F. squadrons has increased, and there has also been an increase in training wastage. It is not, therefore, certain as yet that an adequate flow of recruits will be maintained.

With the above manpower difficulties and complications it was not surprising that the original target of ten squadrons for the I.A.F. had not been achieved by the end of 1943. Eight were ready and two were forming. All ten should be operational by the end of 1944.

Future policy regarding the I.A.F. is not clear-cut though it has been laid down in principle.

Since pilots are scarce, and R.A.F. crews are already employed in I.A.F. squadrons, it is not intended to form further I.A.F. squadrons for some time. The future in peace time of the I.A.F. will best be served by making these squadrons as efficient as possible, and for this purpose the pilots trained under the Empire

Training Scheme, many of whom will gain operational experience in Fighter Command at home, and certain I.A.F. officers who will have gained similar experience by posting on an 'exchange' basis to Royal Air Force fighter squadrons in India, will prove extremely useful.

The next stage in the I.A.F. expansion desired by the Indian Government is the building of I.A.F. maintenance, training and administrative units appropriate to the firstline strength. It would be possible to work in this direction by increasing the Indian element in certain agreed units suitable to the purpose, but no final commitments have been entered into as yet.

41. *I.A.F. Training.*

The actual training of officers and airmen of the I.A.F. has presented difficulties owing to the almost complete absence of R.A.F. officers with a knowledge of India, the general shortage of instructional staff, and inevitable delays over building projects. Elementary and service training for I.A.F. pilots have indeed been carried out, but the wastage rate was alarmingly high, often amounting to over sixty per cent. During the period under review, thirty-seven pilots left for Canada under the Empire Air Training Scheme after completion of their elementary training, and thirty-two successfully passed out of the Service Flying Training School.

Another problem has been the expansion of the ground training establishments. A second recruits training centre for these has been opened in South India, and six new schools of technical training began to function during the period. In addition a third signals school and a second radar school have been opened, and the non-technical training centre at Secunderabad has been expanded.

When the South East Asia Command came into being in November, 1943, and with it the Air Command South East Asia, a separate India Command for the Air (Air H.Q. India) was formed. Into this was merged the Inspectorate General of the I.A.F., a staff that had previously functioned in an advisory capacity in regard to the Indian Air Force.

With the above reorganisation, Air Headquarters, India will be responsible for the control and development of the I.A.F. generally, and for all operations on the North West Frontier. Since 1941, these have in fact been purely I.A.F. commitments. The formation of this new Command will undoubtedly contribute much to the development and efficiency of an Integrated Indian Air Force.

42. *Aircraft Maintenance, Repair and Supply.*

In the process of building up an organisation for these services, the handicaps imposed by India's limited capacity in certain directions must be understood before the nature of the task can be appreciated.

Elsewhere in this Despatch India's shortcomings as a potential base for large scale military operations has been mentioned [11]. The picture from the point of view of aircraft maintenance, repair and supply is as follows.

India is not highly industrialised but has immense natural resources which are only on the threshold of development. Unskilled civilian labour is almost unlimited; there are a few semi-skilled, but practically no skilled, industrial technicians. The use of the available civilian manpower is thus limited, and a heavy load is thrown on service personnel. Even these latter, who form the backbone of the repair organisation, are not skilled technicians as the term is understood in England. The small nucleus of highly trained R.A.F. personnel from which the service has expanded during this war were never accustomed to mass production methods, even on the minor scale which has so far been brought into use in this country. The custom in the United Kingdom that major repairs are undertaken by the makers' working party or returned to the factory cannot apply to this Command. Geographical factors have also complicated the building-up of an efficient repair and supply system. The position in the country of the limited industrial facilities has largely dictated the location of base repair units both civilian and R.A.F., and inevitably long distances separate such units from the squadrons they serve. The over-burdened road, rail and water transport services of India impose heavy delays in transit. Thus, while in a country with good lines of communication a major repair may average a month to six weeks to complete, quite frequently this period elapses in India before the damaged aircraft even arrives at its base repair unit. Climatic conditions affect both material and men, the former by deterioration and corrosion, and the latter by exhaustion.

The "man-hour" depreciates in value some 25 per cent during the hot weather and the monsoon period. Moreover the actual work has frequently been held up for lack of spares and tools. The sinking of one or two ships can, and has, seriously upset the even flow of repair. In November there did not exist in the whole Air Command a single complete base repair kit. Shortage of spares has also led to cannabalisation[12] which, though wasteful, is inevitable.

These difficulties have necessitated an organisation of repair and maintenance units in depth, of which the base units comprise the R.A.F. and I.A.F. maintenance units at Karachi, Ambala, Lahore and Cawnpore, and the civilian maintenance units at Kanchrapara, Trichinopoly, Cawnpore, Barrackpore, Dum Dum, Calcutta and Poona.

The civilian units were organised under the Aeronautical Division of the Department of Supply, which came into being early in 1943, and developed in October into the Directorate General of Aircraft.

During the year, the field maintenance capacity was approximately doubled. The base repair load increased from 42 squadrons and 400 non-operational aircraft to over 60 squadrons and 500 non-operational aircraft. In June 1943, the remarkable totals of 314 air-frames and 210 engines were repaired. This June peak figure was the joint result of a swift expansion of repair capacity, and the culmination of a strenuous campaign for spares carried on both with the United Kingdom and U.S.A. It proved impossible to sustain this level of repair output when the spares position once more deteriorated. The figure fell in October to some 130 airframes and 210 engines. Nevertheless, the outlook is hopeful, for the three Tala civilian maintenance units at Barrackpore, Dum Dum and Poona, and the enormous R.A.F. depot at Cawnpore, have barely commenced production.

43. *Aircraft erection and storage, and the Provision of spares.*
Of the 1,750 aircraft erected in India during the year, 1,120 were assembled between June and November, in a steadily increasing flow. Two units were responsible for the work which was carried on with admirable success in spite of many difficulties. Among these latter may be mentioned aircraft arriving in a badly corroded state through lying for months on wharves, etc.; irregular inflow, the result of shipping vagaries (e.g., when the change from the Cape route to the Mediterranean took place two consignments sent at different times arrived together); and climatic handicaps owing to the unavoidable parking of aircraft in the open. In this connection temperatures up to 170° F. were recorded in the cockpits of aircraft being serviced. Under such conditions the handling of metal parts became a matter of some difficulty.

The aircraft storage programme fluctuated considerably. At the beginning of the year reserves were scarce and the flow through the erection units was rapid. During the monsoon, the aircraft storage units began to build up a larger holding. The total output for the (previous) seven months from December 1942 to June 1943 amounted to 650 aircraft. For the five months from July to November 1943 the total output was 810 aircraft, the monthly figure jumping from 116 aircraft during August to 265 aircraft in October. This total did not merely entail normal routine upkeep services in respect of aircraft held; a very large number of modifications were also continually being carried out.

Almost throughout the first four years of war, the India Command's priority for equipment has been low. Inadequate stocks over most of the ranges of equipment have had a direct bearing on the output from repair units. Tools, certain types of engine spares, dopes, American spares and ground equipment, marine craft spares and practically all items of ordnance supply were short. M.T. spares and domestic and barrack equipment were practically unobtainable. Thus in November there were over 160,000 demands which had not been met.

Although after August a slight improvement appeared, the situation continued poor owing to the demand for spares continuing to increase.

44. *Maintenance and Repair of M.T. Vehicles and Marine Craft of the R.A.F. and I.A.F.*
The administrative difficulties peculiar to the maintenance and repair of aircraft in this Command apply equally in the case of M.T. and marine craft of the Air Forces but in general the problems have not proved so formidable. West of Calcutta (by using the available civilian capacity), it has been possible to decentralise the repair of M.T. to the main towns. East of Calcutta, mobile repair units, known as M.T. Light Repair Depots have been formed and operate as a part of the field maintenance organisation.

The formation of this completely new organisation has been necessary now that the second and third line maintenance of Air Force vehicles has become too large a responsibility for the Army who formerly undertook this task.

As regards marine craft, prior to this period no arrangements existed to deal with their maintenance and repair. Since then, however, contact has been established with the Directorate General of Shipbuilding and Repair, and the naval authorities, and satisfactory arrangements have been made.

45. *Research and Development Work for the Air Forces.*
Research and development work for the Air Forces is now carried out in Air Headquarters, India Command; at the Scientific Industrial Research Laboratories, Delhi, and at the ordnance laboratories, Cawnpore. These bodies deal also with the problem of indigenous manufacture. In addition, research work is carried out at Bangalore for electrical and radar development, at Chaklala for airborne forces, and again at Cawnpore for armament modifications.

Among the achievements of the Research and Development Section of the Air Forces in this Command are:-

The development of new parachute material which has eased the production problem and improved the performance of the supply-dropping parachute.
The production of a new type of supply dropping container.
A roller conveyor for use in supply dropping operations.
An enlarger for microgram negatives.
Substitute proofing lacquer for carburettor floats.
A substitute for duplicator stencils.
Satisfactory aircraft dopes which can be manufactured indigenously.
The manufacture of petrol-resisting tubing in this country which has now been developed to a point where the product is little inferior to that produced in the United Kingdom.
The production of various types of jettison tanks, including one design which utilises locally produced jute and shellac.

In addition the more important India Command Modifications which have been prototyped are:-

Self-sealing long-range tanks inside the wings of Hurricanes Mark IID and IV.
The redesigning of the fuel system on the Vengeance aircraft, and provision for them of jettison tanks.
A bomb-cum-jettison tank modification for Hurricane aircraft.
Compregnated wooden blades for fitting to a propeller.
Certain modifications to Dakota aircraft.
Modifications to the Spitfire VIII pressurised fuel system.

46. *Administrative Development in various Ancillary Services of the Air Forces.*
The Balloon Branch, the Air Sea Rescue, the Meteorological Service and the Flying Control Organisation have all expanded and made important progress. The operational work of the first three has already been referred to above.[13]

All were handicapped in their development by lack of equipment, shortage of personnel and absence of training facilities, while in the Meteorological Service the issue was complicated by the existence already of separate Civil and U.S.A.A.F. organisations working in the same sphere.

THE PROBLEM OF THE MEDICAL SERVICES IN NORTH-EAST INDIA.

47. *General.*

The period covers the annual malarial season, and was therefore one of anxiety. The sick rates as a whole were consistently high. They varied from a maximum of fifty per thousand per week from all causes for British troops in July, to twenty-five per thousand per week for Indian troops – the lowest figure recorded for fighting personnel during the period.

There was no remarkable rise in the autumn rates – indeed for a time in August, when sickness is usually expected to increase, a general fall in the sick rate took place. This was probably due to the widespread and thorough anti-malarial measures that had been in progress since the previous year. At the same time active operations during the period were on a small scale. The worst exposure to infection therefore (i.e., that occasioned by lack of opportunity to take precautions against malaria and other diseases), affected very few.

On balance, taking into account both the encouraging aspects of the problem, and the absence of land operations, sickness remained high, and it must be expected to be high in the future in the operational areas of North-East India and Burma.

48. *Food in relation to Health.*

Elsewhere in this Despatch under the heading of "Supplies" I have mentioned[14] the shortages in India of various foodstuffs. This had a medical aspect at times, in relation to the health of the troops.

Fresh meat was not available in forward areas for Indian Troops, and dehydrated meat could not be provided in any quantity.

For the British Troops in Assam fresh meat could only be issued approximately on one day in each week. Fresh fruit and vegetables were not available for troops in Assam or forward troops in Arakan. Tinned milk (the only logical substitute for meat for Indian troops) was short. Certain important items of diet could not be supplied to hospitals – e.g., chickens or eggs.

The position however, was improving, particularly as regards hospitals, at the end of the period.

49. *Malaria and anti-malarial Measures.*

Our measures achieved over all a great deal of success.

In regard to the anti-malarial engineering projects at such hyperendemic localities as the Manipur Road base and the camp sites on the Tamu and Tiddim roads, an anti-malarially controlled or protected area was set out. In this area the daily sick rate was reduced frequently to two per thousand per day. In certain units partially protected, but outside the controlled area, it has been seven per thousand per day. Outside the controlled area, the sick have been twelve to fifteen per thousand per day. Another major anti-malarial measure which has proved effective was the establishment of controlled malaria harbours along lines of communications at distances suitable to troop movements. In addition, all main routes on the lines of communication in Assam and East Bengal were surveyed, and route maps giving details of malarial incidence were prepared.

Two anti-malarial engineering units were raised; one for the 4th Corps Area and one for Arakan. They are field companies of engineers specially trained in anti-malarial measures, and suitable for undertaking the whole of a large sector of line of communication, or any other comprehensive block of work.

Anti-malarial units of the normal type increased during the period, till the whole Eastern Army Area was adequately served.

Labour for these units was however a difficulty and anti-malarial works had to compete with other demands for labour, of which there was never sufficient for all needs on the lines of communication.

Suppressive treatment for malaria with mepacrine continued to be very effective, but the quantities of the drug involved have been enormous, and at times there was an anxiety as to the supply.

50. *Other Diseases.*

Dysentery, though not extensive, increased during June and July but abated later. The 4th Corps area produced a markedly greater number of cases than Arakan, and the rate among British Troops was much higher than among Indians (treble).

Venereal disease constituted a serious problem. The main sources of infection were in the larger towns, but there was also widespread risk of infection in Assam and Manipur. The Adviser in Venereal Disease instituted a comprehensive campaign against the evil in Calcutta and elsewhere.

Cholera and small-pox have been epidemic in some localities and mass inoculations and vaccinations were carried out. The danger was increased by the widespread famine in Bengal; and in Calcutta an epidemic of cholera has raged among the civilian population throughout the period of this Despatch.

Some sporadic cases of tropical typhus also occurred, causing a number of casualties in one British infantry battalion. This became the subject of investigation and research.

51. *Hospital Development.*

There has been a steady improvement in the condition of all hospitals in North East India. This improvement has been very greatly assisted by the reduction in the number of admissions; so that hospitals have been able to receive, hold and treat patients. Moreover, two-thirds of the hospitals and other medical installations in North East India have been moved east of the Brahmaputra, and this has facilitated the early return of recovered personnel to forward reinforcement camps.

52. *Medical Commitments outside the Military Sphere.*
The influx of large bodies of labourers into very malarious areas inaccessible to ordinary transport necessitated sending additional medical units (including hygiene and anti-malarial sections) to look after them.

Although technically medical arrangements for civil labour are a civil responsibility, in practice especially in forward operational zones, military medical resources had to take over. Indeed, with the great increases in Civil Transport Corps and road-making labour, the problem became serious, and a military medical supervisory chain of officers had to be provided for each of the areas where large numbers of civil labourers were employed.

53. *Evacuation.*
The reduction in evacuations, resulting from the forward-holding policy, greatly eased this problem. An improvement in the accommodation in river hospital steamers also occurred with the provision of suitable fittings.

In Arakan, however, under monsoon conditions the difficulties were great, and caused some unavoidable suffering to patients. The road was closed in the Ramu – Dohazari sector for nearly two months, and the Tambru – Ramu Road, though open, became so bad that serious cases could hardly be sent along it at all.

Conditions for evacuation by sea from Cox's Bazar were also bad. Returning mail and transport vessels were used, but had no accommodation for stretcher cases. Ultimately, one vessel "Nalchera" was allotted entirely for medical use, and was converted into a coastal hospital carrier for fifty lying and seventy sitting cases.

Two other hospital ships in use were the "Wu Sueh" and "Melchior Trueb". The former was unsatisfactory in river evacuation, and had to be fitted with improved cooling plants. The latter was converted during the period into a satisfactory ocean-going hospital carrier with accommodation for two hundred and ninety-four patients.

54. *Training of Medical Personnel.*
This has progressed in spite of difficulties such as low standard of recruits, differences of language, lack of trained instructors, and little time for training.

A medical school of jungle warfare was started in the 26th Division Area (Arakan) in July, which was attended by selected officers from all Divisions in North East India.

55. *Medical Stores.*
During the period, the situation as regards medical stores improved, but there have been temporary shortages at times, of supplies of Mepacrine and Pamoquin (for malaria). Except for this there were no difficulties other than those connected with certain known items of which there is a world shortage.

56. *Incidental Medical Matters.*
Pathology assumes importance when the bulk of sick are suffering from malaria, dysentery or venereal disease, and progress was made in the provision of laboratories and clinical slide-rooms.

Dental facilities improved in all areas, and men were no longer evacuated unnecessarily for dental treatment.

A Facio-Maxillary unit was opened in Calcutta where cases of grave head injuries can receive adequate treatment.

Arrangements for dealing with mental cases also were developed by the formation of a definite network of centres and subsidiary centres in North East India. This will prevent temporary cases being evacuated.

Diversional therapy also received attention, and a Red Cross Diversional Therapy Service has been formed which will extend over the whole of North East India. It should be particularly welcome in forward hospitals where amenities are scarce. In this as in other directions where the Red Cross has extended its invaluable help, our indebtedness to this organisation has continued to be great. I wish to record my gratitude for the assistance it has given.

57. *Welfare among Troops and Families in the India Command.*
With the great increase in the numbers of British personnel in India that took place since the beginning of 1943 their welfare became a matter of increasing concern. It has an obvious bearing on morale, and in this is linked with the soldier's outlook for the future.

Living in a tropical climate under conditions devoid of most ordinary comforts and unable to buy in the ordinary market many of the commodities that make up the every day needs of the civilised mortal, large numbers of British soldiers have had to work under lonely or depressing surroundings in back areas, and without the stimulus of contact with the enemy. It is for these, just as much as for the men in forward zones, that welfare work is of importance, and it has been carried on ceaselessly in spite of many and varied difficulties and handicaps.

One of the difficulties has always been a lack of buildings suitable for welfare activities, and welfare funds were very largely expended in providing them.

A great deal has been done by enthusiastic officers in the field, particularly in the forward areas of Eastern India. The work of the army welfare officers has been supplemented by the efforts of Toc H, the Y.M.C.A., and the Women's Voluntary Services, which have opened many new institutes and canteens in spite of difficulties in obtaining sufficient staff to serve the troops on as wide a scale as is necessary in a country of such vast distances and such difficult climatic conditions, and so undeveloped according to western standards.

In August, 1943, it was possible to appoint welfare officers to all the major areas of the Eastern Army, thus relieving the strain on the few officers who had hitherto borne the whole burden.

Funds were provided for welfare on a per capita basis, but how best to use these funds is ultimately a problem for the unit to decide – a problem which has never been easy in the jungle areas and under the monsoon conditions in which the Eastern Army had to live and fight. In response to requests from units, however, large quantities of books, games, sports gear, gramophones, etc., for both British and Indian Troops were sent out from the Eastern Army amenities depot in

Calcutta. As the volume of the supplies increased it was found necessary to establish two sub-depots to facilitate distribution further forward, and these were accordingly set up at Gauhati and Chittagong.

Supplies of such things as those mentioned above have been generally plentiful, with one major exception. There have never been enough mobile cinema units available in India, and despite persistent efforts to obtain more of them, there are still far too few to cope with the numbers of troops they have to serve. Eastern Army was allotted the major share of those available, but the fact remains that the provision of more projectors and more up-to-date films is a matter of paramount importance and urgency. Entertainment was provided by touring British and Indian concert parties, some organised by G.H.Q. and the rest by the Bengal Entertainment for the Services Association (B.E.S.A.).

Officers were not forgotten, and H.E. the Viceroy generously contributed large sums of money from his War Purposes Fund for the equipping of leave hostels and the subsidization of hotels and the foundation of clubs in Chittagong, Comilla and Gauhati.

The important subject of family welfare, on the British side, was dealt with by the S.S.A.F.A. sub-office set up in Calcutta, and this was followed in July, 1943, by the establishment of a Legal Aid Section which by the end of October had already dealt with 160 applications for legal advice and assistance.

On the Indian side the concern of the fighting man has been the welfare of his family. As the economic situation in India deteriorated and the cost of living rose, the allotments made by serving Indians to their families began to lose their value. At the same time the rise in prices made the cultivator comparatively affluent by comparison with the fighting man. The problem which arose as a result of these conditions was under consideration at the close of the period, and revised rates of pay and allowances were subsequently announced for the Indian soldier.

As regards the personal welfare of the serving Indian, this presents perhaps a lesser problem in that the conditions of life were mainly those to which he is to a great extent accustomed. He benefited, however, in due proportion in the allotment of funds and in the amenities provided in war areas. The welfare of the Indian fighting man will present an ever-growing problem as he becomes accustomed to a higher standard of living.

58. *Welfare in the Air Forces.*

The welfare of Air Force personnel was organised separately, and presented many difficulties in view of the dispersion of detachments and their location in so many inaccessible places. The problem, however, was energetically tackled, and much was done to improve the lot of officers and men. In this work the R.A.F. chaplains of the various denominations gave much assistance, and toured their enormous parishes indefatigably.

In one direction the Air Forces had a great advantage over the other services, and that was in having its own postal service. This more than any other item had a beneficial effect on morale. It dealt with all R.A.F. mails, official and private, inland and foreign, and handled upwards of a million items weekly.

By comparison, the postal communications with the United Kingdom available to the other services, particularly the restricted issue of air letter cards, were a continual source of complaint. Some improvement was made later.

59. *The Canteen Services.*
Apart from the service that they render in areas where actual operations are in progress, the canteens now fill a vital need for military personnel all over the country.

The N.A.A.F.I. does not function in the India Command and the whole weight of the burden has fallen on the Canteen Services (India). This body has built up an organisation to undertake the importation into or purchase, and even in some cases the manufacture in India, of the commodities required. They have also organised storage accommodation, and they carry out the retail work to the troops through the medium of Indian contractors.

Previous Despatches have not so far referred to the work of the canteens. Indeed, it was not till the period now under report that for the reasons indicated above, their activities began to bulk largely. The following review is therefore opportune, and gives some indication of what has been achieved.

In order to appreciate the activities and expansion of the canteens, it is necessary to trace their progress from the inception of the Canteen Services (India) in July, 1942.

Prior to this there was a small body known as the Canteen Contractors Syndicate, who, working under the Q.M.G., organised an approved number of contractors to serve units and formations. The syndicate also had a small organisation for importing commodities which were otherwise unobtainable; or where to import them was profitable by comparison with purchasing in the country. This was, however, only on a limited scale sufficient for the needs of British Troops and Airmen in India at that time.

The following figures give some idea of the expansion that has been necessary:-

The sales for August, 1942 (the first month, of working by the Canteen Services (India)), were Rs. 1,421,696. For June, 1943, they were Rs. 7,100,000, and for November, 1943, at the end of the period of this Despatch, they mounted to Rs. 11,500,000 or about £800,000.

Similarly in regard to warehouses. When the Canteen Services (India) came into existence, there were wholesale warehouses at five large centres including the chief ports. By November, 1943, double this number had been established.

Moreover great development occurred in subsidiary organisations under the Canteen Services (India), and the following came into being during the same period, none of which existed when the Canteen Services (India) were started:-

Canteen Services Personnel Depot, Baroda   1
Base Canteen Depots   4

Advance Base Canteen Depots	7
Canteen Bulk Issue Depots	38
Independent Retail Shops	78
Transhipment Sections	3
Mobile Canteens	17
Tea and Supper Bars	40
Mineral Water Sections	20

It was decided, in agreement with the Secretary of State for India, that the Canteen Services (India) should place its orders direct on all sources of supply with the exception of North America. Indents on the latter would be sent to the Secretary of State for India, who would arrange to procure the supplies required.

As this arrangement was, however, not found wholly satisfactory, an officer representative of the Canteen Services (India) was sent to join the India Supply Mission at Washington, and thereafter indents were sent direct to that body. The latter procured the goods, keeping in touch with the Secretary of State for India, and (in the case of Lease-Lend articles) with the British Ministry of Food also. This system has been working smoothly.

As regards the manufacturing enterprise that has been undertaken by the Canteen Services (India), the following goods have been produced from a factory organised in India:-

Mango Chutney, Cornflour, Custard Powder, Flavouring Essences, Jelly Crystals, Black and White Pepper, Squashes and Cordials, Minolene, Egg Sub-stitute, and Baking Powder.

In addition efforts have been made to augment the supply of alcoholic bever-ages by indigenous production. This applied in particular to beer, of which the supply in India during the present war has always been very much less than the demand.

CONCLUSION.

60. This Despatch has carried the narrative of events in the India Command up to the point when this ceased to be an operational headquarters for the purpose of conducting the War against Japan in this theatre.

The Despatches of my predecessor coupled with this record have told the story of an up-hill struggle. That struggle has been not only against an enemy who attacked us with the advantages of long preparation and special training, but against all the difficulties of staging a campaign on the Eastern Frontier of India.

It has also involved the commencement of the gigantic work of converting India itself into a base, adequate for such a campaign. It is perhaps fitting therefore that this concluding narrative of a series dealing with a somewhat bleak period, should have more to say about the building up of our resources and making our prep-aration in this theatre, than about actual fighting against the enemy.

We have learnt enough about fighting the Japanese to realise that intense prep-aration not only in resources and paraphernalia of war on land, sea and in the air, but in training our men to counter Japanese methods of warfare, are necessary if success is to be assured. Indeed, in this theatre our men have to acquire an almost entirely fresh technique in the tactics and stratagems of jungle warfare. Only thus can they gain complete confidence of being able to beat the Japanese at his own game, and so gain the moral ascendancy over him essential to final success.

Our efforts to organise, equip and train ourselves to this end, with a full realisation of the magnitude of the task ahead, have been indicated in the above review of the monsoon period of 1943. Much remains to be done, but the extent of the progress made and the success already achieved are promising for the future.

The continuance of peaceful conditions both internally and on the North-West Frontier, and the failure of Japanese efforts, to incite subversive elements, and to cause unrest in India by propaganda or through agents, are satisfactory features of the period. The continued flow of recruits for the Indian Services, though slightly reduced in volume, is also reassuring, and indeed remarkable, when it is remembered that every man who joins the fighting forces is a volunteer.

In one direction the period has shown a marked change in our favour. That is in the air. The details recorded of the build-up not only of strength and efficiency of aircraft and aircrews, but of the great and varied supporting organisations behind them, constitute an achievement of the first magnitude. Little less noteworthy was continued successful pursuance of our air offensive over Burma in spite of the monsoon, while the Japanese air effort practically ceased during that period.

Yet another feature of major significance and a milestone in the progress of the air effort in this theatre has been the integration (brought about with the inception of the South-East Asia Command) of the British and American Air Forces in India. With the successful model of the combined Air Forces in the North African and subsequent campaigns, plans are being laid to make the integration in this theatre so effective that it will become a single striking force under unified control. Similar unified subordinate commands will operate the various branches, *viz.* – strategical airforces, tactical airforces, supply dropping and airborne forces, and photographic reconnaissance.

This re-organisation will be no longer my responsibility; but in so far as I can assist with the development of resources and installations in back areas, and the provision and maintenance of efficient communications and supplies, these matters will be my constant concern.

The Indian Air Force which remains my responsibility (except for those squadrons actually operating against the Japanese) is still in its childhood. It is too early yet to try to foretell on what lines it will be organised, or how it will be officered; but it can only be to its advantage that in its early years its growth was amid the storms of war, rather than in the sheltered atmosphere of peace.

61. I have already submitted a list of the names of those officers and men whom I consider deserving of mention and reward for the services they have rendered during the period covered by this Despatch.

I wish, however, to record my special appreciation of and gratitude for the work done by the following officers:-

Air Chief Marshal Sir Richard Peirse, K.C.B., D.S.O., A.F.C., Air Officer Commanding-in-Chief.
Vice-Admiral Sir Herbert FitzHerbert, K.C.I.E., C.B., C.M.G., Flag Officer Commanding Royal Indian Navy.
General Sir George J. Giffard, K.C.B., D.S.O., G.O.C.-in-C., 11th Army Group (later ALFSEA).
General H. Finnis, C.B., M.C., G.O.C.- in-C., North-Western Army.
Lieut.-General A.G.O.M. Mayne, C.B., C.B.E., D.S.O., G.O.C.-in-C., Eastern Command.
Lieut.-General Sir Noel M. de la P. Beresford Peirse, K.B.E., C.B., D.S.O., G.O.C.- in-C., Southern Army.
Lieut-General W.J. Slim, C.B., C.B.E., D.S.O., M.C., G.O.C.-in-C., Fourteenth Army.
Lieut.-General H.B.D. Willcox, C.B., D.S.O., M.C., G.O.C.-in-C., Central Command.
Lieut.-General E.L. Morris, C.B., O.B.E., M.C., Chief of the General Staff.
Lieut.-General Sir C.A. Bird, K.C.I.E., C.B., D.S.O., Master General of Ordnance in India.
Lieut.-General G. Wilson, C.B.E., M.C., M.B., Director of Medical Services in India.

62. I also wish to acknowledge the debt I owe to H.E. The Marquess of Linlithgow, Viceroy and Governor-General of India, for the unfailing support which I have had from him on all occasions of doubt or difficulty.

His wise counsel based on his unrivalled knowledge of the strategy and politics of Asia has been invaluable to me.

Notes
 1. *See* also paragraph 20 below which gives details supply dropping carried out by the R.A.F.
 2. *See* Part I, paragraph 6.
 3. *See* also paragraphs 18 and 19 below under 'Combined Operations, India.'
 4. *See* under the general head of 'Training' above regarding collective training of amphibious formations in both combined operations and jungle warfare.
 5. *See* also paragraph 27 below under 'Transportation Road and Rail.'
 6. *See* also Part II, paragraph 32, The Economic Emergency.
 7. *See* also paragraph 25 above under 'Manpower'.
 8. *See* also paragraph 15 above under 'Training'.
 9. *See* also paragraph 38 below under 'Air Organisation and administration'.
10. *See* paragraph 35 above under 'Engineering'.
11. *See* above Part III, paragraph 20 *et seq.*
12. Breaking up of aircraft to provide spares for other aircraft.
13. *See* Part II paragraphs 14 to 25.
14. *See* Part II, paragraph 32 under 'Economic Emergency and Famine in Bengal'.

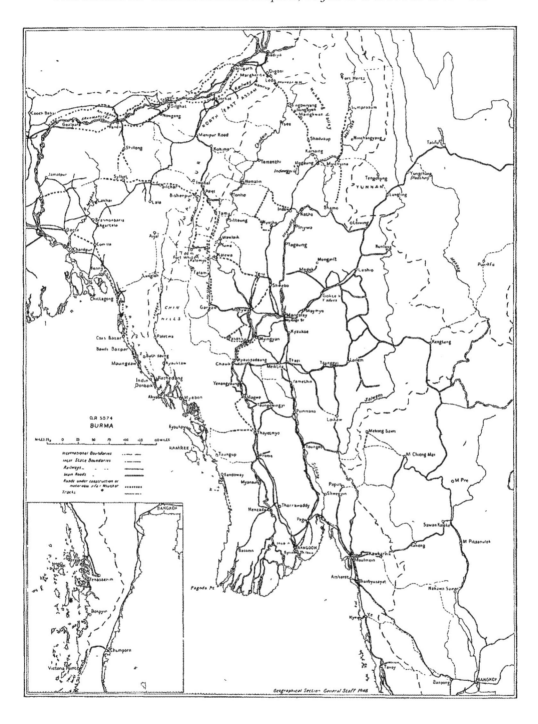

Q.R 5574
BURMA

Geographical Section General Staff 1948

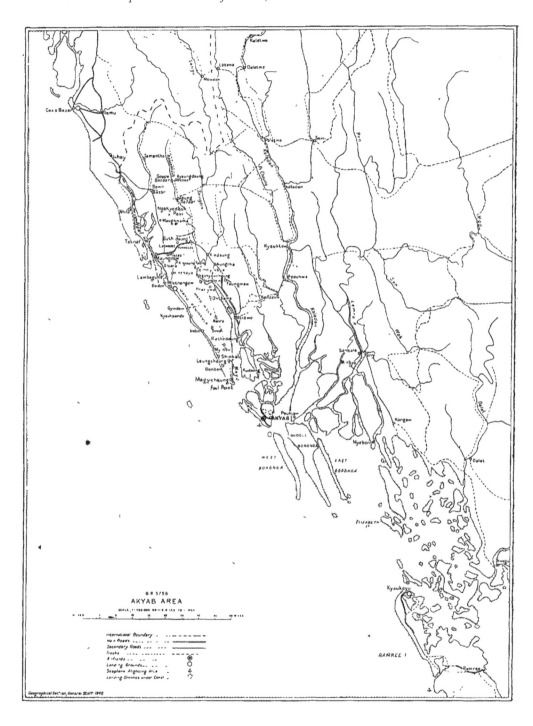

Index

(1) Index of Persons

(2) Index of Naval, Military and Air Force Units